Clientelism, Capitalism, and Democracy

Political parties in the United States and Britain used clientelism and patronage to govern throughout the nineteenth century. By the twentieth century, however, parties in both countries shifted to programmatic competition. This book argues that capitalists were critical to this shift. Businesses developed new forms of corporate management and capitalist organization, and found clientelism inimical to economic development.

Drawing on extensive archival research in the United States and Britain, this book shows how national business organizations pushed parties to adopt programmatic reforms, including administrative capacities and policy-centered campaigns. Parties then shifted from reliance on clientelism as a governing strategy in elections, policy distribution, and bureaucracy. They built modern party organizations and techniques of interest mediation and accommodation. This book provides a novel theory of capitalist interests against clientelism, and argues for a more rigorous understanding of the relationship between capitalism and political development.

DIDI KUO is a Research Scholar at the Center on Democracy, Development, and the Rule of Law at Stanford University, and a Fellow at New America.

Clientelism, Capitalism, and Democracy

The Rise of Programmatic Politics in the United States and Britain

DIDI KUO

Stanford University

CAMBRIDGE UNIVERSITY PRESS

CAMBRIDGE
UNIVERSITY PRESS

University Printing House, Cambridge CB2 8BS, United Kingdom

One Liberty Plaza, 20th Floor, New York, NY 10006, USA

477 Williamstown Road, Port Melbourne, VIC 3207, Australia

314–321, 3rd Floor, Plot 3, Splendor Forum, Jasola District Centre, New Delhi – 110025, India

79 Anson Road, #06–04/06, Singapore 079906

Cambridge University Press is part of the University of Cambridge.

It furthers the University's mission by disseminating knowledge in the pursuit of education, learning, and research at the highest international levels of excellence.

www.cambridge.org
Information on this title: www.cambridge.org/9781108426084
DOI: 10.1017/9781108679923

© Didi Kuo 2018

First published 2018

A catalogue record for this publication is available from the British Library.

Library of Congress Cataloging-in-Publication Data
NAMES: Kuo, Didi, 1983– author.
TITLE: Clientelism, capitalism, and democracy : the rise of programmatic politics in the United States and Britain / Didi Kuo, Stanford University.
DESCRIPTION: New York : Cambridge University Press, [2018] | Includes bibliographical references.
IDENTIFIERS: LCCN 2018009861 | ISBN 9781108426084 (hardback) | ISBN 9781108444439 (pbk.)
SUBJECTS: LCSH: Patronage, Political–United States. | Patronage, Political–Great Britain. | Political planning–United States. | Political planning–Great Britain. | Business and politics–United States. | Business and politics–Great Britain. | Capitalism–Political aspects–United States. | Capitalism–Political aspects–Great Britain.
CLASSIFICATION: LCC JK731 .K86 2018 | DDC 306.20941–dc23
LC record available at https://lccn.loc.gov/2018009861

ISBN 978-1-108-42608-4 Hardback

For my parents, Chung and Josephine Kuo

Contents

Figures

Tables

Acknowledgments

I am grateful to many individuals and institutions who made this book possible. This book began as a dissertation at Harvard University. Peter Hall, my advisor, was extremely generous at every stage of the dissertation process; I first tested these ideas in a paper for his graduate seminar. He spent countless hours reading and commenting on drafts, discussing (and adding clarity to) messy ideas, and providing words of encouragement. He is singularly devoted to his students and his craft, and I am very much in his debt. Daniel Ziblatt served on my dissertation committee and read the book manuscript; his sharp ideas and insightful questions improved my thinking at each stage of this project. Steven Levitsky and Theda Skocpol, the other members of my committee, fundamentally shaped my research with their suggestions and approaches to comparative and American politics. Frances Hagopian was an incredible mentor as I turned this dissertation into a book. She read the manuscript, which was very much informed by her own work on clientelism, provided incisive feedback, and offered professional advice and opportunities.

During graduate school, I benefited from conversations with Robert Bates, Daniel Carpenter, Cathie Jo Martin, James Robinson, Arthur Spirling, Susan Stokes, and Kathleen Thelen. I also had the good fortune to meet and work with Jan Teorell, who taught me a great deal about scholarship as we co-authored a paper on fraud in American elections.

I am grateful to Meg Rithmire, Kristen Looney, Brad Holland, Shahrzad Sabet, Andrea Tivig, Brett Carter, Chika Ogawa, Jane Vaynman, Serene Hung, and Shauna Shames for their intellectual support and camaraderie in Cambridge. Alisha Holland, Amanda Garrett, Amy Catalinac, and Jason Jackson provided indispensable feedback on multiple chapters of my dissertation, as did participants in the Comparative Politics Workshop and the Workshop on the State and Capitalism since 1800.

I spent six months conducting archival research in the National Archives of the United States with the support of the Center for American Political Studies at Harvard University, and with office space at the Centennial Center of the American Political Science Association. The research staff of the Center for Legislative Archives in Washington, DC, particularly Richard McCulley, were immensely helpful, as were the staff of the National Archives in Waltham, MA, and the Baker Historical Library at Harvard Business School. I thank the Krupp Foundation for funding research in Britain, at the History of Parliament Trust and the National Archives of the United Kingdom. Thanks to Daniel Sinnott and Rhona Gaynor for their friendship while I conducted fieldwork. A grant from the Center for European Studies at Harvard University provided me with the time and resources to finish my dissertation.

I am fortunate to call the Center on Democracy, Development, and the Rule of Law (CDDRL) at Stanford University my home. I deeply appreciate the guidance of Stephen Stedman and Francis Fukuyama, who encouraged me to finish this book. I thank them for helping me organize a book conference and for their careful comments and engagement with the manuscript. I am grateful to my other colleagues at the Program in American Democracy in Comparative Perspective, Larry Diamond, Bruce Cain, and Nathaniel Persily, and to many scholars at CDDRL, including Alberto Diaz-Cayeros, Kathryn Stoner, Michael McFaul, and Anna Grzymala-Busse. Whitney McIntosh provided critical research assistance in the book's final stages with her typical acuity. In my time at Stanford I have discussed this project with Isabela Mares, Ira Katznelson, and Nolan McCarty, and thank them for their perspectives. I also received helpful feedback from a talk at the UC Santa Cruz politics department.

I have workshopped and presented various parts of this book with the postdoctoral scholars at CDDRL, all of whom improved it with their critiques and comments. Thanks especially to Kharis Templeman and Katherine Bersch. Kharis participated in the book conference and was a wonderful resource on clientelism and parties. Katherine Bersch deserves credit for the completion of this project. She is both a friend and a taskmaster, dispensing thoughtful and practical advice about career, research, and family, and I am very grateful for our accountability system.

I owe an intellectual debt to my undergraduate professors at Emory University, Richard Doner and Patrick Allitt, for inspiring in me a love of history and ideas, and for so gracefully combining brilliance with humility and kindness. My debate director at Emory, Melissa Wade, taught me the value of research and first encouraged me to consider graduate school. I also thank Albert Weale and Sarah Birch for exemplary teaching while I completed my MSc at the University of Essex.

I thank my editor at Cambridge University Press, Robert Dreesen, for making the publication process so enjoyable. Two anonymous reviewers provided thoughtful and constructive feedback.

Thank you to all the Dryers – Martha, Big D, Eliza, David, and Elizabeth Broadwin – for the stimulating conversations and caretaking. And thanks to Lauren Drayton, Colleen Fogarty, and Meredith Lantz for decades of friendship. My husband, Alexander Dryer, has been a combination editor, sounding board, idea-generator, and panic-defuser. Nothing I write here can adequately thank him for the ways he supported me, with humor and with patience, while this book was under way. Our children were a distraction of the best kind.

Finally, to my parents, who have always supported my efforts with gusto: I never could have finished this without your encouragement and support, and happily dedicate this book to you.

Introduction

You can't keep an organization together without patronage. Men ain't in politics for nothing. They want to get something out of it.
– William L. Riordan, *George Washington Plunkitt of Tammany Hall*[1]

When do political parties reduce reliance on clientelism and patronage, and instead develop programmatic ties to voters? This question has long puzzled scholars of democratization and party organization, since clientelism is an enduring feature of politics across the world. The spread of democracy after the end of the Cold War has shown just how difficult the transition from clientelistic to programmatic politics can be. Programmatic competition – characterized by ideologically cohesive parties and the noncontingent distribution of public goods – is far less common than clientelism, which is characterized instead by the promise of material rewards to voters in exchange for their electoral support.

The process of building democratic institutions is long and arduous, and decades of scholarship indicate that economic and political liberalization can strengthen patron–client ties in the short term. The adoption of competitive elections, for example, creates incentives for local elites to foster dependence and loyalty through the selective distribution of goods. Similarly, the expansion of state agencies at the national and local levels provides politicians opportunities to reward their supporters with public sector jobs or with lucrative state contracts (Chubb 1982; Eisenstadt and Lemarchand 1981; Lerner 1958; Scott 1969; Tarrow 1967). In advanced democracies, on the other hand, leaders and parties mobilize voters through channels of interest representation. Professional staff organize elections and campaigns. Politicians promise distinct sets of policies to voters, and voters hold them accountable to these promises. Civil servants

[1] Riordan 2005, p. 36.

are recruited and promoted through meritocratic rules. How does the transition to programmatic politics arise?

While modernization theorists predicted that rising economic growth would eventually undermine patron–client relationships, clientelism has proven very difficult to eradicate. Clientelism is associated with poverty and can further impede economic growth. It also gives rise to political monopolies and can weaken democratic accountability (Acemoglu and Robinson 2012; Fox 1994; Fukuyama 2014). Because clientelistic strategies are electorally successful, politicians face few incentives to adopt programmatic appeals. In the context of weak states, politicians may not be able to make credible policy promises, since legislatures may have little power to fund or implement them (Keefer 2007). However, there are circumstances under which politicians can transition from clientelistic to programmatic strategies. Huntington (1968, 70) observed that "historically strong party organizations have been built ... by patronage." Recent scholars compare clientelistic distribution to a proto-welfare state, since clientelism generates linkages between politicians and voters that can be strengthened through programmatic policies (Stokes et al. 2013).

This book turns to the historical cases of Britain and the United States to offer a new explanation of the rise of programmatic politics. In the nineteenth century, parties in both countries relied on clientelistic strategies in elections and policy; the formal institutions of democracy existed in tension with highly undemocratic practices. Weak and disorganized political parties used bribes and handouts to win elections. There was little in the way of public policy, since national governments had not yet developed the capacity to implement long-term regulatory schemes. Instead, elected officials used their positions to dole out highly targeted private goods, such as subsidies and land grants. Around the turn of the twentieth century, however, the major parties in both countries – the Republicans and Democrats in the United States, and the Conservative and Liberal parties in Britain – began to lay the groundwork for programmatic competition. They outlawed patronage in the civil service and investigated and punished instances of vote buying. They established party organizations that campaigned using ideological appeals, and touted policy victories in election campaigns. Rather than creating policy through incremental and ad hoc distribution of resources, parties established institutions to regulate the national economy and provide public goods.

How did parties reconfigure their bases of representation over the course of half a century? The shift from clientelism to programmatic politics required new institutions, stronger party organizations, and new norms of interest articulation and mediation. In this book, I argue that economic development alone cannot explain these political outcomes. Instead, changes in capitalism, particularly the rise of managerial capitalism and the creation of a distinct business community composed of new classes of merchants and manufacturers, had a dramatic impact on politics and party strategies.

CAPITALISM, CLIENTELISM, AND PARTY ORGANIZATION

Understanding the rise of programmatic politics requires close examination of the historical processes that influence how parties govern. Many theories of clientelism rely on structural explanations, arguing that economic growth undermines support for clientelism. Higher levels of education may make voters demand greater accountability, for example; urbanization and the rise of the middle class may also produce demands for collective goods. What are the precise political incentives, however, that parties face in choosing new ways to govern? The shift to programmatic politics is both costly and risky. Costly, because it requires building new institutions and devoting limited state resources to significant policy initiatives. Risky, because it requires finding new ways to finance parties and to craft campaign appeals, none of which might succeed.

Changes in the economic sector, particularly in the way businesses and capital are organized, are critical to programmatic political development. It is not simply the case that wealthier societies are less hospitable to clientelism than poorer ones. Instead, capitalism creates a distinct class of economic actors who require different outputs from government. As corporations grow and markets expand, businesses need effective bureaucrats, neutral administration of policy, and predictable party positions, all of which are either lacking or weak in the context of clientelism. The transition from clientelism to programmatic politics is inherently intertwined with transitions in capitalism – from family firms to managerial and hierarchical corporations, and from small, sectoral trade associations to national business lobbies. As the demands of business became increasingly politicized, parties accommodated them by developing new strategies of political engagement and state activity. The result was a decisive shift from a governing strategy based on clientelism to one based on programmatic organization and appeals.

Clientelism in the Nineteenth-Century United States and Britain

Throughout most of the nineteenth century, political leaders in the United States and Britain governed using clientelistic tactics in multiple arenas of politics. In elections, parties used not only outright bribery but also a practice known as "treating," whereby politicians standing for election plied voters with alcohol, transportation, and lodging at the polls. These practices were, in some sense, customary; in the early American republic, George Washington purchased 160 gallons of liquor for electors in his election to the Virginia House of Burgesses (Butler 2000). As the electorates of both the United States and Britain expanded, the two parties competed by offering handouts to voters. According to Bensel (2004, ix), election outcomes in the United States were based on "a shot of whiskey, a pair of boots, or a small amount of money." In Britain, bribery was considered the typical way of conducting business in elections, with the price of a vote varying from £1 to £30 (Gash 1977; Kam 2011; Seymour 1915).

The spoils system in the United States and practices of "Old Corruption" in Britain also allowed parties to dole out civil service jobs to political supporters. After Andrew Jackson instituted the spoils system in 1828 (which, at the time, was considered a democratic measure to wrest control of government from elites), rotation in office became institutionalized. When new presidents were elected to office, there was wholesale replacement of bureaucrats. Patronage appointees were then assessed a portion of their incomes to defray the cost of election campaigns. By the 1870s, civil service workers at the federal and state levels had to donate as much as 10 percent of their incomes to campaign war chests (James 2006; Summers 1987). Patronage politics was even more deeply rooted in Britain, where state offices were considered family property to be handed down generationally. British parties in the second half of the nineteenth century were also extremely generous with patronage appointments (Hanham 1960b). From 1850 to 1883, 532 aristocratic families placed 7,991 of their relatives in 13,888 patronage jobs (Gwyn 1962).

Finally, legislators also used clientelism in policy, through the allocation of resources to specific groups and individuals. The governments of both countries adhered to laissez-faire principles that precluded uniform policies – there was little regulatory or administrative state capacity. Legislators relied on distributional policies that allowed discretionary use of government resources through land grants, subsidies to build roads and canals, and piecemeal allocation of collective goods. Policies were often divorced from ideology or principle, serving only to advance narrow material interests (Gutchen 1961; Lowi 1972; McCormick 1966).

Clientelism served not only the electoral needs of parties, but also their organizational needs. In the United States, patronage appointees were the source of party financing and partisan foot soldiers. In both countries, elections were themselves huge patronage events, with parties paying election agents and administrators. Clientelism also served economic interests by providing state resources to build local infrastructure and facilitate development.

By the late nineteenth century, however, parties were shifting their strategies away from clientelism. In Britain, an effort to modernize party organizations began in earnest in the 1870s, after passage of the Second Reform Bill. The Tories created the National Union of Conservative Constitutional Associations, which brought together local party offices and coordinated the activities of Tories in Parliament with grassroots efforts to mobilize voters. The Liberal party followed soon after with the establishment of a national party organization with a particularly strong presence in urbanizing towns. In the United States, rising levels of patronage after the presidency of Andrew Jackson complemented efforts to build party organizations after the Civil War. Fierce competition for the presidency and Congress led to greater efforts to strengthen state parties and to find ways to cater to the demands of a society in upheaval.

Vote buying peaked in the late nineteenth century and then rapidly declined as parties moved toward issue-based campaigns.

Parties also needed to modernize the state in order to fulfill programmatic campaign appeals. Civil service reforms replaced patronage in public sector jobs with meritocratic recruitment and promotion practices. Britain adopted civil service reforms with the Orders of Council in 1870, while the United States first set aside 10 percent of patronage jobs for merit-based consideration with the Pendleton Act of 1887. Accompanying new practices of civil service hiring were new government institutions. Most patronage positions were in the customs houses and postal offices, both of which expanded significantly after 1800. In the late nineteenth century, political leaders created regulatory commissions and administrative agencies to oversee what were increasingly national problems, such as railway transport. American historians describe this period as the "organizational synthesis," when governments expanded bureaucratic capacities by adopting hierarchy and technical expertise.

Over half a century, parties transformed the way they governed their societies. While clientelism had helped parties craft electoral majorities and serve narrow elite interests, the expansion of professionalized parties and greater state capacity ushered in a new form of representative politics. Parties developed means to integrate and respond to pluralist demands rather than cater to individual interests. The expansion of government's administrative capacity also ensured that parties would serve integral links among competing groups, making politics the arena of contestation over a variety of economic and distributive claims.

Capitalist Interests and Political Development

In the late nineteenth century, Britain and the United States faced national challenges that were similar in kind and daunting in scope. Rapid population growth, advances in communications and transportation technology, and new sources of industrial wealth were reshaping once provincial and isolated landscapes. Until this point, the role of the state in the economy had been minimal. But around the turn of the twentieth century, the governments of both countries needed to devise institutional solutions to economic and social problems. This presented a host of political challenges, including how the state could best facilitate and oversee economic development.

Beginning in the mid-nineteenth century, there was explosive growth in the transport and industrial sectors of the British and American economies. The rise of the modern corporation led to new forms of economic management, as corporations increasingly stressed values of efficiency, hierarchy, and order. Corporate values of scientific expertise and bureaucratic administration stood in stark contrast to national laissez-faire approaches to market regulation. Businesses became increasingly frustrated by incompetent patronage-appointed bureaucrats and inconsistent policy positions between the two major parties. Corporations therefore sought influence in politics through financing political campaigns, testifying before congressional committees, and lobbying for federal regulation of the market. Businesses also created trade, employers', and producers' associations to share information and eliminate competition. Corporate calls for regulation were self-serving; businesses believed that by influencing regulatory laws, they could monitor their own industries and craft friendly policies.

Rather than perpetuating corruption, the demands of business organizations ushered in significant political changes that resulted in a decline in clientelistic politics. Political parties became more ideologically consistent, in that they developed overarching ideological commitments from which they could derive implementable national policies. Political leaders also adopted corporate requests for national regulation by creating executive agencies and a meritocratic civil service.

Capitalism and democracy share a relationship that is simultaneously cooperative and tense, since capitalism creates benefits for society – economic growth, wider tax bases, and jobs, for example – while also creating costs that governments must regulate and mediate. Capitalist interests have historically been excluded from the literature on clientelism, which assumes that business interests are static over time and that businesses use corrupt or personal ties to political leaders to extract rents and advantageous policies. Businesses in capitalist economies are powerful political actors, and their preferences often diverge from other organized interests, including agricultural and landed interests and, of course, those of labor. It is often the case that parties respond to the needs of business over the demands of other groups.

However, clientelism has consequences for economic development: When parties do not govern based on predictable, ideologically consistent policy positions, and when state institutions are too ineffective to implement policies, businesses cannot rely on parties to effectively oversee complex economic arrangements. The primary aggrieved class in clientelistic exchange is often the business class. As the industrial economy became increasingly competitive and chaotic, businesses demanded reforms that would create predictability and standardization in national policy. Further, they demanded greater state capacity in regulation and administration of policy, which then helped parties develop bases of programmatic claims. The historical origins of business involvement in politics is one of political organization and is integral to understanding how representative government changes in response to economic demands.

BUSINESS DEMANDS AGAINST CLIENTELISM: THE ARGUMENT IN BRIEF

This book examines how parties in the United States and Britain changed over the period of 1870–1900. It finds that in the final decades of the nineteenth century, two political processes influenced the transition from clientelism. First, industrialization produced a distinct business class that began to organize against patronage and the perceived corruption of distributive policy.

The needs of new merchants and manufacturers required skilled bureaucrats, reliable services at post offices and customs houses, and effective revenue collection agencies. As capitalism developed, a division emerged between heavy industries with fixed assets (such as railways or extractive industries) that engaged in monopolistic practices and merchants and manufacturers who shipped supplies and goods. As a result, the latter group developed a distinct political identity and turned to the state for protection in the form of strengthened regulation and bureaucracy.

Second, expanding the administrative capacity of the state was critical to the transition away from clientelism, since parties used these new institutions to satisfy competing interests and build programmatic policies. Further, the timing of party organization relative to the organization of business interests is important in determining the nature of programmatic competition. In Britain, where parties organized prior to the organization of business groups, state reforms were not unduly influenced by economic interests. In the United States, on the other hand, the relative weakness of party organization and relative strength of business organizations gave economic interests a powerful voice in the state-building process. While parties successfully reduced patronage and clientelism, they created opportunities for new forms of clientelistic politics through regulatory and rule-making institutions.

Using the cases of the United States and Great Britain, I illustrate two possibilities for transitions to programmatic politics. In both cases, political parties were organized to serve clientelistic outcomes as they mobilized voters for most of the nineteenth century. In both cases, business interests coalesced against reliance on patronage and demanded that parties reform the state to serve economic interests by improving bureaucratic quality and regulatory oversight. And in both cases, parties engaged in a period of state building that ultimately provided a foundation upon which they could build programmatic messages and policies. Where they differ is in the level and timing of party organization, which then determined how parties responded to capitalist pressure.

In Britain, parties began to develop national associations after passage of a bill extending suffrage in 1867.[2] The Conservative and Liberal parties hired professional party agents, created hierarchical organizations that connected parliamentary party leaders to party offices in the districts and also developed ties to workingmen's associations, unions, and religious groups to extend social bases of support. As a result, the party actively sought to mobilize specific interests, rather than cater to demands from particular constituencies. The effort to centralize state institutions and develop administrative capacities was conducted without significant input from business interests, as parties replaced patronage with policy appeals.

---

[2] This was the Second Reform Act; it was preceded by limited suffrage extension through the Great Reform Act of 1832 and succeeded by the Third Reform Act of 1884.

In the United States, however, where parties were less organized than they were in Britain, business interests assumed a significant role in the state-building process. As the Republican and Democratic parties implemented civil service reforms, they turned to capitalists for monetary, organizational, and informational resources. Decades of reliance on patronage without a concomitant effort to build cohesive parties at the state, local, and national levels – and without organizational ties to increasingly class-conscious or sectoral interests – left parties less organized than business groups when building programmatic linkages. As both parties developed national organizations and issue-oriented campaigns, the concerns of other groups, including labor unions and farmers' associations, took a back seat to the concerns of business.

By focusing on party organization, this book conceptualizes clientelism as a set of related strategies – in elections, as well as legislative and bureaucratic politics – that constrain the ability of parties to develop programmatic appeals. Using historical and archival data from Congress and Parliament, I measure clientelism across distinct arenas of politics. As parties faced pressure from the newly organized business community to reform the state and assume a more significant regulatory role, parties developed new methods of policy making and organization that became the basis of programmatic competition. By elucidating how the interests of businesses and politicians changed as capitalism evolved, this book develops an argument about how parties accommodate interest groups' demands through new channels of interest representation. Finally, it shows how the sequencing of business organization, party organization, and state reforms influences the trajectory of clientelistic politics.

CONTRIBUTIONS

In revisiting the institutional reforms of the late nineteenth century, this book takes up a broader debate concerning business interests in capitalist democracies. It challenges the idea that corporate interests always diverge from those of public interests; it also challenges the notion that only societal actors who are losing relative to corporations can mobilize to enact regulation. To be sure, politics is a battle of competing interests. But for more than a generation, academics have assumed that the interests of one of the critical players in capitalist democracies – that is, business – have been fixed. Lindblom wrote in 1977 that business "occupies a privileged position in politics": It faces fewer barriers to collective action and, of course, wields almost exclusive access to and control over capital. This has influenced our understanding of epochs of social reform, including the Progressive Era and New Deal.

However, recent literature has challenged the presumptive structural power of business. Culpepper, defining structural power as "the ways in which large corporations and capital holders ... gain influence over politics without necessarily trying to," argues that the structural power thesis is overly deterministic (2015, 405). It cannot explain why policies are often passed over the objections of business, or why states have been able successfully to regulate business and markets. Vogel (1987) also shows that business is just an interest group like any other: It often fails to keep issues off the political agenda, and its power waxes and wanes. More importantly, the structural power hypothesis is vague about the precise interests of business. Business may prefer labor repression, lower tax rates, and higher corporate profits, generally speaking. But there are many cases in which business may need a trained and comfortable labor force, a social safety net, and a robust regulatory environment. There are historical cases in which business has worked "against" its own interest or when trade-offs between different goals lead business to support policies it otherwise might not. In other words, it is simplistic to assume that business is inherently opposed to wholesale categories of public policy.

As Smith (2000, 452) has argued, "the study of business remains a niche area in political science" given the assumption of raw corporate power in American politics. Instead, this book shows that careful attention to the historical origins of business power can shed light on critical ways that capitalist interests shaped the evolution of state institutions and party organization. In particular, it shows that early tensions between capitalism and democracy led to the accommodation of business interests through strengthening the administrative capacity of the state. The rise of corporations and the concentration of capital, combined with a volatile market prone to panics and depressions, left industrialists clamoring for stability and predictability. Further, although the late nineteenth century is remembered for the rise of monolithic industries such as the railways, industrialization was driven by merchants and manufacturers whose business activity and trade made their interests antithetical to those of monopoly. It was these interests that were best served by collective action and by mobilizing in favor of regulation.

These changes to the state led parties to shift their governing tactics. Rather than relying on clientelism, parties could now rely on bureaucrats and agencies to carry out policies with long time horizons, impacting multiple sectors of society. They shifted from policies of narrow distribution to public policies. Further, parties took on new responsibilities of interest aggregation and mediation. As other groups, such as farmers, laborers, and moral and religious societies, sought to influence politics, they adopted strategies created by businesses to promote their political agendas. Parties then needed to craft policies that accommodated these interests, while cognizant of trade-offs in public support in the electorate.

It is too simple to say that economic development produced programmatic politics in the United States and Britain. The aim of this book is to uncover heterogeneity within capitalist interests and to show how new developments in capitalist organization led business preferences to evolve in favor of programmatic reforms. It then traces the historical process of party organization to show precisely how parties dismantle clientelism in consecutive arenas of politics. Far from arguing that programmatic parties were immune from undue

business influence, this book instead traces the political processes that lead parties to develop systematic linkages to organized interests rather than nurturing
clientelistic linkages with firms and individuals.

This book speaks to debates about clientelism and party development and
offers a novel explanation of the decline of clientelistic politics. It unites diver-
gent strands of research on clientelism that examine vote buying, on the one
hand, and resource distribution, on the other, by instead focusing on the way
parties reform the state in order to reduce reliance on clientelistic strategies across
different arenas of politics. In doing so, it stresses the importance of looking at
how precise interests change over time with respect to how parties govern.

This research also shows that business plays a crucial role in many aspects
of programmatic politics, including the timing and form of institutional reform.
In the postwar period, the political power of the business lobby shows evidence of clientelistic relationships between business and parties. But it does not
follow that business-political ties are inherently clientelistic. Within the literature on party systems and clientelism, there has been relatively little attention
paid to the historical origins of business power. Political scientists who work on
nineteenth-century associations have explicitly privileged voluntary and citizens'
organizations to shed light on the relationship between citizens, civil society,
and the evolution of national policy (Crowley and Skocpol 2001; Hansen 1991;
Sanders 1999; Skocpol et al. 2000). As it stands, "the literature on the relationship between firms and political parties is sparse" (McMenamin 2012, 4).

ORGANIZATION OF THE BOOK

This book is organized around an empirical puzzle, namely, why and how did
parties in the United States and Britain transition to programmatic politics in
the late nineteenth century? This question is inadequately addressed by existing
theories of clientelism, since economic development alone does not explain why
political parties modernized their organizational apparatus and implemented
state reforms. Given the importance of these cases in particular to clientelistic
debates about democratic accountability, economic development, and governance, this book aims to provide a new explanation of the transition to programmatic competition. It draws on interdisciplinary work in the political economy
of development, American political development, business and economic history, and interest group politics. Using archival data on elections and policy,
it provides measures of clientelism over time. It then uses comparative case
studies to elucidate the historical processes underlying the rise and politicization
of business interests, as well as the adoption of new party strategies.

Chapter 1 explicates a theory of the political mobilization of business interests against clientelistic politics. After critiquing and engaging with dominant
theoretical approaches to clientelism, it argues that changes in capitalist organization, particularly the development of managerial capitalism, lead business
elites to develop preferences against clientelistic politics. As business becomes

more organized across firms and industries, businesses develop linkages with political parties and make demands for predictable policy programs and effective public administration.

Chapter 2 details the extent of clientelism in the nineteenth-century United States, when clientelism was "the exclusive type of national domestic policy" (Lowi 1964, 689). I show that parties used clientelism in multiple arenas of politics, including elections campaigns, policy decisions and resource distribution, and appointments to the civil service, and argue that these were part of an overarching governing strategy. I use data gathered from six months of archival research at the Center for Legislative Archives in Washington, DC, to construct a measure of clientelism over time (Kuo and Teorell 2016). Party reliance on clientelism provided a way to ensure electoral victory and to build party organization, making a transition to programmatic politics electorally risky as well as politically costly.

Chapter 3 segues to changes in the economic arena, showing how changes in modes of capitalism in the nineteenth century led to a coalition of businesses opposed to clientelism. This chapter focuses on the shift from small-scale family firms to large-scale managerial corporations. It traces business interests over time using archives of local and national business groups, such as the National Board of Trade, to show how business leaders used the language and strategies of managerial capitalism to advocate political reforms. Once organized, businesses pioneered lobbying techniques that included congressional testimony, campaign finance, and interest group pressure. This created a new politics of interest articulation and pluralism, and parties responded by building programmatic organization and using policy to cater to the demands of diverse groups, including citizens, farmers, and labor. The chapter concludes by tracing the historical development of policy-oriented parties at the turn of the twentieth century.

Chapter 4 turns to the British case, showing that clientelism peaked in the mid-nineteenth century, a few decades earlier than the United States. Using data on parliamentary elections and hearings, as well as civil service appointments, I show that the Conservative and Liberal parties relied extensively on clientelism as a governing strategy. This is substantiated by a novel measure of clientelism using public and private bills, a feature of parliamentary legislation that reveals how parties shifted from distributive, targeted policies to public and regulatory policy over the course of the nineteenth century. The data from this chapter are drawn from six months of research in Britain's Parliamentary Archives and British Library.

In Chapter 5, I turn to business influence in politics in the United Kingdom. Using archives from the Association of British Chambers of Commerce, I show how British business interests also crystallized in favor of programmatic reforms. Although managerial capitalism was less pronounced in Britain, a similar pattern of firms operating in a more bureaucratic fashion influenced the political demands of business. This chapter traces deeper political linkages that developed as business leaders influenced national railway regulation and meritocratic civil service reforms (first outlined in the Northcote–Trevalyan report of 1853 and implemented by the Orders of Council in 1870). It then uses records from the National Union of Conservative Constitutional Associations and National Liberal Federation to show how political parties became more programmatic in orientation.

Finally, the book concludes by comparing the legacy of clientelism in British and the United States. In the United States, parties instituted reliance on capitalist input in policy making in a way that the British did not. British administrative reforms created more effective state capacity than similar reforms in the United States, showing how the decline of clientelism in some arenas – such as elections and policy – does not necessarily entail a lack of clientelism in new administrative institutions. The Conclusion also discusses the book's theoretical and empirical contributions, particularly to scholars working on clientelism in contemporary politics. By linking the historical roots of programmatic reforms to changes in capitalist organization, this book challenges the presumptive structural power of business and argues instead for nuanced examinations of capitalist interests in understanding democratic reforms.

I

Clientelism as a Failure of Governance

A Theory of Business, Parties, and Programmatic Demands

Clientelism has long been a defining feature of democratization, and scholars have developed different approaches to understanding why clientelism is more prevalent in some places than others. Structural approaches, such as modernization theory and its contemporary variants, argue that clientelism is more likely at low levels of economic development. These theories explain clientelism as a result either of scarce resources or of individual preferences for handouts. Institutional approaches, on the other hand, focus instead on political variables. Party competition theories examine the level of electoral competition between political parties, arguing that close elections make programmatic reforms more likely. Another school of thought suggests that the timing of bureaucratization and suffrage determines party use of clientelism. When suffrage precedes the development of a meritocratic, Weberian bureaucracy, parties will develop clientelistic ties with voters.

CLIENTELISM: CONCEPTS AND THEORIES

Clientelism refers to a form of democratic accountability that is highly particularistic: Political officials appeal to voters solely on the basis of the material benefits they will provide in exchange for ongoing support. In elections, clientelism is synonymous with vote buying. Candidates offer voters money, food, or jobs if they cast their votes a certain way. In policy making, clientelism typically refers to situations in which political officials direct rewards – government contracts, subsidies, land grants, qualifications for benefits – to specific individuals, firms, or districts. Clientelism is distinct from outright corruption, since it does not entail violation of the law or misappropriation of government resources for purely private gain. Nor is it the same as rent-seeking, whereby public officials tack on extra costs to government services for their own benefit.

Clientelism is instead contrasted with programmatic politics, which refers to democratic competition along ideological and policy grounds. However, the two forms of politics may operate concurrently, and there is debate about the extent to which clientelism presents an actual problem for democracy. Some argue that clientelism "vitiates democracy by undermining the equality of the ballot, allowing some voters to use their votes to communicate policy preferences while others use their votes only as an exchange for minor side payments" (Stokes 2007, 604). Alternatively, clientelism can be seen as "entirely compatible with democratic commitments and pluralist competition," since it helps parties to mobilize voters, deliver goods, and create administrative loyalty and popular support (Grzymala-Busse 2007, 35). When clientelism is open and publicly accepted, voters in democratic settings may even prefer it to programmatic politics (Kitschelt and Altamirano 2015). Vote buying may run counter to democratic norms of holding politicians accountable for their policy promises, but it nonetheless ensures that some voters – especially those who are low income or politically marginalized – receive benefits from the state.

While clientelism is also often used to describe any deviation from democratic expectations of bureaucratic neutrality in rule-making, meritocratic hiring to state office, or competitive bidding for state contracts, some level of politics is always discretionary. There is no example, in other words, of a purely programmatic polity in which political leaders never use their office to ensure that some segment of their base is better off. A leftist politician is expected to pass policies favorable to labor unions, for example, while a politician of the right may be inclined to eliminate trade barriers for favored industries.

Scholars of clientelism have adopted two theoretical approaches to explaining the decline of clientelism in democracies. The first is modernization theory: As states become more economically developed, political officials are far less likely to distribute clientelism in exchange for votes or to pad state offices through patronage appointments. The second set of theories relates to political and institutional causes of clientelism. Some argue that the timing of bureaucratization and suffrage determines clientelistic politics, while others suggest that the competitiveness of major parties is a better predictor.

By failing to distinguish between varieties of clientelistic politics in elections and policy, many of these theories explain only a narrow subset of types of clientelism. As a result, the theories do not adequately explain a shift toward programmatic party competition across multiple areas of politics. Additionally, few existing theories provide mechanisms for the transition between clientelistic and programmatic modes of exchange. We therefore have a limited understanding of how the interests and preferences of different actors influence political reforms.

Modernization Approaches to the Study of Clientelism

The most prevalent causal explanation of the decline of clientelism relates a country's level of economic development to the likelihood and extent of clientelistic politics. Modernization theorists have offered two mechanisms for the relationship between development and clientelism. The first is the rise of the middle classes: Poor voters are more likely to value the handout they receive in clientelistic exchange. Rising per capita incomes, however, decrease the relative value of a bribe. Middle-class citizens are also likely to see clientelistic exchange as illegitimate and to hold candidates accountable for their campaign policy promises. The second mechanism is that clientelism becomes too costly as the population grows; parties cannot afford to continue offering money and jobs to enough voters.

In the 1950s and 1960s, as many countries achieved independence, scholars sought to explain the political consequences of economic development. Many tribal areas had longstanding practices of tribute – an informal institution of gift giving between tribal chieftains and subjects (van de Walle 2007). Clientelism naturally developed from this instrumental dyadic relationship "in which an individual of higher socioeconomic status (patron) uses his own influence and resources to provide protection or benefits, or both, for a person of lower status (client) who, for his part, reciprocates by offering general support and assistance ... to the patron" (Scott 1972, 72). Many aspects of the patron–client relationship were transferable to democracy. As premodern societies adopted universal suffrage and competitive parties, preexisting hierarchies became "effective channels for the delivery of votes from the newly enfranchised lower classes" (Chubb 1982, 4). This pattern – whereby elections became vehicles for conditional exchanges between political leaders and poorer citizens – was documented extensively throughout the developing world (Eisenstadt and Lemarchand 1981; Gellner and Waterbury 1977; Schmidt 1977; Scott 1972; Tarrow 1967).

Patronage politics, often considered a subset of clientelism, was also the subject of empirical investigation in the 1970s. Relying heavily on case studies, scholars found that political officials often used their access to state bureaucracies to provide jobs to their family and friends. States with weakly developed institutions seemed particularly susceptible to abuse by democratically elected officials (Chubb 1982; Shefter 1977; Tarrow 1967). Therefore, clientelism was originally presented as a way to understand how social and political obligations functioned in underdeveloped areas. Through ethnographic research, scholars documented patterns of obligation and reciprocity unique to specific regions. There was an underlying assumption in this literature that social and economic development would reduce clientelism by undermining traditional practices in premodern societies.

Because much of this early scholarship saw patronage as fundamentally intertwined with social class, scholars also highlighted the beneficial effects of clientelism. Functionalist accounts of the machine offered by Merton and Schmidt described how clientelism was a more effective governing strategy in urban areas than programmatic politics. Because bosses could use clientelism to create heterogeneous coalitions, they could quell social unrest that might otherwise arise between different populations (Merton 1968; Schmidt 1977).

Machine leaders also reached out to marginalized groups and racial minorities, which politicians outside of cities were often reluctant to do. Therefore, the machine guaranteed that marginalized citizens would receive some state benefits – even if they were monetary or transactional – from electoral participation. Those who advanced this "rainbow theory" were concerned not as much with the nefarious outcomes arising from patronage, but rather with documenting a different form of politics that succeeded in creating accountability and delivering goods to citizens (Erie 1988).

Recent literature also links economic development to clientelism and asks whether clientelism necessarily obviates political accountability. Low levels of economic development are correlated with higher levels of electoral fraud (Lehoucq 2003), rent-seeking by public officials (Treisman 2007), weak and ineffective bureaucracies (Montinola and Jackman 2002), and similar indicators of corruption. Much of this literature explains clientelism as the result of the preferences of political actors. But unlike earlier waves of research, these arguments are not based on the cultural attitudes of poor voters. Instead, these theories argue that clientelism is the product of rational preferences of voters and politicians alike. Poor voters may prefer payoffs to policies due to shorter time horizons: The expected utility of a handout may be greater than that of a probabilistic policy outcome (Hagopian 2007; Keefer 2007; Kitschelt and Wilkinson 2007; Stokes 2007). But clientelism could also be the result of politicians' preferences; they may target the lower classes with clientelistic benefits as a form of redistribution. In a survey of Argentinean voters, Stokes (2005) found that parties were far more likely to target poor people "for whom the payoff of even a small reward outweighs the expressive value of voting for one's preferred party" (p. 325).

Economic development is also tied to cultural arguments advanced to explain the emergence and persistence of clientelistic politics, particularly the political machine, in the United States. Noting the high immigrant population of many machine cities, including New York City, Boston, Philadelphia, and Cincinnati, scholars argued that the low incomes or "backward" cultures of immigrant groups necessitated patronage. Moynihan (1963), for example, contended that the Irish were accustomed to rural tradition and religious hierarchy, and therefore preferred patron–client relations. And Banfield and Wilson (1963) argued that due to their "private-regarding ethos," immigrants preferred highly targeted goods rather than broad, redistributive policies. This was said to be in contrast to Americans from Anglo-Saxon Protestant backgrounds whose values of efficiency and honesty led to public-regarding motivations. The classical theory of patronage therefore linked social status to politics: "[I]mmigrants, displaced peasants, and the poor are especially likely to demand patronage in exchange for their votes, and ... voters who belong to the middle class and to the industrial working class are more likely to respond favorably to parties that offer collective or programmatic benefits" (Shefter 1994, 24).

It could be the case that economic factors play an important role in a short-term decision to use clientelism; poverty and inequality may also create conditions favorable for patronage. However, the relationship between income and clientelism remains unclear. Clientelism could be the only form of politics available in poor areas, which often suffer a paucity of state resources. The choices attributed to low-income voters or political candidates may therefore be highly constrained. In these areas, clientelism serves as an effective form of redistribution, guaranteeing that citizens receive some benefits, however marginal, when broader policies are ineffective. In turn, this locks in clientelistic practices. When the economy declines, voters may be even more inclined to turn to patrons for some sort of financial assistance; officials then drain already cash-strapped state coffers. Below certain levels of development, programmatic politics may be nearly impossible since resources may simply be too scarce for any form of accountability to emerge (Kitschelt and Freeze 2010; Stokes et al. 2013).

As incomes rise with economic development, levels of clientelism may actually increase before a middle class emerges that prefers programmatic competition. There is some debate about the monotonicity of the relationship between development and clientelism. Stokes et al. (2013) imply that the relationship is linear and that clientelism represents a proto-welfare state; Weitz-Shapiro (2014) also finds that clientelism is lower in districts with more nonpoor voters. But other evidence indicates that the relationship may be curvilinear, with rising incomes actually facilitating clientelistic transactions. In a study of Pronasol, an antipoverty initiative enacted in 1989 that distributes spending on both public and private goods in Mexico, Magaloni et al. (2007) find that municipalities at middle levels of development received the most clientelistic transfers – more than the very poor areas and more than wealthy areas. This suggests that "modernization does not erode clientelism until it surpasses a sufficiently high threshold" (p. 195). In India, as voters became more educated, they demanded greater clientelistic goods from politicians, including subsidies, loans, housing, and clothing (Wilkinson 2007, 112). Kitschelt and Wilkinson (2007) also note that modernization may increase the salience of ethnic mobilization and opportunities for clientelistic distribution as groups compete for resources (p. 26). This pattern also seems to hold cross-nationally. Results from the Project on Democratic Accountability, a set of global expert surveys used to measure national levels of clientelism, show that neither clientelistic nor programmatic distribution is pervasive in extremely low-income countries. Instead, opportunities for clientelism rise with economic development (Kitschelt and Kselman 2013).

As incomes rise, politicians try to buy off voters with ever-increasing bribes or offers of state benefits. Over time, however, middle-class voters come to value public goods and policy. Not only does the marginal benefit of a handout decline with income gains, but also middle-class voters may find clientelism an insufficient way to hold politicians accountable. As they vote against politicians who rely on clientelism, candidates face audience costs that force them to evaluate trade-offs between clientelistic and programmatic strategies (Weitz-Shapiro 2014).

Another account of the relationship between development and clientelism focuses on demographic change and politicians' willingness to buy votes. Comparing the United States and Britain, Stokes (2013) argues that population growth, mass communication, and urbanization explain the decline of clientelism. In Britain, the Liberal and Conservative parties had relied on vote buying as an electoral strategy for the better part of the nineteenth century. But as the right to vote was extended in a series of Reform Acts (1832, 1867, and 1885), parties could no longer afford to rely on bribes. A historian of Britain also argues that the growth of the electorate to 5,000,000 after 1884 made "persuasion ... prohibitively expensive" (Ingle 2008, 14). And Cox (1987), writing about the expansion of the British electorate, surmises that "one suspects ... that candidates in the larger and more independent boroughs engaged in the politics of opinion more thoroughly than their colleagues in the smaller towns" (p. 57).

However, while the size of the electorate does increase the cost of bribes, parties continue to provide clientelism in nations with full suffrage, and these arguments do not articulate a threshold after which parties switch to programmatic politics. Changing demographics did not deter politicians in other advanced democracies such as Italy and Japan, where politicians expanded pork-barreling and patronage as the electorate and economy expanded in the postwar period. Indeed, economic development can often provide political officials with even more resources to distribute to voters, in which case the growth of the electorate simply leads to more clientelism. Demographic change more often than not leads to competitive clientelism, whereby parties simply outbid each other for votes (Keefer and Vlaicu 2007).

Some modernization theories also advance functionalist accounts of public goods provision, arguing that socioeconomic change creates new demands for government intervention. Industrialization entailed large social and economic costs, as urban population density, poor sanitation, and public health crises were making clear (Lizzeri and Persico 2004; Reid and Kurth 1988). Citizens therefore placed a rising value on public policies that could alleviate these costs (Aldrich 1979). Given that prereform "political institutions were dominated by clientelism and patronage ... the extension of the franchise caused a shift away from special-interest politicking toward a more public-oriented legislative activity" (Lizzeri and Persico 2004, 709). Lizzeri and Persico predict that as public goods become more valuable, politicians support franchise extension in order to secure those goods (p. 713). State intervention, however, increases opportunities for patronage and clientelism (Bratton and Walle 1997; Chubb 1982; Rauch and Evans 1999). As the price of bribes rises with demographic change, provision of state services may transfer opportunities for clientelism to new state agencies.

While explanations focused on economic development may be able to tell us about the probability that politicians will use electoral clientelism, they are not entirely persuasive about the emergence of programmatic politics or the decline of clientelism. While the focus on the supply side rather than the demand side is useful in pointing out that population growth can greatly increase the cost of clientelism, it does not then follow that rational politicians seeking to win elections will unilaterally transition to cheaper programmatic appeals.

Ultimately, economic variables tell us little about the actual supply and demand of patronage. Who lobbies for goods from the government, rather than payoffs? And when are politicians in a position to provide collective goods rather than side payments? While modernization and industrialization undoubtedly shape the preferences of social and political actors, they may not do so in homogeneous and predictable ways.

Nor does development provide a mechanism for the decline of clientelism. If public goods become more valuable, do politicians actually distribute more of them? If bribes become too expensive, how do parties mobilize and persuade voters by combining policy-oriented campaign messages with other forms of organization? How do actors change state institutions to allow effective implementation of programmatic policy? We need to understand the explicit political processes that allow parties to rely increasingly on programmatic competition over time.

The problem with the modernization literature is that it is difficult to make predictions about how changes in a party's ability to supply clientelism – owing to enlargement of the electorate or rising incomes – affect the actual distribution of clientelism. There are no thresholds that determine when parties decide that vote buying or patronage is no longer sustainable. More importantly, what these explanations lack is an empirically accurate description of the process by which parties shift to programmatic campaigns and distribution of public goods. What is needed is a demand-side story that specifies the actors seeking alternatives to clientelistic linkages with parties.

Overall, these economic explanations seem deterministic, revealing little about the actual supply and demand for clientelism. Poor voters may prefer handouts to programs, but middle-class voters' need for public goods does not necessarily exceed that of poor voters. In other words, few studies articulate the point at which nonpoor voters make demands about the specific policy goods and programs they prefer to handouts. Further, economic development alone cannot explain variation in the supply of clientelism. Politicians may not be able to provide policy goods under certain institutional constraints. As I will argue below, more attention to political and institutional variables is necessary to explain the emergence of programmatic forms of exchange.

Finally, perhaps the most surprising or stark oversight in the literature on clientelism is that, while many explanations rely on economic development, few explanations actually discuss economic *actors*. Structural approaches divide the electorate by income, rather than by economic activity. Different sectors of the economy require different goods from the state. The development of industrial capitalism leads to segmentation between labor, agriculture, and business interests, for example. And within business, different sectors also need distinct forms of government protection. Extractive industries may want strong property rights and low labor costs, while merchants and manufacturers may want protective tariffs, skilled labor, and effective regulation. Capitalism requires a state that effectively implements policy and parties that signal meaningful policy differences in elections. Businesses develop interests for programmatic politics because their ability to trade and produce effectively relies on the state.

Institutional Approaches to the Study of Clientelism

Institutional theories emerge to address the shortcomings of modernization theory. There are two sets of institutional explanations for the use of clientelism. The first, associated primarily with the work of Shefter (1977; 1994), argues that patronage is a function of the timing of bureaucratization and democratization. The second focuses on the level of electoral competition among political parties. Both of these theoretical approaches are attentive to the proximate causes of clientelism, although neither theory presents a satisfying account of how programmatic politics arise.

Shefter (1977) argues that the sequencing of democratization and bureaucratization explains why parties in some nations rely more heavily on patronage than parties elsewhere. Shefter compares parties in Germany, Britain, Italy, and the United States. He finds that historically, when countries extended universal suffrage prior to the emergence of what he terms a coalition for bureaucratic autonomy, parties relied on patronage to win votes. Such was the case in Italy and the United States, where mass democracy arrived prior to a meritocratic civil service. In Germany and Britain, on the other hand, elites protected bureaucratic institutions through civil service reforms that prevented politicians from dispensing civil service jobs to party loyalists. Shefter (1994) defines the coalition for bureaucratic autonomy as a group of individuals with "a stake in the system that is sufficiently powerful to prevail over competing forces" (p. 28). He is not clear about the origins of the coalition for bureaucratic autonomy. But he assumes that politicians are predatory: When state resources are available to them, they use those resources to build and maintain parties.

Although Shefter's theoretical point that a robust and meritocratic state apparatus can prevent clientelism has been extremely influential, it has not withstood empirical scrutiny. Cross-national studies show a relationship between functioning bureaucracies and programmatic parties (Bustikova and Corduneanu-Huci 2017; Keefer 2006). However, these models fail to explicate the precise causal relationship between bureaucratic strength and programmatic politics. It is unclear whether functioning bureaucracies are a product or a cause of programmatic parties. Ultimately, these models observe that programmatic politics begets itself, almost a tautology. Case studies have also challenged Shefter's arc of the timing of bureaucratic autonomy and suffrage. In Western Europe, countries such as Austria, France, and the Netherlands extended suffrage after bureaucratic reforms but still developed patronage-based parties (Piattoni 2001).

While able to explain some of the advanced democracies, Shefter's thesis also does not travel well. Many political parties that once relied on patronage were able to shift to programmatic competition over time. And in the context of contemporary democracies, it seems unlikely that countries with weak institutions prior to democratization will never be able to develop programmatic linkages. Further, parties rarely rely solely on either patronage or programmatic policy. There may be instances in which they rely on one strategy more than the other, but there are also cases of reversal in which patronage has been discouraged but later used again. Even in the cases that Shefter discusses, parties continued to use multiple strategies to win votes.

Another theory relating political parties to clientelism focuses on the level of electoral competition between parties. One way that competition affects clientelism is through the arrival of new parties in the electoral arena. Parties differ in the level of access they have to state resources, which influences their use of clientelism. Following Duverger, Shefter (1977) distinguishes between internal parties – those that grew out of legislative factions – and external parties, which mobilized outside the electoral arena. Shefter argues that the only way to compel internally mobilized parties to adopt programmatic strategies is when externally mobilized parties, typically Leftist parties that rely on mass mobilization and have no access to state resources, become electorally viable. Because externally mobilized parties can offer only programs, they force other parties to compete on programmatic grounds. Historically, socialist and workers' parties, as well as religious parties, organized around ideological principles. They were explicit about the policies they would adopt if elected to govern. In order to remain competitive, internal parties therefore had to engage with the programmatic campaigns of their rivals. However, this theory does not specify that externally mobilized parties are necessary for programmatic outcomes; programmatic politics can develop in countries without robust external parties. Ziblatt (2016) finds that conservative parties, for example, were much more important to the decline of patronage and consolidation of parties than socialist or religious parties. Nor can Shefter explain why many externally mobilized parties in Europe also used clientelistic strategies once elected to office.

More intense interparty competition may also help existing parties overcome the collective action problems inherent in political reform. New parties can motivate elites to build up state institutions, for example, in order to foreclose patronage options to future political leaders. In her work on post-Soviet Europe, Grzymala-Busse (2007) finds that competition encouraged postcommunist parties to build robust states in order to insulate institutions from partisan control. O'Dwyer (2006) also finds that robust party competition constrained patronage-led state building. Geddes (1996) provides a somewhat more nuanced view, arguing that parties can overcome the collective action problems facing civil service reform only when they share roughly even access to patronage (for example, when two parties have about equal seats in the legislature). Competition can also turn corruption into an election issue by allowing candidates and voters to sanction corrupt officials (Montinola and Jackman 2002; Przeworski et al. 1999). However, Keefer and Vlaicu (2007) find evidence of competitive clientelism – as competition rises, parties simply outbid each other to win votes. Further, much of this work applies to polities dominated by one party for an extensive period. In countries where two or more parties have experienced frequent alternations in power, the threshold for competitiveness is unclear. This literature does not explain when clientelistic parties that have been competitive for decades choose instead to implement programmatic reforms.

Finally, the literature on distributive politics seeks to explain whether politicians are more likely to use clientelism to target specific types of voters (core voters vs. swing voters) or to target specific outcomes (turnout vs. persuasion).[1] Rather than looking at the content or nature of electoral appeals, these theories seek to understand how and to whom parties distribute goods in elections. Cox and McCubbins (1986) predict, for example, that parties will distribute discretionary benefits to their core supporters in order to maintain their bases of support. In Argentina, parties monitor voters in an effort to reward core voters (Stokes et al. 2013) and ensure turnout on election day (Nichter 2008). Dixit and Londregan (1996) and Lindbeck and Weibull (1987), on the other hand, hypothesize that parties distribute clientelistic benefits to swing voters. In Sweden, for example, Dahlberg and Johansson (2002) found that incumbent governments tactically provided grants to local governments with many swing voters in order to shore up electoral support.

But these analyses do not predict how parties change their strategies over time, as the attitudes of voters evolve. What is needed is a more explicitly political account of how parties decide among competing clientelistic and programmatic strategies, and how parties use their successes in office to change the content of electoral campaigns.

Clientelism and the State: Toward a Unified Approach

Modernization and institutional approaches to understanding clientelism are not mutually exclusive. It could be the case that economic development affects the willingness of parties to protect their bureaucracies from patronage or to engage in different forms of distributive politics. However, current theories have not examined the way these approaches might be related.

---

[1] These are only examples of a wider literature on partisan distributive strategies; see Cox (2009) and Golden and Min (2013) for a more thorough review of this literature.

One of the challenges in synthesizing the literature on clientelism is that clientelistic strategies pervade distinct arenas of politics. Most work on clientelism focuses on vote buying, but there are many other examples of clientelism that include patronage, pork-barrel policies, and manipulation of public resources (e.g., conditioning welfare on partisan support). Further, these strategies are often used together. To understand why and how these strategies are combined, we need to move toward an understanding of clientelism as an overarching strategy of governance rather than simply a set of narrow, isolated political strategies. One of the drawbacks of current empirical and theoretical approaches is that disaggregating clientelism in elections and in policy obscures the interrelationship of these tactics.

Clientelism in Multiple Arenas of Politics

Clientelism is often understood as an iterative, dependent relationship between patrons and clients. However, most studies of clientelism focus exclusively on vote buying and the short period of election campaigns and election day. This may not capture the entire picture of how clientelism works, since clientelism usually endures – indeed, is often strengthened – over multiple election cycles. Looking at vote buying alone can only tell us about clientelistic moments at one moment in time, rather than how politicians use power while in office. As Kitschelt and Freeze (2010) have pointed out, linkages "do not exhaust themselves in politicians' talk and posturing, but necessitate implementation through ... resource flows. And ultimately for politicians the key is whether talk and action translate into votes at subsequent elections" (p. 25).

Recent work reveals how prevalent clientelism is in policy, particularly in distribution of state resources (Diaz-Cayeros et al. 2016; Kitschelt and Wilkinson 2007; Stokes et al. 2013; Weitz-Shapiro 2014). In fact, clientelism in policy creates deeper ties of clientelist dependence, because supporting a specific candidate is the only way voters may be able to ensure access to government resources. While voters may not need a small cash bribe before elections, they are more vulnerable when they rely on politicians to keep their jobs or their access to welfare benefits and social programs (Mares and Young 2016).

Conceptualizing programmatic and clientelistic resource distribution is more complicated than determining whether or not candidates buy votes in elections. Traditionally, scholars tried to categorize specific policies as either programmatic or clientelistic. Subsidies, for example, were considered clientelistic, while progressive taxation was considered programmatic. But this quickly becomes tricky. Many pork-barrel projects are programmatic in that they supply districts with public goods, such as bridges or postal routes. However, pork is often considered clientelistic because its benefits are geographically limited while its costs are shared collectively. The logic linking pork to clientelism dates to Lowi (1964, 390), who argued that "patronage in its fullest meaning of the word can be taken as a synonym for distributive." Clientelistic policies were therefore distinguished from public goods and policies that "distribute benefits and costs to all citizens regardless of whether they voted for the government of the day" (Kitschelt 2000, 845).[2]

Perhaps unsurprisingly, given the difficulty in delineating between clientelistic and programmatic policy, scholarly efforts to measure the "amount" of clientelism in a polity have not been very effective. In cross-national studies of clientelism, scholars proxy for clientelistic policies using government ownership of newspapers, secondary school enrollment, and infant mortality rates, all of which theoretically indicate some commitment to social policy or public goods (Bustikova and Corduneanu-Huci 2017; Keefer 2007). These outcomes, however, do not tell us anything about how goods are distributed. Studies have also used the amount of public investment as a fraction of GDP to indicate the degree of pork-barrel politics (Cruz and Keefer 2015; Samuels 2002; Wilkinson 2007). In work on the political economy of redistribution, redistributive taxation is considered programmatic, while regressive taxation is considered clientelistic (Cox and McCubbins 1986; Dixit and Londregan 1996). These classifications are conceptually unsatisfying, though, since any policy good – education, taxation, infrastructure – can be distributed in either clientelistic or programmatic ways.

Newer research on clientelism shifts from thinking about which policy goods signal programmatic commitment. Studies turn instead to looking at how policies are allocated. Hagopian (2015, 14), for example, distinguishes patronage "not on the basis of the nature of what is being offered – after all, programmatic appeals are often ultimately about a redistribution of resources toward a targeted constituency – but by the *criteria* according to which resources will be distributed, and specifically, the excludability and reversibility of the goods."

In their study of distributive politics, Stokes et al. (2013) classify policies according to the criteria of distribution employed. Programmatic policies are those with formalized, public criteria of distribution. Nonprogrammatic policies describe those whose publicized rules do not shape their actual distribution – such as pork-barrel policies or partisan policies in which benefits flow only to specific districts or groups. Finally, they classify clientelist policies as those that condition benefits on political support. Clientelist benefits include patronage (when benefits flow to party members) and vote buying (when benefits flow to voters). This categorization of different modes of distribution is a significant conceptual step forward. However, their empirical analysis relies exclusively on data about vote buying; the authors do not explain whether the factors that drive bribery also drive clientelistic policies.

In her study of an Argentinean food distribution program, Weitz-Shapiro (2014) privileges clientelism in policy over vote buying alone. Similarly to

---

[2] See also Lizzeri and Persico (2004), who contrast redistribution (which has "ad hominem benefits") with public goods (which instead have diffuse benefits).

Stokes et al., Weitz-Shapiro also argues that clientelism is a *"mode* of distribution ... [that] does not fit neatly into conventional distinctions between private and public goods." She provides an illustrative example:

Food stamps are clearly private goods by any definition of the term ... Yet, without knowing how a food stamp program is administered, it is impossible to say whether it is indeed distributed using a clientelist logic. Are recipients chosen on the basis of need alone, or do they believe that their continued receipt of benefits is contingent on their political behavior? If need governs distribution on an ongoing basis, then, although a private good is being distributed, some public end is also served. In contrast, if the continued receipt of these benefits is contingent on the recipient's political behavior, the benefit is not only private, but clientelist practices are in place. (p. 81)

Viewing policy goods through a lens of clientelistic distribution is not a matter of categorizing some policies as programmatic and others as clientelistic. The works reviewed here reveal just how manipulable policy instruments are, even those governed by universal criteria or neutral political principles.

Conceptually, the idea of policy clientelism remains slippery, and it is nearly impossible to draw a clear line between a clientelistic and programmatic policy. Scheiner (2006) shows that in Japan, pork is a significant vehicle for clientelism, given the parties' connections to local businessmen and construction groups. Pork therefore serves many private interests, particularly in rural areas, while underserving urban voters. Weitz-Shapiro's (2014) analysis shows that decentralized policies that allow local implementation are vulnerable to clientelism, but can also be vehicles of programmatic service delivery. As Stokes et al. (2013) point out, "reports of programmatic distribution have a dog-bites-man quality," leading to disproportionate attention to cases of biased resource distribution (p. 9). This research has gone a long way toward identifying clientelistic and programmatic policy strategies, although it remains difficult to generalize about these strategies across dissimilar political contexts.

Finally, there has been little attention to the myriad ways in which programmatic and clientelistic strategies are combined, as there might be "different compromises for the protection of particular interests and the promotion of the general interest" (Piattoni 2001, 3). Without more careful theorizing about programmatic politics, we risk conceptual slippage. If clientelism refers to even mundane political decisions in which there are winners and losers, then almost any type of distributive politics can be clientelistic. The concern with clientelism is not just that there are policy losers, however, but that politicians take advantage of their relationship with (often less-advantaged) voters in order to deny them benefits they deserve. The incentives that politicians face to provide clientelism in some arenas, like policy, and in other areas, like elections, may differ. The next section therefore turns to ways institutions constrain the ability of politicians to provide policy goods.

Clientelism and State Institutions

In Stokes's (2013) account of the decline of machine politics in Britain, clientelistic election strategies such as bribery and treating (providing voters with transportation, alcohol, and food) peaked in the mid-nineteenth century. They declined as population growth made brokers too expensive for parties to use. Economic development and its concomitant changes, such as improved education and faster communications, also could have made voters less tolerant of clientelistic practices.

But an element missing in this account, and in most recent accounts of clientelism, is how political strategies are enabled and constrained by state institutions. There are two reasons that the relationship between parties and the state is important. First, the extent to which parties can use patronage – the exchange of public sector jobs for party support – influences the decision to engage in other forms of clientelism. When parties can buy enough influence through patronage, they may be able to persuade without resorting to outright vote buying. Looking only at vote buying can therefore obscure deeper, more pervasive clientelistic relationships. Second, the reciprocal causation between reliance on patronage and low state capacity presents a significant barrier to programmatic reforms. Parties often use clientelistic appeals because they cannot credibly commit to programmatic ones. Reliance on patronage then further weakens state institutions. In the context of weak state capacity, programmatic politics becomes even more elusive.

While patronage may seem like a strategy to use in addition to vote buying, providing political officials with the option of persuading voters either through bribes or through promises of employment, patronage can actually increase or decrease the use of vote buying. The supply of patronage jobs is usually too limited to buy a significant amount of votes; patronage is a useful tool of political manipulation precisely because jobs are limited. Providing someone with a public-sector job allows more control of these supporters, creates more dependency on the patron, and allows politicians to wield enormous influence through controlling all instruments of local policy distribution.

Current clientelism literature looks primarily at vote buying, ignoring a range of negative electoral inducements that serve as substitutes for handouts. Vote buying is a positive inducement, but voters can reject a bribe that will only make them slightly better off, while they may not be able to ignore coercion or threats that will leave them far worse off (Mares and Young 2016). Patronage gives politicians the ability to leverage the threat of unemployment to ensure political loyalty, and therefore to turn state employees into party brokers. In the heyday of machine politics in American cities, parties maintained power precisely through the appointment of friends to positions collecting taxes, granting licenses and permits, and procuring lucrative construction and infrastructure contracts. In southern Italy, the Christian Democrats similarly secured support through their control of not only all local state offices, but also jobs in banks, hospitals, the public housing authority, and key business and trade associations (Chubb 1982; Tarrow 1977). Mares and Young (2016) show that the same dynamic can be found in contemporary developing countries, where parties deploy an array of state employees – police officers, tax collectors, and social policy administrators – to help parties persuade voters in elections. They do so through selective enforcement of the law and through favoritism and special access to state resources.

Reliance on patronage often limits the ability of politicians to provide policy goods. The current literature's focus on vote buying assumes that parties can offer programs but choose not to. However, reliance on patronage, unlike vote buying, can increase demand for public largesse, leading to bloated public sectors and reducing the provision of public goods (Calvo and Murillo 2004; Robinson and Verdier 2013). Patronage can also lead to overemployment and overpricing in public works, further undermining local economies and labor markets (Roniger 2004). In urban areas governed by political machines, parties are known for governing through favoritism, partiality, and exceptions in the administration of the law (Stone 1996; Wolfinger 1972). Some scholars of comparative politics therefore see clientelism and machine politics as synonymous since they both rely heavily on discretionary and targeted behaviors (Gans-Morse et al. 2014). While vote buying may not be endogenous to poverty, patronage often is, since the institutions required to ensure economic development remain weak.

State capacity also affects the distribution of clientelism. Most of the new work on clientelistic service provision analyzes variation within countries, controlling for national state capacity (Diaz-Cayeros and Magaloni 2016; Weitz-Shapiro 2012). Decentralization or delegation of policy to local units creates opportunities for clientelistic politics. In work on mayoral manipulation of cash transfer or food transfer programs, there is evidence of widespread variation in the partisan provision of social policy (De La O 2015; Diaz-Cayeros and Magaloni 2016; Weitz-Shapiro 2014).

The broader finding of this literature is that the weakness of state institutions can increase opportunities for clientelism. Keefer (2007) and Keefer and Vlaicu (2007) argue that young democracies rely on patron–client networks because building credible policy institutions is costly. Clientelistic parties are also less likely to perform oversight of the executive branch, which reduces effective policy implementation (Cruz and Keefer 2015). In weak institutional contexts, voters may be less likely to believe programmatic campaign promises. Lyne (2008) argues that voters face a dilemma when they prefer programs but do not believe that the parties will enact them. Parties need long periods of building up reputations for bureaucratic effectiveness and public goods provision before they can offer credible programmatic promises (Bustikova and Corduneanu-Huci 2017; Hicken 2011; Lizzeri and Persico 2004).

In the context of weak state institutions, vote buying and patronage are often linked. Parties may need patronage to ensure electoral success as well as campaign funds. And because patronage further weakens state capacity by filling bureaucratic posts with poorly trained political appointees, parties may continue to buy votes since they cannot persuade voters that this weakened state will enact beneficial policies.

UNDERSTANDING PROGRAMMATIC POLITICS

This chapter has argued that clientelism is a strategy that parties use in multiple arenas of politics and that there is a need to integrate approaches that focus on economic development with those that focus instead on state institutions. One way to do this is to look at the emergence of programmatic politics with respect to capitalism, particularly the mobilization of business interests against clientelistic politics.

Specifically, changes in the organization of capitalism within and across firms – such as the shift from personal capitalism to managerial capitalism, and the shift from sectoral business groups to national trade associations – creates a distinct class of merchants, manufacturers, and capitalists whose interests are directly tied to programmatic policy. Where parties rely on clientelism as a strategy of governance, it generates economic costs. Parties are unable to make policy commitments; once in office, reliance on distributive policy creates an ad hoc, disadvantageous playing field for businesses who need effective and predictable administration of policy. Patronage-appointed bureaucrats are unable to carry out routine state activity, not to mention implement long-term policies.

Conditions for Programmatic Politics

Political parties are considered programmatic when they adopt ideologically cohesive and distinct policy platforms, carry issue-oriented messages consistent with these platforms in elections, and try to implement these policies once elected to office (Hagopian 2015). Programmatic party competition is also indicated by the strategies that parties use to distribute resources: They are programmatic when they offer policies that benefit voters collectively, rather than when they offer specific benefits to individual voters. Trying to explain the emergence of programmatic parties requires looking not just at how parties maintain support with individual voters during campaigns, but at how these linkages with voters and groups get accommodated and reinforced in policy making.

Conceptualizing programmatic competition through party strategies also forces us to examine the institutions that foster or preclude programmatic politics. Bureaucracies may be weak, for example, and lack safeguards against predation by political parties. Or state administrative capacity may be too poorly developed to implement broad national policies. But the ways that parties govern society (through the laws they pass and the institutions they create) in turn condition the ways they seek votes. A theory of the decline in clientelism needs to take into account not only the grounds on which parties compete and the strategies they use in elections, but also the institutional environment in which parties operate.

The Economic Costs of Clientelism

When parties that rely on clientelistic strategies win elections, they are unlikely to unilaterally abandon clientelism for programmatic politics. Instead, parties "will construct a strong, broadly based party organization only if it is necessary for them to do so in order to gain, retain, or exercise power" (Shefter 1994, 5). Further, parties are likely to develop nonclientelistic strategies only if their electoral losses can be attributed to opposition to clientelism.

Using this logic, we can hypothesize that even in countries without electorally viable external parties, powerful interests can also compel parties to adopt broad-based programmatic organization. Organized and powerful political opposition to patronage can emerge from new sources of political and economic power that are disadvantaged by clientelistic politics. Capitalist interests can be crucial to programmatic reforms when they stand to benefit from predictability and uniformity in policy. When business acts as the equivalent of an externally mobilized group that enters politics with a strong policy agenda, this decreases the efficacy of clientelistic appeals and forces parties to compete on policy grounds (Shefter 1994). When the state does not serve the interests of business (defined here as the owners and managers in capitalist systems of production) business interests become increasingly politicized. Industrialization leads to "the development of a competitive and differentiated society ... [which] provides the necessary preconditions for the emergence of the politics of individual opinions and interest" (Nossiter 1975, 107).

The costs of clientelism come in the form of unpredictability and inefficiency in policy making and governance. Where patronage is widely used, the bureaucracy cannot be trusted to implement policies successfully or to develop expertise in policy areas. Parties that rely on patronage do not build effective institutions to administer policy. The interests most affected by weak administrative apparatuses are those that require uniformity and standardization over time, in order to carry out business transactions and facilitate trade. Clientelistic strategies such as patronage or distributive policy impose broad social costs while narrowly directing private benefits, so "no constituent group may be able to organize effectively" to oppose them (Goldin and Libecap 1994, 10). Business is far more likely than disparate citizen groups to be able to delineate, and articulate, the negative effects of clientelism.

Any sector that relies on long-term predictable policy is negatively impacted by poor governance, although some more so than others. Those in extractive industries may only need to ensure monopolistic access to land and a plentiful and cheap supply of labor. Complex manufacturing processes, however, that rely on the supply and transport of raw materials and that require distribution of finished products across a national consumer market are far more likely to depend on government services – infrastructure, transportation, regulation of pricing, efficient capital markets – to operate successfully. In the finance sector, business needs to trust the government for reliable contract enforcement and predictable monetary policy. Therefore, although business is not a universal actor, the sectors that emerge in industrial economies are likely to require governance and policies distinct from agricultural and extractive economies. To the extent that clientelism precludes the development of coherent national institutions and policies, the clear losers are actors who need to predict the ways in which policies will impact business cycles, market failures, and depressions. Over time, these losers come to articulate alternatives to the status quo in order to secure more effective forms of service delivery and more consistent national policies.

The conventional wisdom about business and clientelism, or democratic reforms in general, at least in the postwar period in advanced industrial democracies, is that business is perhaps the foremost recipient of favorable policies from the government. Business is often assumed to pursue its own interests at the expense of labor; through the military-industrial complex or public-private partnerships, business may also profit at public expense. Of the many competing interests in democratic societies, capitalist employers, producers, industrialists, and financiers have privileged, if not exclusive, access to politics. Business interests also often align with conservative political forces against trade unions, government regulation, and social or welfare policy. In contemporary politics, the myriad links between the private sector and political officials have been a defining feature of national politics.

Scholars of business and politics often focus on how "the structure of capitalism advantages all business actors in the same way against non-business actors," without attention to the mutual dependencies between business and the state (Culpepper 2015, 391). In contemporary politics, there is ample evidence that business is a powerful political actor. Through lobbying and campaign finance, business interest groups can wield significant influence in many aspects of policy.

However, the political influence of business throughout history has often been assumed rather than empirically demonstrated. Capitalism and democracy have evolved together for over a century, yet there has been relatively little scholarly attention to the historical development of linkages between business and parties. Attention to nonbusiness actors can lead us to overlook the times when business interests converge with the public interest. More importantly, it overlooks the way that business preferences shape democratic institutions.

Most analyses of business's privileged role employ a framework of interest group politics. Interest groups make claims for the "establishment, maintenance, or enhancement of forms of behavior" implied by shared attitudes

(Truman 1951). Their strategies rely on "close consultation with political and administrative leaders" through financial resources, substantive expertise, and inclusion in congressional constituencies (Walker 1991). Businesses face fewer collective action obstacles to organizing – they are economically and geographically concentrated and relatively small in number. They also marshal hefty financial resources to hire lobbyists and public relations experts to manage their political ties. Pluralist democracies therefore inevitably give rise to powerful, concentrated business interests.

CAPITALIST DEMANDS FOR PROGRAMMATIC REFORMS

In theory, state building is a prerequisite for programmatic politics, which relies on the promise and delivery of public goods. The most basic state institutions are perhaps obvious – tax collection, statistical and auditing agencies, and agencies designed to oversee and implement policies in specific areas, including defense or social welfare. As states oversee increasingly complex economies and societies, they also create regulatory agencies that impose direct constraints on private actors (Lowi 1972) and development agencies to assist the health and welfare of the population.

There is a variable that has yet to be rigorously integrated into the study of clientelism: capitalism. Of course, there is a robust literature on economic development and clientelism in the form of modernization theory, which argues that economic growth and its attendant trends – urbanization, literacy, communications technology, education – spur democratization and demands for cleaner governance. There are numerous empirical findings demonstrating that higher incomes are associated with less bribery and patronage. However, modernization theory is not explicit about the way economic development happens. Further, it is agnostic about the precise interests that produce demands for public goods.

The demands of capitalists are likely to be important to political incentives to reform the state. Capitalism creates a distinct business class with a vested interest in effective governing institutions, since businesses require different outputs from the state than average citizens. They need protection of property rights, enforcement of contracts, mediation of competing interests, and predictable long-term policy arrangements. Once capitalism is established, its success becomes integral to other interests in society. Labor benefits from higher wages; agriculture benefits from greater consumption; politicians benefit from higher tax receipts. Capitalism then generates competition for redistribution through the political arena, with labor and citizens' groups demanding redistribution or protection, and capitalists vying for lower tax rates or favorable policy. As Khan (2005) shows, parties are then forced to make a *public* case for policies that benefit collective interests, whether those interests are "class, regional, or sectoral" (p. 716). Similarly, Grzymala-Busse (2008) notes that where feedback from the capitalist sector is weak, the state faces less pressure to provide public goods.[3]

For these scholars, capitalism provides a way to build state capacity and to place the burden on parties to mediate competing political interests. Two outcomes are possible. The first is that capitalism can play a fundamental role in generating programmatic competition. Capitalist interests are systematically disadvantaged by reliance on clientelism, which weakens state capacity and relies on highly discretionary, targeted relationships with politicians rather than predictable and efficient institutional arrangements. The second possible outcome is that capitalists capture state institutions in the process of reform and rely on corrupt ties to the state to engage in capitalist rent-seeking and extraction (Hellman 1998).

The relationship between capitalism and clientelism is attenuated – it works through state institutions. Because patronage and weak state capacity often go hand in hand, the argument here is that capitalist interests are distinct from those of the amorphous "wealthy." Merchants and manufacturers in the capitalist class attach a different political value to general services. They require "services of an indefinite duration, covering somewhat nebulous fields" (Wiebe 1967, 184), including effective provision of goods, regulation to protect against monopolistic practices, and protection from the exigencies of the market (Reid and Kurth 1988).

Capitalist Support for Social Policy

Landmark social policies such as collective bargaining and workers' insurance represented a triumph over business interests. In debates about the origins of the welfare state and variation in social policies across advanced democracies, business is often assumed to be opposed to national regulation and prolabor policies. Power resources theory, for example, argues that it is the strength of the political left (relative to conservative business forces) that determines how expansive welfare policies are. In the United States in particular, business has resisted progressive social policies in banking, conservation, and regulation (Carpenter 2001). The reasoning behind business opposition to social policy is rather intuitive: Businesses pursue twin goals of extracting rents and repressing labor, both of which are undermined by the welfare state.

However, comparative historical research has shown that business has been critical in coalitions behind social policies and the welfare state (Mares 2003a; Martin 2000). In a debate over New Deal policies, Swenson, rebutting Pierson

---

[3] As Swenson (2002) and Mares (2003a) have shown, capitalists have also supported social welfare policies and centralized industrial relations institutions. While these policies seem to go against capitalists' material self-interest, a sector or firm's export orientation and exposure to risk make greater regulation or redistribution advantageous. In other words, it is important to examine variation within capitalist interests.

and Hacker's claims about business hostility to the welfare state, has shown that many New Deal policies were carefully crafted with the approval, if not the outright assistance, of business (Swenson 1997; 2002). He finds that employers support regulatory policies when there is little risk or even a net benefit, and "interests often quickly dissolve ideological sentiments against government regulation" (Swenson 2002, 2).

There are notable cases in Scandinavia and Western Europe in which employers prefer to centralize bargaining arrangements between capital and labor and prefer generous welfare states. Business preferences are *sector specific*: Depending on a firm's exposure to risk and vulnerability to labor conflict, its preferences may dovetail with those of labor. Swenson argues that sectors that are more exposed to the market, rather than sheltered, prefer to centralize industrial relations institutions. Export-oriented firms need both to attract labor from sheltered producers who offer higher wages and to insulate themselves against conflict with labor (Swenson 1991). Large manufacturing firms in Denmark and Sweden, for example, historically supported centralized bargaining arrangements (Thelen 2001). Mares (2003a; 2003b) also shows that intersectoral conflict over risk redistribution and skilled labor explains variation in business support for specific types of national insurance schemes.

Business is also crucial in *cross-class alliances* that support social reforms. In his study of the New Deal, Swenson (1997; 2002) finds that business leaders in the United States supported wage and hour regulation, social security, and protection of unions. Rather than place direct pressure on politicians, business leaders instead signaled to political officials that they would support the industrial arrangements brought on by New Deal reforms. Gordon (1994) also shows that businesses called for the New Deal as a solution to the private sector's inability to manage industrial relations in the early decades of the twentieth century.

The social welfare literature shows that business organization can create preferences for centralized institutions and government regulation, rather than private, market solutions. Writing about the United States, Mizruchi (2013) also finds that the unification of the business elite in the postwar period led to political moderation and pragmatism. Business leaders used their political power to lobby for public goods, such as national infrastructure and expansion of the social safety net. They accepted the legitimacy of federal regulation and labor unions and focused on legislative compromise rather than political opposition to government policies. The literature on industrial relations and social policy reveals that business is hardly a consistent opponent of reform. Although firms may have to pay more for national insurance schemes, or provide concessions to labor when the state centralizes industrial relations, these policies can also advance the material interests of business.

Just as the welfare state should not be seen as indicating a decline of capitalist power, institutional reforms to regulate the private sector should not be seen as antithetical to business interests. Although reformer groups sought regulatory laws as well, regulation was not simply a byproduct of mass support, since capital can "regroup and shift the sands of electoral and parliamentary support" (Swenson 2002, 2). Gordon (1994) also finds that groundbreaking labor legislation in the United States was modeled on the private policies that businesses had established. For decades before the New Deal, business had pursued recovery politics at the state level, or even simply among themselves. But they remained dogged by market chaos and uncertainty, ultimately lobbying for national labor legislation. In Britain, Hay (1977) finds that businesses were early drafters and supporters of British health insurance, largely because it would resolve inefficiencies and mitigate crises.

Capitalist Mobilization against Clientelism

Clientelistic strategies, unlike welfare and redistributive policies, do not always reward socially defined groups, nor do they align with preindustrial cleavages of laborers and producers. Indeed, part of what makes clientelism so effective is that parties can construct haphazard coalitions among diverse sets of interests to secure electoral victory. While individual businesses may benefit from clientelistic relationships with parties, entire sectors are better served by programmatic politics. Organization helps businesses overcome collective action problems inherent in clientelism, and the development of new forms of business organization changes what the voice of business seeks. Businesses therefore become proponents of not only programmatic reforms and progressive policies, but also regulation, since "regulation is acquired by the industry and is designed and operated primarily for its benefit" (Stigler 1971, 3).[4] Regulatory policy helps businesses control market entry, shift costs to the state, and promote critical infrastructure. Firms often see legislation as a way to "'buy' justice relative to individuals and smaller businesses" by shifting the arena of political contestation from costly litigation battles to the legislature and bureaucracy. (Glaeser and Shleifer 2003, 413).

The private sector stands to gain from coherent development outcomes in policy. In the context of patronage, elected officials only serve the material interests of specific groups and voters. This has an impact on governance, since it limits the state's administrative capacities and obviates the creation of robust economic and political institutions. Given that businesses pursue social and democratic reforms when it is in their interest to do so, it seems logical that businesses might have an interest against clientelistic modes of governance. Businesses therefore can serve as a critical promoter of programmatic reforms (Figure 1.1).

However, business preferences for programmatic politics alone cannot change party strategies. Therefore, we turn to the mechanisms that underlie

---

[4] See also McChesney 1987; Peltzman 1976; and Posner 1974.

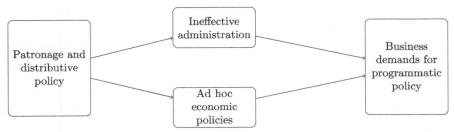

FIGURE 1.1 The economic costs of clientelism.

the relationship between business preferences for programs and programmatic reforms. In order for businesses to effect a decline in clientelism, they must (1) be organized enough to wield political power – to serve as a bulwark against parties – and (2) demand specific types of reforms that facilitate programmatic competition.

Business Organization

Industrial economies do not require specific forms of commercial organization; industries may be composed of small, family-owned firms or can be organized by corporations in which a class of managers oversees labor and production. The corporate form became widespread in the United States in the late nineteenth century, when railways rationalized their business methods. Within corporations, new classes of professional managers developed technical expertise and adopted principles associated with scientific management to solve problems. Corporations also created new means of organizing competitive markets through pooling and mergers. By developing new principles of hierarchy and efficiency among themselves, the industrial sector generated models that could be applied to government administration.

Businesses also seek to coordinate their activities in periods marked by economic instability and market competition. Trade associations, for example, allow firms to share information on production and prices. This can help stabilize markets and establish entry requirements for new firms. And across sectors, voluntary business associations aim to aggregate and articulate interests for the commercial community as a whole.

Business organization is therefore necessary for businesses to coordinate their goals and to identify as a group of actors with common interests. Whiskey producers may not share much in common with textile manufacturers or oil refiners, but organization allows them to advocate for policies that facilitate trade and economic growth irrespective of industry. And when business becomes interested in politics, it begins to assume the contours of an interest group, which Clemens (1997, 2) defines as a "political organization mobilized around specific issues or policy demands and sustained not only by financial resources but by extra-partisan voting blocs."

The level of employer coordination is another important determinant of capitalist support for social policy. When firms are organized across sectors into national associations, and therefore speak with a unified voice on matters of national policy, there tends to be greater centralization of industrial relations institutions. Employer coordination through national peak associations is also correlated with higher levels of redistribution.

The scale of the organization shapes the likelihood that it can succeed in fulfilling its political goals. In literature on coordinated and liberal market economies, scholars have found that corporatist arrangements – in which the state negotiates with representatives of nationally organized peak associations of laborers and employers – can lead to more redistributive and social policies. In liberal market economies, on the other hand, disparate groups representing different sectors of business and labor must compete for political power. This literature predicts that reforms are probably more likely under coordinated market economies than their liberal counterparts. However, recent work by Martin and Swank (2012) and Iverson and Soskice (2009) sheds light on the relationship between industrial relations and electoral politics between 1870 and 1950. Both find that when business interests were organized into national associations, they were critical to redistributive and egalitarian policies. Business organization is therefore critical to advancing programmatic reforms, since businesses need to articulate their demands collectively (Figure 1.2).

Businesses are best served by reforms that generate efficiency, standardization, and predictability in government. If business simply wants advantageous economic policy, it can lobby for specific laws, such as tariffs, trade policies, and patent protections. But when business requires more effective government on the whole, it instead demands institutional improvements such as meritocratic bureaucracy and expansion of regulatory capacities (Wiebe 1967). Trade associations and business organizations cannot effectively monitor and regulate markets when they cannot predict state policies or trust that policies will be administered impartially.

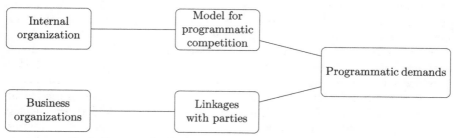

FIGURE 1.2 Capitalist organization.

In the twentieth century, business came to occupy a privileged position among interest groups in advanced industrial democracies (Lindblom 1977), but this position was not the inevitable result of economic power. Business became an important political player by organizing collectively and then using political channels to persuade political parties to adopt new strategies. As Hart (2004) has observed, business is not in itself an interest group. Business is instead a class of economic actors composed of producers, bankers, merchants, and other interests that may run counter to each other. I therefore argue that organization is a critical component in this account of how business becomes politically involved. As Mathias (1983) explains, "national associations were very often at their most active just when the structure of an industry was changing most rapidly" (p. 356). That is, organization was a solution to the chaos of the market; businesses organized not in response to labor, but instead when "factions of an industry seek government aid or protection from their competitors" (Walker 1991, 29).

Managerial Capitalism

The idea that business provides a model for government institutions is not new; Weber, for example, included modern capitalist enterprises in his study of bureaucracy. Corporations, like governments, have different principles of organization: Large family firms may privilege personalistic recruitment, promotion, and ownership, while managerial firms are organized by hierarchical, meritocratic management. Innovations in the corporate form are often tools of effective administration that translate easily to government institutions. Therefore, strengthening state capacity and building a bureaucracy are ways that business can enact administrative coherence in government policy.

For most of the nineteenth century, industry had been small scale and run not by firms, but by families. This "personal capitalism," as noted business historian Alfred Chandler (1977) termed it, could not produce manufactured goods on a large scale. Large industries became dominated by corporations that attached increasing value to efficiency, hierarchy, and management. Soon these corporations dominated industry, replacing (or purchasing) many regional and family firms. Managerial capitalism entailed mass production and distribution, multifunctional and integrated departments, and capital-intensive, rather than labor-intensive, practices. By the early twentieth century, corporations had national reach, "transcend[ing] any specific place – to be centered nowhere in the process of being everywhere" (Blumin 2000, 859).

Corporations were not simply larger versions of family firms, though. The critical change that occurred among firms was the use and expansion of management. Managerial capitalism entailed the rise of the large-scale corporation, which "dominated major sectors of the economy ... alter[ing] the basic structure of these sectors and of the economy as a whole" (Chandler 1977, 10). Through emerging management practices, firms developed new standards for production. Professional managers used scientific principles and technocratic approaches to ensure the consistent application of solutions rather than ad hoc problem solving. Management also allowed for vertical and horizontal integration and streamlined business practices across departments and industries.

Corporations adopted distinct operating units, administered by a hierarchy of salaried, middle-, and top-level managers. Management allowed corporations to adapt to competitive pressure, source raw materials, and find new markets for finished goods. Management became a profession in itself, as managers sought promotion and advancement based on performance and skill rather than personal connections to owners – indeed, one of the critical distinguishing features of management was its wholesale separation from ownership and financiers. Management expanded to a field complete with formal training, educational programs, professional journals, and associations (Chandler 1977). The structure of corporate organization was increasingly hierarchical and centrally managed.

The shift from personal to managerial capitalism, as practiced by large corporations, reflected an administrative logic that transferred easily to the political arena. The use of professional managers meant that expertise was increasingly seen as a product not of experience on the shop floor but, instead, of know-how in scientific principles and technocratic rationality. Further, emphasis on hierarchy created accountability and predictability in management decisions. These values influenced models of government institutions and administration. Through principles of expertise and bureaucratic administration, businesses developed ideas for how to govern complex economic areas (Tarr 1984). Managerial capitalism also created demand for such governance; as firms became national in scope and expanded to new markets, they needed to secure inputs across wider territories and became more dependent on infrastructure. Put simply, through new management practices, corporations developed their own forms of bureaucratic administration and saw in them a model for government institutions (Galambos 1970; Walker 1991).

Party Institutionalization

Both clientelistic and programmatic politics require a significant organizational investment from parties; there is not a straightforward relationship between the strength of a party's organization and the type of linkages it fosters with voters. As Hagopian et al. (2009) point out, "party strength, of course, can be based on different things, and the emergence of party-oriented legislators provides no assurance that party competition and party–citizen linkages will become more programmatic" (p. 367). Political machines, such as the Peronist party in Argentina and Tammany Hall in nineteenth-century New York, spent enormous resources on local brokers and monitors to keep tabs on voters and to distribute goods to party supporters (Levitsky 2007; Stokes et al. 2013). Kitschelt and Wilkinson (2007) also argue that it is entirely possible for parties with robust platforms and policies to engage in clientelistic appeals, noting that parties in Italy, Japan, and Austria maintain deeply embedded clientelistic ties to their base.

Programmatic parties are also embedded in society. They have distinctive platforms and spend their resources aggregating and mediating competing interests in society, enacting legislative programs, and providing information and constituency service to voters. These mass parties have professional staff and offices at the local and national levels. Building programmatic party organization requires maintaining ties to a variety of civic, economic, and religious groups, since parties become coalitions of interests brought together by some measure of ideological coherence.

How do parties recruit volunteers and activists, and how do they establish professional party organizations? In much of the literature on clientelistic brokers, reliance on brokers as independent agents signals low organizational party capacity, while parties that use partisan brokers are somewhat better organized. Brokers can serve as conduits of clientelism, and reducing party use of brokers can signal a shift to programmatic politics (Stokes et al. 2013). There is an element of uncertainty in relying on brokers, since information asymmetries prevent parties from knowing whether or not brokers will deliver votes. Programmatic parties, however, develop ongoing relationships with organized interests. They use their connections to these groups, including workplace unions, religious communities, and neighborhood associations, to develop policy messages (Hagopian 2015). Parties can then absorb brokers into rank-and-file members, such as party volunteers or local party leaders, signaling a socially embedded party.

Therefore, party linkages with society are necessary to understand how parties build organizational bases of support. Shefter's (1994) account of why competition was important was based on the fact that different types of parties – particularly those that emerged from societal institutions, such as labor groups and religious organizations – could use their ideological appeals to persuade voters. This emphasis on policy, combined with these parties' ties to social groups, mounted a serious challenge to clientelistic parties that could offer only handouts or jobs to voters. Therefore, it is not enough to show that competition increases or decreases opportunities for clientelism. Recent findings from the new wave of literature show that there are cases in which competition increases clientelism and cases in which it decreases clientelism. It is more important to focus on party attributes to explain how competition matters for programmatic and clientelistic outcomes.

As parties reconfigure state institutions to accommodate programmatic policies, their incentives to use clientelistic vote buying or patronage change. Once parties can tout their policy successes, they can "buy" votes more cheaply through promises of policy change. Further, they become invested in strengthening the institutions of the state so as to ensure that policies are carried out.

Contemporary examples show how the interrelationship of programmatic strategies leads parties to pursue alternatives to clientelism. In Latin America, for example, neoliberal reforms of the 1980s provided political parties with opportunities to reconfigure strategies across multiple levels of politics. In Brazil, the Party of Brazilian Social Democracy (PSDB) and the Workers' Party (PT) passed civil service reforms, depoliticized state assistance through conditional cash transfers, reformed pensions, and adopted budgets with caps on government payrolls. The cumulative effect of legislative and state reforms was to deprive parties of many traditional clientelistic appeals and to create incentives for parties to adopt programmatic platforms (Hagopian 2015).

In new democracies, where the political landscape is highly uncertain, politicians will not be able to make programmatic electoral commitments. State institutions are underdeveloped, economic performance fluctuates unpredictably, and external actors make policy recommendations for which domestic parties cannot claim credit. But middle-income countries have larger states and tax bases that parties can tap into and an industrializing society with laborers who need public sector employment (Kitschelt and Kselman 2013, 1461). As industrialization proceeds, states with established administrative institutions and diversified economies that can weather price shocks lend themselves to programmatic competition.

Testing a theory of the relationship between capitalism and programmatic politics therefore requires close examination of the way parties *respond* to capitalist demands against clientelism. Where parties try to build both programmatic policy and professional organization, they can successfully accommodate business demands for reform.

EMPIRICAL STRATEGY

Using the cases of the United States and Great Britain, I illustrate two possibilities for transitions to programmatic politics. In both cases, political parties were organized to serve clientelistic outcomes as they mobilized voters for most of the nineteenth century. In both cases, business interests coalesced against reliance on patronage and demanded that parties reform the state to serve economic interests by improving bureaucratic quality and regulatory oversight. And in both cases, parties engaged in a period of state building that ultimately provided a foundation on which they could build programmatic messages and policies. Where they differ is in the level and timing of party organization, which then determined how parties responded to capitalist pressure.

I use data gathered on clientelistic politics in the nineteenth century, as well as archives of political parties and business groups. I explicate the relationship between business and clientelism over a similar period of time in both countries to demonstrate that the same phenomena were at work. Britain and the United States are usually considered similar with regard to clientelism: Stokes (2013) shows that vote buying declined earlier in Britain than in the United States but that the patterns were similar in both countries. Further, Britain and the United

States often cluster together in the literature on the political economy of advanced democracies. They share institutional similarities (first-past-the-post, two-party electoral systems) as well as ideational and ideological ones (laissez-faire policies, pluralist rather than corporatist industrial organization). As liberal market economies, they exhibit similar outcomes with respect to social policy and redistribution.

While many studies of clientelism examine the immediate context of vote buying, such as the income level of voters or the level of electoral competition in a district, this analysis examines how parties come to rely on clientelism as an overarching strategy of governance: how parties use clientelism not only to win votes, but also to shape policy, to distribute state resources, and to staff state offices. Clientelism is not simply a one-shot transaction, and politicians do not choose between clientelistic and programmatic promises in each election cycle. Instead, moving away from a clientelistic mode of governance involves a process of reforming state institutions, expanding state capacity, and developing coherent and ideologically differentiated policy programs. While these are not outcomes that easily lend themselves to measurement, I use archival materials from congressional and parliamentary investigations to measure the rise and decline of clientelistic strategies over time.

In order to test a theory of business preferences for programmatic reforms, this book compares the cases of Britain and the United States. It elucidates the strategic interaction of businesses and parties, and the timing of party organization relative to the development of the political organization of business, to explain how parties move away from clientelistic modes of governance over the course of decades. This theory is best tested using comparative historical analysis, a method of analysis that is attentive to the dynamic nature of political reforms (Pierson and Skocpol 2002). This method allows examination of the changing relationship between organized business and parties, with particular focus on the sequencing of political reforms. I use archival materials from business organizations to trace the politicization of business preferences and to show how capitalists came to see themselves as a distinct class of political actors in pursuit of reform. I then document how parties responded to demands from these new interests in society. The comparative historical method allows the relationship between business and parties to be seen as contingent, rather than fixed, and the evolution of this relationship over time to be traced.

The theory advanced here is less about institutions per se than about strategic interaction between political parties and organized interests (Capoccia and Ziblatt 2010). Rather than viewing history as a set of institutional outcomes determined by distant historical correlates, I instead try to offer a microfoundational account of the relationship between politically mobilized actors and the strategies adopted by parties. I therefore depart from scholars of historical institutionalism who focus on critical junctures or distinct moments of legislative reform, because a few *episodes* of reform are less important in this analysis than the incremental *processes* by which emerging politically powerful actors helped parties create new linkages with citizens. Institutions serve as a mediating factor, rather than an outcome.

Like many scholars working in the tradition of comparative historical analysis or American political development, the approach in this book privileges the specific dynamics of each case rather than the pursuit of a generalizable theory of clientelistic reform. However, the analysis shows that a business class that is nationally organized, with preferences for effective government, can pressure clientelistic parties to adopt programmatic reforms. The theory's general precepts can be reduced to the idea that when economically powerful actors seek more effective governance, they can serve as bulwarks against clientelistic governance. This conclusion can travel to countries besides the United States and Britain – to any polity in which economic actors require effective state services.

By using a comparative historical approach, the rest of this book lays out how the interests of important actors – new classes of capitalists, as well as party leaders – changed over a few decades. It shows how capitalist organization helped businesses overcome sectoral and regional divisions to articulate collective, national needs. Finally, it shows how the legacy of clientelistic politics can survive in administrative institutions when parties rely too heavily on business input.

2

Clientelism as a Governing Strategy in the United States

In a congressional election in Pennsylvania in 1868, an election agent working for a Democratic candidate to the House of Representatives went to a railway foreman for help securing votes. The agent paid the foreman both to get the voters drunk and to cover the voters' railway fees to travel to and from the precinct. When the foreman cautioned that such tactics were "too barefaced" to avoid detection, the agent replied, "Pshaw! What is the ballot box but a farce?" (Bensel 2004, 162). American electoral history is replete with accounts of raucous election campaigns, with candidates supplying generous amounts of food, alcohol, and entertainment for voters.

Widespread clientelism in elections throughout the nineteenth century reflected a similar lack of policy priorities in governing. Parties relied on clientelism not only to win votes, but also to distribute government resources. After Andrew Jackson was elected president in 1828, both the Democratic and Republican parties engaged in clientelism, both in elections and in staffing state offices through patronage. Historians refer to this period of electoral competition and party building as the Second Party System, when suffrage expanded and elections became more competitive. Clientelism provided a way for parties to develop national organizations, mobilize loyal bases of support, and provide for their constituents through handouts and jobs. Clientelism was also an effective way to govern the nascent industrial economy, providing a consistent, even if not ideological, way to allocate state resources. Senators and representatives legislated through private bills, granting funds and contracts to local individuals and corporations for development projects. Just as party competition after Jackson resulted in more vote-buying, parties also expanded state activity through patronage and pork. Both strategies provided ways for parties to facilitate economic development given the limited administrative capacities of the state. But clientelism became part of broader debates about the role and size of government, and toward the late nineteenth century, the pitfalls of relying on pork and patronage were becoming pronounced. This chapter describes how American parties increasingly relied on, and adapted, clientelism as a governing strategy.

VOTE BUYING AND CLIENTELISM IN NATIONAL ELECTIONS

At the time of the nation's founding, there was widespread variation in the franchise. Each state set its own voting requirements based on considerations such as property ownership, residency, income, and mental competency. Because party labels in the early republic fluctuated, elections were governed by local, often unaffiliated party organizations. The administration of elections also varied – some elections were conducted *viva voce* and others through ballots. Election administrators were drawn from local judges and magistrates and were responsible for registering voters, protecting ballot boxes, and tallying vote results. The context of elections is important to understanding why clientelistic tactics were widespread and why they are difficult to uncover. Given the lax environment in which elections took place, it was easy for candidates and election officials to monitor the choices of voters.

The election of Jackson in 1828 ushered in a new period: one of feverish excitement over elections, marked by high levels of voter turnout and newspaper readership. Elections became celebratory events, and the period of the 1840s–1880s is considered a "golden age" of popular participation (Gienapp 1982; McCormick 1966; Renda 1997; Williamson 1960). This period was dominated by the Democratic and Republican parties at the state level. Many states loosened their suffrage restrictions; by 1840, most non-property-owning white males could vote.

However, this was also a period of widespread electoral abuse. Successful candidates secured victory through bribes and manipulation of ballots (Altschuler and Blumin 2000; Bensel 2004). To the extent that candidates campaigned on issues, they relied on personal vituperation and character attacks or on symbols to invoke national pride and appeals to virtue (Aldrich 1995). It is difficult to ascertain the extent of clientelistic practices, since they "tend to be reported anecdotally, concealed whenever possible, and seldom studied systematically" (Silbey et al. 1978, 138).

The secondary literature on nineteenth-century electoral politics focuses on outright cases of fraud, such as stealing ballot boxes or padding registration lists, alongside cases of clientelism. The distinction is important, because whereas election fraud is a criminal perversion of the democratic process, clientelism involves transactions and accountability between politicians and voters. Accounts of distributing money and alcohol for votes appear as early as the pre-Revolutionary period, in elections to the Virginia House of Burgesses. Not only did George Washington dispense liquor to voters, but James Madison also appealed an election loss upon learning that his opponent had offered free whiskey. (He lost his appeal.)

Jacksonian politics inaugurated decades of vote buying, which peaked in the late nineteenth century. In a sweeping study of newspaper accounts, local histories, and court cases, Argersinger finds "incontrovertible evidence" of vote buying in the nineteenth century, particularly during the Gilded Age (Argersinger 1985). Up to 90 percent of voters in Adams County, Ohio, sold their votes in the 1890s, for example, and a third of voters in New Jersey consistently sold their votes as well (Reynolds 1980). In 1880, an Indiana Democratic chairman instructed party workers to "organize some plan to keep even with" the fraudulent activities of Republicans, while a Republican party leader advised candidates about the "large purchasable element among the voters" (Argersinger 1985, 678).[1] In rural areas, many reports of vote buying were concentrated in the 1880s and 1890s, and Sikes (1928) concluded that practices such as bribery and intimidation were less prevalent in the late 1920s compared to a couple of decades earlier.

Further, clientelism was not confined to specific areas of the country, although vote buying is often associated with political machines. The political machine emerged in the late nineteenth century; by 1890, machine bosses controlled half of the largest cities in the country (Erie 1988, 2). Machines were distinguished by one political party "captur[ing] the local governing apparatus and centraliz[ing] power in a given jurisdiction," and they were associated with reliance on patronage and spoils to ensure loyalty (Trounstine 2006, 881). Because machine bosses controlled hundreds of local and municipal offices, they could exchange jobs for votes and could use control over offices to ensure high turnout in elections (Wolfinger 1972). Patronage was so widespread that civil service wages were significantly higher in cities governed by machines than they were in similarly sized cities around the turn of the century (Troesken 2009).

In addition to dispensing jobs, machine bosses were also known for their largesse during elections, providing food, alcohol, and money to voters. George Washington Plunkitt, a well-known boss of Tammany Hall, remarked that "some people say they can't understand what becomes of all the money that's collected for campaigns. They would understand fast enough if they were district lead-em. There's never been half enough money to go around." In cities, embedded patronage networks led machine bosses to extort money from local businessowners and to grant favorable contracts and legal exceptions to party supporters (Banfield and Wilson 1963; Erie 1988; Stone 1996).

While machines lasted for decades in many American cities, they peaked around the same period that contested elections peaked in Congress, roughly the 1870s through the 1890s. In the presidential election of 1868, the Tweed

---

[1] Many first-hand accounts of electoral politics in the nineteenth century use "fraud" and "bribery" interchangeably. Most states had proscriptions on electoral bribery, although it was also common practice.

machine in New York naturalized 50,000 ineligible aliens, and New York State went Democratic by 10,000 votes. The House created the Select Committee on Alleged New York Election Frauds in the 40th Congress (1870), and in 1871, the second of the Enforcement Acts allowed federal regulation of elections in cities with more than 20,000 people. The act allowed citizens (or parties) to petition U.S. Circuit Courts for federal marshals and deputies in polling places where fraud was likely. Between 1871 and 1894 (when the law was repealed), it was enforced in cities run by machines such as Boston, New York, Brooklyn, Jersey City, Baltimore, Philadelphia, Chicago, and San Francisco (Burke 1970, 17). Records from the Department of Justice show widespread vote buying on the part of city bosses.

Contested Elections to the U.S. Congress

Because descriptive accounts of the extent of clientelism vary so widely, they are unreliable as sources of systematic data for electoral clientelism (Kuo and Teorell 2016). Skeptics of nineteenth-century bribery have noted, for example, that "the evidence to demonstrate the existence of election fraud in the literature is not only anecdotal, it is unsystematic, impressionistic, and by and large inconclusive" (Allen and Allen 1981, 167).

While the very nature of electoral clientelism makes it difficult to capture empirically, contested elections to the House of Representatives provide a previously overlooked source of data on electoral clientelism. The House is tasked with seating its own members; issues that arise in elections to the House are resolved by the House itself, rather than through the courts. A contested election is "the filing of proceedings to bar the right to a seat of a Member-elect based upon a question concerning the electoral process." The Committee on Elections was the first standing committee established by the House of Representatives during Congress's inaugural session. The committee's duties included overseeing certificates of elections, qualifications of members, and "such matters as shall or may come in question." From 1789 to 1989, there were 590 contests in the House; in 20 percent, the contestant, or individual disputing the election, eventually won the seat. Most contests concern electoral fraud, irregularities, vote buying, and improper ballots or ballot counting (Martis 1989).

Many scholars have utilized contested elections as a promising source of data on electoral abuse outside the United States. Seymour conducted an exhaustive study of contested elections in Britain; more recently, Kam and Stokes used election contests to estimate the extent of bribery in Victorian elections (Kam 2011; Seymour 1915; Stokes 2013). Contests have also been used to study elections in Costa Rica (Lehoucq and Molina 2002), Germany (Anderson 2000; Ziblatt 2009), and Sweden (Teorell 2016).

In the United States, the number of election contests began to rise in the mid-nineteenth century, peaking with the 40th–60th Congresses (1867–1907). Candidates alleged many instances of vote buying, intimidation, and influence in national elections. The Committee on Elections, which was responsible for seating members of the House of Representatives, had to be divided into three separate committees, as its caseload dramatically expanded in the 54th Congress (1895–97), with a record thirty-eight petitions filed. The evidence from these contests has been used to detail the venal nature of elections in the late nineteenth century (Altschuler and Blumin 2000; Argersinger 1985; Bensel 2004). Candidates offered whiskey, bacon, and cash to voters; in areas dominated by landlords or large businesses, voters were also threatened with loss of housing or employment for failing to vote the right way. These cases, which undoubtedly underrepresent the instances of clientelism in the late nineteenth century, indicate that many candidates persuaded voters not with issues but with material rewards.

Contested election cases are comparatively better than sources measuring clientelism through media reports or biographical accounts. First, they are based on a procedure that does not differ across the country, and that at least for most stretches of history has been fairly unified across time. The first election contest, filed in 1789 by David Ramsey against William Smith, concerned naturalization – specifically, whether the British-born Smith had been a citizen of the United States for the seven years the Constitution requires. Committee members took evidence from both contestant and contestee (the original winner of the election), including birth records, copies of state laws, and documents from the South Carolina Commissioners of the Treasury. They found that Smith was entitled to his seat and, in doing so, established rudimentary procedures to govern election contests.

For each contest thereafter, the committee therefore collected evidence and reported back to the House a recommendation in favor of the contestant, the contestee, or neither, in which case the seat was vacated. In 1851, the House established a uniform procedure governing election contests. Under these provisions, the contestant had to notify the contestee in writing, within thirty days after the announcement of the election result, of his intention to contest the election, stating all the grounds for the contest. The contestee then had thirty days to respond to the charges, which meant that the issues under consideration were to be articulated within at most sixty days after the electoral contest. The contesting parties then had sixty days to take testimony and gather other forms of evidence, a period of time that was extended to ninety days in 1873. To speed up the handling of these affairs, it was further enacted in 1887 that the briefs of the contestant and contestee, including all relevant evidence, had to be printed and filed with the clerk of the House before the meeting of Congress. After this, no major changes in procedure occurred until the passage of the Federal Contested Election Act in 1969. As a result of this unified federal procedure, the "rules of the game" concerning contested election cases are comparable across time and space for most of the nineteenth and twentieth centuries. They do not vary by state-specific legislation, the access and proliferation of media outlets, or other local peculiarities that could affect other potential sources of election fraud.

The contests are also adjudicated and litigated similarly to judicial trials. In 1929, the Supreme Court ruled that the Houses of Congress acted as "judicial tribunals" in deciding election contests (Dempsey 1956, 42). These contests rely heavily on evidence, witness testimony, hearings, and congressional investigations in order to reach a verdict. Although other considerations may also weigh on the matter, the evidentiary basis of these rulings has been adhered to in principle since the first efforts to regulate the taking of testimony in contested election cases in the late eighteenth century.

Until the mid-nineteenth century, only about three elections per congressional session were contested. Contests steadily increased following the Civil War, and in 1895, the House split the Committee on Elections into three committees to handle its increased caseload (Figure 2.1). While the sheer number of contests peaked in the late nineteenth century, the percentage of seats contested was at its highest in the Reconstruction period, with up to 10 percent of seats challenged from 1865 to 1890.

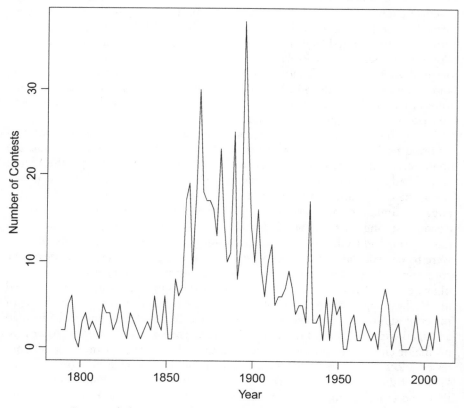

FIGURE 2.1 Contested elections to the House of Representatives, 1789–2011.
From the Center for Legislative Archives; author's calculations.

Because each state passes its own election administration laws, there are no set grounds on which contestants can claim their right to a seat. But the vast majority pertain to some aspect of electoral corruption. There were 609 contests between 1789 and 2010, and the records from these contests (contained in the holdings of the Committee on Elections in the National Archives) are voluminous. Each case includes official documents, beginning with the contestant's official notice enumerating his right to the seat.

Since the committee adheres to precedent when evaluating contests, clerks of the House created digests of contested elections as quick references for committee members. The digests summarize the reports issued by the committee and describe the grounds that the House considered most important when determining cases. Subsequent scholars have relied on these digests when classifying election contests. Dempsey sorted contests into fifteen categories, and Jenkins and Green adapted these categories in their analyses of contested elections (Green 2007; Jenkins 2004), distinguishing cases of corruption, fraud, or bribery, and cases of procedural irregularities with no intent of fraud. Their research focuses on the partisan makeup of Congress and the demographics of Southern districts in the Reconstruction period, rather than examining the extent or types of electoral corruption. In this period, Dempsey, and therefore Jenkins and Green, classify 36 percent of all cases as corrupt, and another 22 percent of cases as involving irregularities.

The digests that previous scholars relied on do not capture the full extent of contestants' claims about the conduct of elections. First, there are many more contests in the legislative archives than the digests cover. As Figure 2.2 indicates, while the proportion of contested seats was highest in the Reconstruction period, there were contests well into the first few decades of the twentieth century. Materials from these election cases, including contestants' claims and witness testimony, offer rich descriptions of electoral clientelism. The reports from the committee do not capture the extent of clientelism because House members were very reluctant to take charges of corruption into account when deciding election contests. In the report for the case of Gill versus Dyer in the 63rd Congress (1913), in which election judges forged ballots and falsely claimed that voters were illiterate or disabled in order to vote on their behalf, the committee wrote that "conspiracies and fraud are frequently not susceptible of direct or positive proof. They usually are connived at and concocted in secret." And when candidates had paid voters, the committee simply subtracted the number of bribed voters from the total vote count to reach a decision, rather than ruling primarily on grounds of bribery.

These contests reveal a great deal about clientelism in the nineteenth century. One of the earliest cases alleging bribery occurred in 1831, in the 22nd Congress. James Gadsden, a candidate for the House in the then-territory of Florida, contested the seat of Joseph White. Gadsden argued that White's party used "federal and local patronage of the Land office, Post office, Surveyor General's and Executive offices, General Land and Post office Departments ... to enable

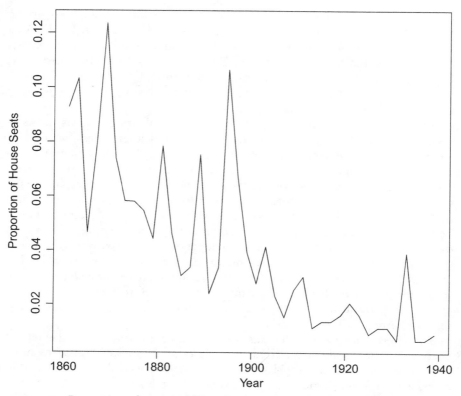

FIGURE 2.2 Proportion of contested House seats, 1860–1940. From the Center for Legislative Archives; author's calculations.

the Party to deal out doses of political quaker" and also that "grog shops were purchased, stalls set up, bets made, whiskey barrels opened, and every other corrupt and corrupting influence employed against me that malice could invent or ingenuity devise."[2]

In 1863, in the Pennsylvanian election of John Kline versus Leonard Myers, Kline alleged that "large sums of money were expended ... in procuring for you the votes of persons who were not qualified, and in inducing persons to vote who would otherwise have voted against you, and for me; and that a large number of persons were induced to vote for you by promises of gifts and rewards and by promises and offers of appointments, employment, and pecuniary benefits, and by threats of loss of appointments, employment, and pecuniary benefits."[3]

[2] HR 22A-D6.1, *Gadsden v. White*. Center for Legislative Archives.
[3] H. Misc. Doc. 26, 38th Congress, 1st Session, *Kline v. Myers*, December 8, 1863.

In an 1881 election in the Dakota territories, the Republican candidate for office, M. K. Armstrong, was accused of distributing cash and sacks of flour to voters. One witness also admitted to helping the candidate distribute whiskey.[4] In that election, members of local mills were instructed to deliver sacks of flour to specific citizens and areas of the congressional district. There was even a rumor that one man who brought in nineteen voters received two steers as a reward.[5] In the 44th Congress, in the 1875 election of Bromberg versus Haralson, generous amounts of food were provided to voters during campaigns, including bread and coffee. But the "Government Bacon" played a particular role; candidates offered voters large amounts of bacon and salt meat at many different locations around the town, and promised a barbecue on the day of the election.[6] Witnesses estimated that the offer and delivery of bacon greatly increased turnout – by up to 800 or 900 votes. When investigating this case, the House found clear evidence from shipping receipts that large amounts of bacon had been delivered to the district, but they could not determine whether or not the bacon influenced turnout.[7]

Thomas Reed, the famed Speaker of the House, was accused of bribing voters in the 1881 election to his seat. Witnesses reported being offered cash bribes, and his opponent, Samuel Anderson, accused him of asking employers to threaten their workers with loss of employment if they did not vote for Reed.[8] This case illuminates the way clientelism assisted parties and voters alike, with voters describing the quid pro quo relationships involved in clientelism. A few witnesses admitted to having received patronage positions from Reed, and one Republican supporter justified his vote on the grounds that "as long as I have lived here in Biddleford, I have never got a favor from a democrat, and I will never vote with them."[9] Another witness complained that "the Democrats were so damned mean they wouldn't pay anything."[10]

In 1883, the Committee on Elections found rampant evidence of bribery in the Indiana case of Kidd versus Steele; election volunteers were paid to distribute whiskey and money (between $3 and $5) to voters. Although the committee cited witness testimony admitting to being bribed, it refused to overturn the election.[11] A few years earlier, in 1880, the House had allowed the winner from the third district of Minnesota to retain his seat despite overwhelming evidence of electoral manipulation. Witness testimony revealed not only that the winner, William Washburn, had provided large amounts of cash and flour, he also paid

---

[4] H. Misc. Doc. 47, 42nd Congress, 2nd Session, *Burleigh v. Spink*, January 22, 1872.
[5] Ibid., p. 152.
[6] H. Misc. Doc. 47, 44th Congress, 1st Session, *Papers from the Case of Bromberg v. Haralson*, January 14, 1870.
[7] H. R. 294, 44th Congress, 1st Session, *Bromberg v. Haralson*, March 23, 1876.
[8] H. Misc. Doc. 13, 47th Congress, 1st Session, *Anderson v. Reed*, December 27, 1881.
[9] Ibid., p. 456.   [10] Ibid., p. 102.
[11] H. R. 4142, 49th Congress, 2nd Session, *Kidd v. Steele*, February 21, 1887.

railway workers a day's salary for turning out to vote.[12] In a Rhode Island election in 1885, voters received $2 to $3 for their votes; election agents circumvented the secret ballot by printing some ballots in a slightly different color.[13] In an election in 1900, in Kentucky, a candidate entered into a deal with local whiskey distillers and liquor dealers to bribe over 800 voters.[14]

These contests reveal how political candidates used clientelistic election tactics; in some cases, they also show how voters saw elections as opportunities for material transactions. Candidates from both parties used vote buying, and these tactics were common in both urban and rural areas. While contested elections do not constitute a perfect measure of clientelism – sometimes contests were filed for partisan advantage, and not all of them included allegations of vote buying – they nonetheless supplement the secondary accounts of widespread clientelism in the late nineteenth century.[15] By 1920, few elections to the House of Representatives were contested on claims of vote buying. Clientelism persisted at the local level, particularly in cities run by urban machines, but was far less widely used in congressional elections.

CLIENTELISM IN POLICY: PATRONAGE AND THE PORK BARREL

Most of the literature on clientelism in elections assumes that vote buying and programs are substitutes. Politicians choose to use clientelistic appeals with some voters, and programmatic ones with others (Wantchekon 2003). In debates about partisanship and redistribution, scholars have hypothesized that parties reward some voters with pork and other voters with programs. Cox and McCubbins (1986), for example, theorize that parties reward core supporters with favorable tax rates or patronage jobs, while Dixit and Londregan (1996) find that moderates and swing voters are more likely to receive pork. These studies indicate that distributional policies are part of partisan strategies to recruit or maintain support. They also assume, however, that politicians have a choice between programmatic and clientelistic strategies.

What these studies overlook is that political decisions to offer programmatic goods are constrained by the policies that the state can implement. One of the critical differences between clientelistic and programmatic strategies is that the timing of the distribution of benefits varies; in clientelistic exchange, voters often derive benefits at the time of the election, whereas in programmatic exchange, voters receive benefits as a result of electing politicians to office and securing policy goods. Voters will prefer clientelistic benefits if the probability that they will

---

[12] H. R. 1791, 46th Congress, 2nd Session, *Donnelly v. Washburn*, June 16, 1880.

[13] H. R. 3617, 49th Congress, 2nd Session, *Contested Election from Second District of Rhode Island: Page v. Pirce*, January 15, 1887.

[14] H. R. 1182, 62nd Congress, 2nd Session, *McLean v. Bowman*, August 13, 1912.

[15] See, e.g., the debate between Jenkins (2004) and Green (2007) concerning partisan motivations in filing election contests, and partisan decision making in the House Committee on Elections.

receive policy benefits is quite low. In other words, when politicians cannot credibly commit to policies, voters and politicians alike opt for clientelism.

Politicians in the nineteenth-century United States combined clientelistic campaign strategies with distributive legislative policies – those that targeted resources to discrete populations – not only as a way to recruit and to reward voters, but also as a broader policy of economic development. Expansion of the postal service, for example, not only provided a way to increase the delivery of goods, but also provided a politically expedient way to reward voters (with positions in the postal service) and districts (with new post offices). Similarly, providing federal grants to canal corporations fostered both trade and development while also promoting local partisan interests. By using distributive policies and patronage, clientelism became a "strategy for the acquisition, maintenance, and aggrandizement of political power" (Piattoni 2001, 2).

Clientelism persisted from the Jacksonian period through the late nineteenth century since parties engaged both in vote-buying and distributive politics. A shift to programmatic competition, though slow to develop, had increasing returns for parties, since it became more efficient to pass broad policies that appealed to large segments of voters rather than continue to use ad hoc, distributive policies. Cleaning up the civil service, a key element of programmatic reforms, also allowed politicians to credibly commit to policies that could be implemented by skilled bureaucrats.

Distributive Politics and Pork-Barrel Legislation

Lowi (1964, 690) famously observed that until the 1870s, American parties did not employ governing strategies related to discernible ideologies. Rather, they used distributive policy, which was

a term first coined for nineteenth-century land policies, but easily extended to include most contemporary public land and resource policies; rivers and harbors ("pork-barrel") programs; defense procurement and research and development; labor, business, and agricultural clientele services; and the traditional tariff ... These are policies that are virtually not policies at all but are highly individualized decisions that only by accumulation can be called a policy.

Lowi distinguishes distributive policy from redistributive policy, which transfers resources from some segments of society to others, and from regulatory policy, which targets groups rather than individuals and concentrates costs. These types of policy do not easily map onto programmatic and clientelistic categories, but distributive policy is often clientelistic – either on its face or in practice. Regulatory and redistributive policy, on the other hand, may still benefit some groups over others, but are nonetheless public policies. Although political scientists differentiate between these types of policies in general, it is difficult to quantify the extent to which congressional policy falls into different categories. Katznelson and Lapinski, in a 2006 study on the substance of legislation, lamented the lack of better systematic data on different types of congressional policy.

To approximate the extent of clientelism in policy making, we can distinguish between the types of legislation that Congress passed in the nineteenth century. "Public acts" of Congress are those that legislate on nonindividual matters. In the nineteenth century, distributive policies were nonetheless public. Congress used public acts to erect post offices, to authorize ports of entry, to expand railway lines, and to deepen harbors. But Congress could also legislate through private acts. Private legislation in Congress aids specific individuals on issues like naturalization, pensions, and patents. Private legislation allowed members of Congress to address the needs of specific individuals.

Patterns of private and public bills tell us something about how legislating evolved from 1870 to 1920. In the nineteenth century, not only did Congress primarily deal with distributive policy, but it also devoted a great deal of time to private bills. In Figure 2.3, we see that the number of private and public acts was relatively equal until private acts spiked at the turn of the century.

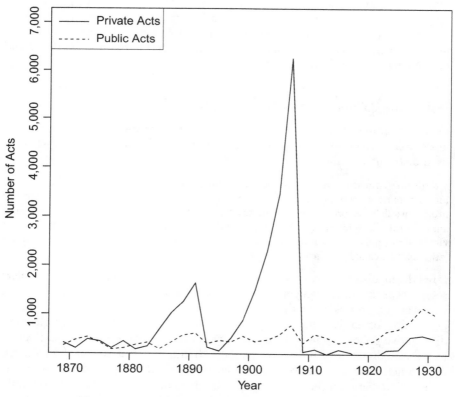

FIGURE 2.3 Public and private legislation in Congress, 1870–1930. From McIvor (2006).

FIGURE 2.4 Proportion of private legislation in Congress, 1870–1930. From McIvor (2006).

In 1900, the large rise in private bills was due to naturalization of immigrants. After 1910, however, public acts greatly outnumber private ones.

Another way of visualizing this change is by looking at the proportion of private bills to all congressional legislation (Figure 2.4). While private bills constituted the bulk of congressional activity in the nineteenth century, we can see that the proportion declines drastically after 1900. This indicates that members of Congress were devoting more time and attention to public matters. Demands of citizens had often been of a discrete or highly particularistic nature, as evidenced by calls for local developments throughout the nineteenth century (McCormick 1986). As demands of citizens changed, and as parties reduced traditional means of rewarding supporters, congressional activity reflected new attention to national issues.

The role of the legislator prior to 1900 was highly constrained. Aside from matters such as national security and tariff policy, members tended to the interests of their district primarily through targeted pork projects and private, individualized legislative matters. After the turn of the century, however, congressional activity shifted to become less oriented toward specific constituencies and local interests. This shift is explained by the rise of regulatory politics. Rather than relying on ad hoc distributive policies, parties instead adopted general precepts for governing. Rather than asking whether or not the federal government should oversee the industrial economy, the question became how the federal government could best craft policies that benefited voters collectively, and govern relations among broad classes of individuals (Higgens-Evenson 2003; Lowi 1964).

Regulatory trends began at the state level, with railway policy. Soon after the Civil War came to an end, the Western Pacific Railroad Company, the Central Pacific Railroad Company, and the Union Pacific Railroad Company joined their rail lines to complete the First Transcontinental Railroad. This had been made possible through congressional Railroad Acts during the Civil War, which provided government bonds and piecemeal land grants – both of which are hallmarks of distributive politics – to railroad companies. As railways brought together disparate communities of farmers, producers, and consumers, they became essential for producers and traders. But in the 1870s and 1880s, the railway industry became dominated by corporations that set arbitrary and discriminatory rates. Congress was reluctant to regulate the railways; it had little precedent for entering the economy in such a direct way. Individual states, however, began creating their own regulatory commissions. By 1887, twenty states had railway commissions that could regulate rates.

In 1887, Congress enacted the Interstate Commerce Act. Although it was passed "well before the advent of the Progressive movement ... it was almost typical Progressive reform" (McConnell 1966, 281). The Interstate Commerce Act created the Interstate Commerce Commission (ICC), a five-member body tasked with overseeing railway rates and standards. The ICC was designed to allow nonpartisan experts to monitor and provide recommendations for transportation policy. The ICC was an early effort at government intervention on behalf of the public interest, which served as a model for regulatory politics in the early twentieth century (McCraw 1975). The ICC did not have tremendous regulatory power at first, since the Supreme Court ruled that it could not fix rates. But the Commission itself signaled an end to laissez-faire politics and a new federal role in overseeing commerce and trade. Prior to the ICC, the only regulatory schemes included the Patent and Trademark Office (1836) and the Copyright Office of the Library of Congress (1871). After the ICC, Congress also created the Federal Trade Commission (1914), the Tariff Commission (1916), the Federal Power Commission (1920), and the Federal Radio Commission (1920). The relationship between parties and organized business was central to the expansion of the federal government's regulatory capacity, and will be discussed in subsequent chapters.

By turning attention to policies that could benefit citizens collectively, parties in Congress could reduce reliance on distributive policies. This meant that parties lost some of the "tangible benefits they had once had at their disposal to reward voters" (Balogh 2003, 223). Whereas parties once saw elections as a way to extend "hegemony" over government to control the distribution of benefits to local party networks, they shifted to the adoption of national policy agendas (Johnson and Libecap 1994; Skowronek 1982, 39). The national parties began devising effective government programs, including new forms of regulatory oversight, ushering in programmatic policy. Chapter 3 goes into further detail about how distributive policies helped parties both cultivate political support and encourage economic development, and why parties then transitioned to national policy.

PATRONAGE POLITICS AND THE FEDERAL BUREAUCRACY

Patronage is often considered an electoral strategy, since elected officials provide jobs or access to employment in exchange for voters' support. However, patronage was so widespread in the nineteenth century that it constituted a governing strategy, reflecting ideas about how and by whom the state should be managed; patronage went hand in hand with pork-barrel politics as a political strategy to maintain electoral support (Silberman 1993, 232). Prior to 1828, the US bureaucracy was modeled after that of Britain. It was concerned primarily with foreign affairs; the first departments were the State Department, the Department of War, the Treasury, the Post Office, the Office of the Attorney General, and the Navy. Early on, "recruitment for civil office . . . was conducted through social networks of elites, networks that were anchored by the leader of the state" (Carpenter 2005, 48). But when Andrew Jackson instituted the spoils system in 1829, it was designed not only to reward party supporters but also to staff state offices. The spoils system was seen not as nefarious, but rather as a way to ensure government was accessible to the common man and not only to elites. Patronage promoted ideals of equality and mobility, since it provided the average citizen with access to public office (Riper 1958).

Patronage also functioned to finance the activities of local party organizations and campaigns. Civil servants "were expected to contribute their votes and a portion, often substantial, of their time, energy, and income to the political party to which they were indebted for their employment" (Riper 1958, 46). By 1860, when rotation in office had been firmly established, assessments of civil service workers – whereby a marked percentage of incomes was returned to the party – provided the vast majority of party funds. Patronage was therefore vital to the development of national parties, providing the resources for extravagant campaigns, and with resources that went to voters in the form of bribes.

The size of the civil service rose steadily from the mid-century, dovetailing nicely with the expansion of political parties (Table 2.1). State-level party organizations were motivated to mobilize voters for national elections because of the reward of presidential patronage positions (Chambers and Davis 1978).

Patronage became increasingly burdensome to incoming presidents as more and more voters expected positions and as the state expanded. In 1840, when William Henry Harrison was elected president, there was such a large crowd of

TABLE 2.1 *Growth of the federal bureaucracy*

Year	Civil Servants	Competitive Positions
1816	4,837	
1821	6,914	
1831	11,491	
1841	18,038	
1851	26,274	
1861	36,672	
1871	51,020	
1881	100,020	
1891	166,000	33,873
1901	256,000	106,245

From Wallis (2006).

job-seekers in his office that he could not attend his first Cabinet meeting (White 1954, 304). President Polk entered office as a Democrat in 1844; he wrote a year after being inaugurated, "will the pressure for office never cease! ... I most sincerely wish I had no offices to bestow" (ibid.). And later he complained that the office-seekers "hold the balance of power between the two great parties." Because parties relied so greatly on patronage to ensure electoral victory and party financing, civil service and party had become inextricably tied by the end of the Civil War (Silberman 1993, 247). By some estimates, the federal government provided one job for every hundred voters (Kornbluh 2000, 52).

In 1881, President Garfield was assassinated by a man who had been promised, but had not received, a post in the New York customs house. By this point the incompetence of the civil service had been widely documented by investigative commissions created by the Department of the Treasury and the House of Representatives. The Jay Commission of 1877, for example, investigated inefficiencies in customs houses and found losses of over $36,000,000 alone at the port of New York. Civil servants frequently engaged in fraud, "creating delays and mistakes, imperilling the safety of the revenue and the interests of importers, and bringing the service into reproach."[16] Further, investigators argued that these frauds were due explicitly to patronage – "inefficiency, peculation, partisan intrigue and needless expense have characterized every period in post-office affairs ... from Jackson's administration."[17]

Civil service reform had been under consideration as early as the Civil War. In 1864, Senator Charles Sumner (R-Mass.) introduced twenty-one bills to extinguish patronage in the civil service, but failed. In 1868 Rep. Thomas Jenckes (R-R.I.) commissioned a report on the civil service that discussed Chinese,

[16] Annual Report of the Secretary of the Treasury on the State of the Finances for the Year 1885, Vol. II: Collection of Duties, p. 557.
[17] Report of the United States Civil Service Commission, Fifteenth Annual Report, 1899. Citing Eaton House Ex. Doc. No. 94, 46th Congress, 3rd session, p. 19.

Prussian, French, and English civil service procedures. His legislative proposals integrated lessons from these comparative findings, including examination-based entry and promotion by merit, but they were defeated in Congress.

It was not until 1883 that Congress implemented the first stage of civil service reforms, with passage of the Pendleton Act. The Pendleton Act created a Civil Service Commission to create rules for appointments and to implement regular examinations, investigations, and reporting. The act immediately set aside 10 percent of civil service jobs – about 6,000 jobs throughout the country – for competitive examination. It also provided that the president could set aside more offices for merit through executive order. The act also banned forced assessments of civil service employees, whereby a part of employees' salaries was remitted back to the party, and also banned coercing employees into political action. It further specified that only two members of a family could have positions in the federal service. By 1920, over 80 percent of the civil service was hired through examination rather than patronage (Figure 2.5).

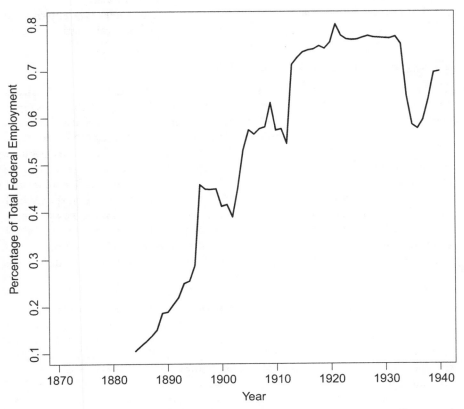

FIGURE 2.5 Proportion of competitive civil service positions, 1870–1940. From Wallis (2006).

Even though the Pendleton Act granted the president discretion to classify patronage jobs as merit or nonmerit, Congress also reduced patronage offices that were reserved for Congressional appointments. Congress administered patronage positions through Rural Free Delivery, a program that allocated more than 77,000 rural postmaster jobs. This program was the single largest patronage pool for the federal government. In the early twentieth century, Congress reduced patronage appointments to this service, opting instead for more universal hiring standards (Kernell and McDonald 1999). Teddy Roosevelt eventually incorporated these postmasters into the meritocratic civil service during his presidency, but even before then, the parties had effectively curtailed their use of patronage.

By the early decades of the twentieth century, parties in the United States were able to tout policy successes and to present distinct programs to voters. The years of 1870–1920 have been described as a period of organizational synthesis in which political officials sought to reduce uncertainty produced by clientelistic, ad hoc policies through the development of institutional solutions (Hays 1957; Hofstadter 1955; Wiebe 1967). Not only did the types and instances of electoral clientelism decline through the early twentieth century, but policy making also underwent a significant shift. The next chapters will explore the role of business groups in effectuating the adoption of programmatic reforms.

Clientelism and the "Weak" American State

The relative weakness of the federal government is often used as an explanation for the United States' long history with patronage. For most of the nineteenth century, legislative authority was limited, and there were few executive agencies aside from those related to the military. The American state was, in Skowronek's (1982) terms, one of "courts and parties." To the extent that there was any sort of public policy, it was created through the common law decisions of the courts, rather than the legislatures. In the twentieth century, the American state lacked a robust welfare state, even after many Western European counterparts had established strong social safety nets (Alesina et al. 2001; Hartz 1955; Lipset 1996; Smith 1993). The diminished scope of the American state is attributed both to institutions and to ideology. Federalism ensures that policy making is decentralized, and liberal, laissez-faire ideologies made American leaders wary of overstepping constitutional powers.

We might therefore expect that the United States was inherently prone to clientelistic politics. Perhaps because American parties, which needed to win votes of a large electorate, had a weak state, parties capitalized on access to state resources to distribute spoils to voters. Britain, on the other hand, with its strong administrative institutions and centralized political power in the Ministry, was less reliant on patronage. This comparison has been asserted most convincingly by Martin Shefter (1977), who attributed different levels of patronage in the civil service to the sequencing of universal suffrage and bureaucratization.

Much of the discussion of weak or strong states is largely unhelpful when it comes to explaining clientelism, however. Clientelism can be employed by parties with very strong states. Japan, for example, is a strong state whose parties also rely extensively on clientelistic strategies (Golden 2003; Scheiner 2006). By disaggregating the state into component institutions, we can get past restrictive conceptions of the American state as inherently weak. Even in the nineteenth century, the federal government was present in many aspects of American life: It established the postal service, connecting disparate towns and communities (John 1995); regulated public space and public safety (Novak 1996); and implemented uniform legal and judicial procedures through the federal courts (Horwitz 1992). The misconception of the limited role of the American state has prevented deeper understandings of how state activity affected various realms of policy, since American "infrastructural power is and always has been extensive" (Novak 2008). Similarly, although British institutions were strong in general, Members of Parliament used their office to distribute spoils and local grants rather than overseeing programmatic policies. Comparing Britain and the United States shows that the strength of specific institutions matters far more to clientelism than the state as a monolithic entity.

This analysis tries to show instead that parties became committed to clientelism as an ideological principle that served nascent democratic interests as suffrage expanded in the 1800s. In Congress, elected officials used their office to distribute goods to their districts and to serve individual constituent needs. The spoils system instituted by Andrew Jackson and Martin Van Buren in 1828 provided a way for ordinary citizens to participate in government and to contribute to party organization. Patronage and pork, combined with vote-buying in elections, provided effective ways for parties to mobilize and reward voters.

CONCLUSION

Throughout the nineteenth century, parties and candidates routinely engaged in clientelistic tactics in elections. They offered voters not only cash bribes, but also alcohol, food, and access to employment (or, in some cases, threats of employment termination). In the United States, electoral clientelism reflected expectations on the part of voters that they would be rewarded by candidates. Elections were less about issues and policy than they were about securing short-term handouts. These patterns were similar to those in the developing world, where village hierarchies replicated themselves in elections and voters considered food, drink, and remuneration to be tokens of appreciation. As the number of voters expanded in the first half of the nineteenth century, due to suffrage expansion as well as population growth, elections became increasingly costly, with candidates and local parties providing parades, rallies, and tremendous amounts of alcohol and food to voters.

Clientelistic strategies proved adaptable and useful to parties over the course of the nineteenth century. Clientelism was impervious to reform, surviving bans on bribery in elections in the mid-nineteenth century. Even the secret ballot, which was introduced in the United States in the 1890s, could be circumvented; parties paid voters not to turn out, for example (Cox and Kousser 1981). But around the turn of the twentieth century, candidates reduced their use of vote buying, relying instead on issue-oriented campaigns and party slogans to win votes. As subsequent chapters will show, programmatic election strategies were the result of broader changes in the ways parties connected with voters. Specifically, I argue that as parties adopted new strategies of governing – by embracing regulation, legislating through public policy, and reforming the civil service – they also changed the landscape of electoral politics. The role of the politician evolved from that of a mere patron to that of a member of a party that created national policy.

The story of American political parties and clientelism accords well with recent findings that clientelism and development are not linearly related, but instead that clientelism is a product of early stages of development. Just as modernization theorists found that increasing economic opportunities and expansion of suffrage would lead parties to patronage, so too has recent work found that democracies tend to become more clientelistic as incomes rise, since the developmental state provides opportunities for clientelism (Kitschelt and Altamirano 2015, 8).

This finding can be explained by clientelism as a governing strategy, since politicians who have access to newly available state resources and offices will use them to reward supporters. In the absence of robust state institutions that legislate and implement broad policy matters, parties will rely on vote buying in elections. Once parties are able to shift to more programmatic forms of distributive policy, however, they pursue new linkages with citizens that create accountability based on adherence to policy goals.

3

Business Organization and the Push for Programmatic Parties

In the nineteenth century, industrialization fundamentally reshaped the social and economic landscape of the United States. In 1850, 64 percent of the U.S. workforce worked in agriculture, while only about 13 percent of the workforce worked in manufacturing. There were over 1.5 million farms compared with about 123,000 industrial establishments.[1] By 1890, however, the share of the workforce in agriculture had declined to 43 percent. Meanwhile, the manufacturing sector grew 660 percent in the three decades between 1870 and 1900. The construction of roads, canals, and, by the mid-nineteenth century, railways, greatly shortened the distances between scattered towns and cities. Technological advances streamlined the production of raw materials and goods. National consumer markets emerged, firms grew in scale and scope, and urban areas became densely packed with laborers and immigrants. The structural changes brought on by industrialization ushered in new political cleavages between farmers and manufacturers, laborers and producers, and urban and rural dwellers. These cleavages often underscored sectional differences, with the interests of the agricultural South and Midwest increasingly aligned against those of the urban manufacturing centers in the Northeast.

The emergence of the railway, steel, and oil industries created unprecedented economic growth and gave rise to monolithic corporations of the 1880s and 1890s. Standard Oil, U.S. Steel, and numerous regional and transatlantic railroad companies were led by robber barons such as John Rockefeller, Andrew Carnegie, and Jay Gould. As these corporations accumulated market power and wealth, and as their unscrupulous business practices became public, social movements coalesced around opposition to corporate power. Discontent had many sources: Farmers balked at inconsistent and exorbitant transportation rates, labor unions

---

[1] Atack and Bateman 2006.

protested unfair working conditions and wages, and intellectuals decried the corrupting effects of monopoly and agglomeration. The overarching narrative about late nineteenth-century America is that it was dominated by corporate interests, with all other economic sectors allied against them.

What this narrative misses is that it subsumes all businesses into a few large industrial corporations. In the 1870s, however, business *itself* was a nebulous and diverse group of interests that was coming into its own, not only as a vibrant economic sector, but also as a set of economic actors. By the twentieth century, what was important about the American economy was not that it was controlled entirely by monolithic corporations, but instead that it had become so greatly influenced by managerial capitalism and corporate organization. Business practices changed dramatically over the latter half of the nineteenth century, with the foremost change being the adoption of managerial capitalism. This described a new mode of conducting business through the use of managers and administrators. By separating ownership from management, corporate leaders could delegate increasingly complex production and manufacturing processes to a core group of men whose expertise lay not in technical skills but rather in oversight and technocratic procedures.

As business evolved in its corporate practices and competitive strategies, its relationship with government was also continually in flux. Over the course of the nineteenth century, the relationship between business and the national government went from one of relative laissez-faire benign neglect to one of mutual benefit, if not mutual dependence. Specifically, evolving business preferences for state intervention in the economy led business to develop new linkages with political parties. Businesses sought solutions in government – centralized administration, consistent application of neutral principles, formulation of long-term policy – that were adaptations of the functions of managerial capitalism.

As business practices evolved, business leaders developed new preferences toward government activity and intervention. This chapter traces the history of business–state relations from the founding period to show how the adoption of managerial capitalism, combined with the damaging effects of patronage politics, slowly gave way to demands for coherent and programmatic government policies. Historical records of national trade associations show that manufacturers, transportation owners, and finance capitalists alike required rationalized and standardized services from the government. Business organizations then created new political strategies to achieve programmatic goals. They sought influence in the political process, testifying before Congress and articulating specific reforms and administrative principles on which legislators could craft policy. As parties reduced their use of patronage, they looked to other groups for financial support, and businesses began contributing significant sums to political campaigns. These new linkages between business groups and parties paved the way for programmatic competition.

PARTY–BUSINESS LINKAGES BEFORE 1870

Before the 1870s, the relationship between the federal government and corporations was poorly developed. Given that there was little industry to speak of at the time of the nation's founding, national institutions were not designed to oversee a complex, industrial economy. The early nineteenth century was a period in which political parties were growing at the state and national levels, and a period in which suffrage expanded. By 1840, all states had eliminated property requirements for voting for white men. Therefore, parties needed both to court votes and to implement policies that would expand economic opportunities.

As discussed in Chapter 2, congressional policy consisted almost exclusively of distributive policy in the nineteenth century. Rather than reflecting state weakness, distributive policies actually arose out of ideas from the founding period of how the state should intervene in economic affairs. In the decades following the founding of the American Republic, politicians debated the extent to which government would be involved in "internal improvements," which were synonymous with public works, but broadly referred to "all kinds of programs to encourage security, prosperity, and enlightenment" (Larson 2001, 3). The primary way the federal government could foster economic development was not through public ownership and funding of projects, but instead through helping to integrate the otherwise isolated communities of the new nation. Proponents of what was termed constructive liberalism felt that "government, by building infrastructure itself, or by aiding in its private construction, could provide a context which would release private energies" (Aldrich 1979, 5). Private enterprises were seen as too small to carry out major infrastructural improvements on their own, and private capital to fund public works projects was scarce (Goodrich 1960).

The federal government first authorized appropriations for public works in 1802, with a congressional allocation of $30,000 to build inland waterways from the Delaware River. The same year, Congress set aside 2 percent of land sales from the state of Ohio to build roads in that state; it later did the same for many new Midwestern states. In 1806, the federal government began surveys for a national road from Maryland to Wheeling, West Virginia; the first portion opened in 1813. In 1808, Albert Gallatin, President Jefferson's Secretary of the Treasury, produced a Report on Roads and Canals – a scheme for national transportation. It called for federal construction of a chain of roads and canals along the Eastern seaboard. Although never adopted, Congress did begin to appropriate funds for development projects. In 1824 Congress passed the first of many rivers and harbors bills, and work began on ports for the Great Lakes.

In 1817, President Madison vetoed the "Bonus Bill" – an Act of Congress that created a permanent fund for internal improvements by setting aside $1.5 million from the Second Bank of the United States. However, Congress was empowered by the Supreme Court decision of 1824, *Gibbons v. Ogden*, which held that Congress's power of interstate commerce was broad. The decision "paved the way for federal improvement of rivers and harbors for navigation" (Goodrich 1960, 40). That year, the General Survey Act created the Army Corps of Engineers to assist with infrastructure projects. While the construction of public works was occasionally divisive, owing to tensions over class, agriculture, sectionalism, and wariness of federal overstep, Congress continued to appropriate funds for road, harbor, and canal construction. From 1820 to 1840, federal expenditures on internal improvements constituted 11 percent of the federal budget. Local contractors built the projects, while states and localities supplemented capital. Early transportation projects such as turnpikes were also built by small private corporations chartered exclusively for specific projects, but after the success of the Erie Canal in 1825, corporate capital was not sufficient to finance transportation (Chandler 1977, 34). Instead, the "greatest American public works ... were built with massive infusions of federal aid" (Aldrich 1979, 15).

While national transportation and regulatory schemes failed in the early nineteenth century, Republican and Democratic congressmen increased their expenditures of local infrastructure projects (Minicucci 2004). In the 1850s, the federal government overtook the states as the primary source of investment funds in transportation (Aldrich 1979). After this, federal funding increased dramatically, with subsidies going to roads, lighthouses, harbors, and land surveying. Congress also became more involved in determining the location of projects, allocating over 22 million acres of land to private projects. Politicians "learned to encourage improvements in general but not to commit themselves either to public investment or to the principle of activist government" (Larson 2001, 5). For most of this period there was no delineated business sector to speak of. Industry was small scale and limited to traditional guilds as well as textiles, leather, lumber milling, flour and grist milling, and limited production of iron and steel.

The substance of policy was less important than the extent to which policies could distribute and apportion resources. As party competition increased after Jackson's election to office, parties ensured electoral majorities by using congressional funds for district projects (Kornbluh 2000). Reliance on distributive policy only declined with the growth of regulatory and redistributive policy of the twentieth century, which allowed parties to develop – and claim credit for – broad public policy (Goodrich 1960; Sylla 2000).

Although the Republican and Democratic parties differentiated themselves on national issues (such as slavery and tariffs) during the nineteenth century, ideology did not govern the choices of distributive policies. McCormick argues instead that nineteenth century "'policy' was little more than the accumulation of isolated, individual choices, usually of a distributive nature" (McCormick 1986, 206). Lowi, using congressional annual session laws, finds that while Congress had very little to do in the nineteenth century, "99% of what it did do was what we nowadays calls subsidy or patronage politics" (Lowi 1979, 272).

Federal subsidies and land grants were particularly important to the railways, which began interstate construction in the 1850s.[2] As the railroads grew, public funds came to account for more than half of the construction of the Union Pacific and Central Pacific railways, which would eventually unite the coasts. After completion of the transcontinental railways, however, private capital overtook public funds as the way to invest in and to grow industry. There was a shift from public to private provision of transportation, which spilled over to other industries and led to a reconfiguration of the federal government's role in the economy.

Industrialization in new areas, such as steel, coal mining, tobacco, chemical processing, oil refining, and food and meat processing, expanded dramatically after the Civil War. Traditional forms of firm ownership and management no longer sufficed to keep pace with industrial output. The American economy had been organized around family firms, which adapted organizationally as industries grew. Each state was responsible for its own incorporation laws, and the states of the Northeast, particularly Delaware and New York, facilitated the rise of corporate ownership. Corporations became larger and developed elements recognizable to us today: boards of directors, stocks, limited liability. Technology, transportation, and cheap labor from a growing urban and immigrant population made it easier for corporations to streamline production chains.

Industrialization rendered inadequate traditional business practices. Market volatility and depressions wreaked havoc on firms. In response, businessmen reconfigured traditional modes of capitalist organization, resulting in new levels of market coordination and cooperation. The critical change that occurred among firms was the use and expansion of management. Managerial capitalism entailed the rise of the large-scale corporation, which "dominated major sectors of the economy ... alter[ing] the basic structure of these sectors and of the economy as a whole" (Chandler 1977). Table 3.1 shows some of the key differences between personal and managerial capitalism.

Managerial capitalism made the modern business enterprise possible. Firms adopted distinct operating units, administered by a hierarchy of salaried, middle- and top-level managers. Management allowed corporations to do what previously had been left to the market: control competition, source raw materials, find new consumers, and set prices. Managers established new procedures for production and distribution, and developed applications of scientific principles to corporate problems. Management became a profession in itself, as managers sought promotion and advancement based on performance and skill rather

[2] The first commercial railroad was the Baltimore and Ohio Railroad, which was chartered by Maryland in 1827.

TABLE 3.1 *Changes in capitalist organization*

Personal Capitalism	Managerial Capitalism
Owners = managers	Professional managers
Small-scale production	Mass production
Outsourced distribution	Multifunctional and integrated departments
Labor intensive	Capital intensive
Ad hoc solutions	Technocratic solutions

than personal connections to owners – indeed, one of the critical distinguishing features of management was its wholesale separation from ownership and financing. Management expanded to a field complete with formal training, educational programs, professional journals, and associations (Chandler 1977). The structure of corporate organization was increasingly hierarchic and centralized. Corporations developed their own forms of bureaucratic administration, and saw in them a model for government institutions (Galambos 1970; Walker 1991). This allowed firms to broaden the scope of their outputs and the scale of industrial processing.

Salaried managers were first employed in the transportation and utility sectors. Railways, for example, were difficult to coordinate across far-flung regional networks of tracks and trains. Telegraphy and cable also spread quickly, requiring coordination and organization of messages. Managers were soon found to be useful in other sectors. The Standard Oil trust used managers to determine which refineries to maintain or close down, where to build new ones, and how to streamline transport of oil from field to refinery to consumer. In mass retailing, Sears, Roebuck expanded its mail-order business by adopting management practices; by 1905, it was filling more than 100,000 mail orders per day, which was more than a traditional family retail shop could fill in a lifetime (Chandler 1984).

Sectors with fixed manufacturing processes, such as lumber, publishing and printing, and apparel, continued to thrive without managerial capitalism. But new technologies, which hastened economies of scale in production, made the role of skilled management all the more important. Technological innovation led to new production of foodstuffs, textiles, and chemical and metals processing. The 1880s saw growth in the manufacture of cigarettes, soap, paint, drugs, vegetable oil, and grain milling. Food canning led to the creation of companies such as Heinz and Campbell's. Automated assembly, mechanized production, and the rise of machine manufacturing – sewing machines, harvesting machines, office machinery such as typewriters and cash registers – went hand in hand. Managerial capitalism was therefore adopted in industries with mass production and economies of scale, allowing companies to create and maintain quality controls in manufacturing and distribution.

As industrial sectors expanded, the economy suffered depressions and panics, including a deep depression in 1873 and a widespread wave of labor strikes through 1877. Efforts to mitigate the boom-and-bust cycles of cutthroat competition led firms to pursue more aggressive strategies, including pooling, mergers, acquisitions, and trusts. The pool was a gentlemen's agreement to establish minimum prices and allocate markets. Firms could not enforce pooling agreements, however, so they began to consolidate with one another. From 1894 to 1914, thousands of small firms were absorbed into corporate conglomerates. Corporate reorganization was so widespread in the United States that from 1898 to 1904 alone there were more than 300 industrial consolidations overseeing more than $7 million in capital (Sklar 1988). In this period, 1,800 companies disappeared through mergers (Cassis 2007). Organization among corporations was partly a result of the chaos of market competition, as corporations sought to guard against business cycles, crises, and disequilibrium. And these consolidations created "regulatory trends in the private sector ... that immediately called into play proposals for government regulatory authority" (Sklar 1988, 17). The next section therefore turns to political solutions that businesses pursued to generate long-term market stability.

THE ESTABLISHMENT OF NATIONAL BUSINESS ORGANIZATIONS

The primary vehicle for the politicization of business interests was the trade association, which aimed to represent business interests irrelevant of sector specificity. Peak associations formed with the explicit intention of engaging with politics and influencing matters of commercial policy. The foremost business associations in the United States – the National Association of Manufacturers (NAM) and the Chambers of Commerce – have their roots in the early twentieth century. The former was a voluntary association, established in 1895 by concerned members of the business community. The latter was a federation of many local and state Chambers of Commerce, convened by President Taft in 1912.

By the time NAM and the Chambers of Commerce were created, many regional and sectoral trade associations had already been established. The first Chamber of Commerce in the United States, in New York, was chartered by King George in 1770. Local boards of trade originally established to buy and sell grain also evolved into Chambers of Commerce. In 1800, there were only four Chambers of Commerce in the United States: Philadelphia, Pennsylvania; Charleston, South Carolina; New York, New York; and New Haven, Connecticut. This number expanded rapidly over the course of the nineteenth century. Businesses were beginning to see advantages to cooperating rather than engaging in cutthroat competition. Over the next century, the number of localities with these associations grew exponentially. As business leaders addressed issues that were now national in scope, the purpose of trade associations became more political in orientation. Members of business organizations saw themselves providing services to the business community, and donated time and money toward year-round activities (Carrott 1970; Foth 1930).

The organization and management techniques revolutionizing corporations also influenced the organization of the business community itself. From 1890 "efficiency and cooperation were bywords of business ... the spirit of business cooperation was embodied in the ... flourishing trade associations" (Haber 1964). By 1900, there were 2,944 commercial organizations in the United States, and 100 national commercial bodies (Sturges 1915, 45). The National Board of Trade represented an early effort to unify the business community and engage in national politics.

The National Board of Trade: 1868–1890

The National Board of Trade (NBT) was a national, cross-sectoral trade association that convened immediately after the Civil War. Records from the NBT illuminate not only the primary concerns of businessmen in this period, but, more importantly, the way these concerns changed over time. It was the Boards of Trade that called on members to influence politicians, as NAM and the Chambers of Commerce would do to great effect later. These records reveal business preferences for reform, and how the nature of organization itself shaped these preferences over time.

The NBT represented the first effort to develop not only a distinct merchant class, but to derive a set of commercial interests that could shape national policy. Importantly, it was the first time that the commercial class attempted to reconcile their material interests with those of the public good. It also revealed that businessmen were realizing the importance of formal organization as a vehicle to advance political goals. As Davis (2014, 762) explains, the creation of a "'business' interest ... tapped into republicanism by positioning merchants as stewards of an economic commonwealth." By focusing on cross-cutting economic policy concerns, the businesses and individuals who joined the NBT were actively trying to tamp down sectional and regional divisions that had fractured the commercial class prior to the Civil War.

The Board of Trade began in Philadelphia in 1868 as a coalition of various chambers of commerce. The idea for it dated to 1859, when the secretary of the Boston Board of Trade, Lorenzo Sabine, issued a report calling for direct recognition of merchants by the government. A commercial convention was held in Detroit in 1865, when businessmen representing locally established commercial organizations met to discuss a treaty with Canada.[3] Representatives came from across the United States, from Albany to Detroit to New Orleans. At this meeting, businessmen expressed concern that their expertise

---

[3] Hill 1885, 8.

on commercial and financial matters was lost on Washington. They also lamented that they were not as influential in congressional matters as they ought to be. Even as early as the Detroit meeting, businessmen began to float the idea of a Cabinet-level department "devoted to trade, navigation, transportation, and related interests; and, also, there should be a closer and more intimate connection with each other of the commercial bodies of the country."[4] Citing the Board of Trade of England, which was established in 1636, Lorenzo Sabine called on his fellow merchants to come together and demand deeper interaction with the federal government, since "many of the questions which these Associations are required to entertain are . . . national in their character" (Davis 2014, 778).

Membership leaned heavily toward industrialists and merchants. Frederick Fraley, its president, was the head of the Lehigh Coal and Navigation Company; one of its vice presidents, William Henry Baldwin, Jr., worked on the Union Pacific Railroad, while another vice president, Ambrose Snow, was a ship-builder who later joined the American Shipping League. There were also lawyers and politicians, such as William Morrow, who later became the Attorney General of California, and James Buchanan,[5] who was later elected to the House of Representatives.

In order to influence matters of policy relevant to the business community, the NBT met in 1868. In the first meeting, the board elected an executive council and also drew up a constitution. The NBT declared itself an organization devoted to commercial purposes to "secure unity and harmony of action in reference to commercial usages, customs, and laws; and especially, in order to secure the proper consideration of questions pertaining to the financial, commercial and industrial interests of the country at large."[6] While the foremost goal was therefore to standardize preferences of businessmen themselves, the organization quickly expanded its scope to include politics.

The Executive Council emphasized that the board would aim to be nationally representative and free of sectarian and partisan considerations. Over the next few decades, the NBT met annually, discussing the year's progress (or lack thereof) in securing favorable political outcomes and drawing up resolutions that would guide the organization's activities. The foremost goal of the NBT was to standardize the preferences of businessmen nationwide. Their deliberations indicate that businessmen long preceded reformists and Progressives in agitating for federal regulation. Not only did businessmen see federal intervention and regulation as the key to economic growth, but they also demanded expansive, broad policies and predictability in the policies advocated by the parties.

---

[4] Hill 1885, 8. [5] No relation to President James Buchanan.
[6] *Proceedings of the Third Annual Meeting of the National Board of Trade* (Boston: Barker, Cotter & Co., 1870), p. vii.

Another explicit goal was to influence legislative outcomes. In 1870, the board noted that "the vote of the Board on a given subject, being recommendatory only and not authoritative, may or may not lead to immediate legislation ... but its thorough and candid examination by practical and experienced men is sure to lead, in the first place, to harmony of opinion ... and to the creation of a commercial public sentiment which sooner or later will secure the desired result."[7] For many years this meant the board helped to secure federal funds for public works, such as canal and harbor construction, but this proved unsatisfying. By 1878, the board instead transitioned its efforts toward "the consideration of questions of general policy and principle, and for dealing with issues in which, by common consent, all parts of the country and all classes, have more or less concern."[8]

The NBT proceedings also reveal a disdain for partisan politics. In the Fifteenth Annual Meeting, in 1885, the NBT debates show a concern about the economic depression of 1882–85. They worried that economic problems would worsen under the newly elected Democrats "until the new administration shall have foreshadowed its policy."[9] They also bemoaned that it was too unpredictable for presidents to rotate out of office every four years, finding that presidential campaigns "unsettle and confuse the general business interests of the country, thereby entailing vast losses, with their accompanying results of failure among merchants and manufacturers."[10]

Civil Service Reform

By the 1880s, the drawbacks of patronage had been well documented. In reports issued by the Department of the Treasury and the House of Representatives, business owners complained that patronage produced unreliable customs and postal agents. Patronage appointees could not carry out routine transactions, and business owners enumerated the loss of revenues that patronage entailed. They argued that they could not support patronage because they adhered to "principles common among honorable business men" – those of professionalism, efficiency, and transparency.[11] Further, given that employment turned over with each new administration, businessmen argued that there were enormous delays in service delivery when new civil servants took office.

There was therefore agitation for civil service reforms. In the first meeting, the board noted that "it is to the great regret of the business men of the United States [that] Mr. Jenckes's great measure for promoting Civil Service Reform

---

[7] Ibid., vi.

[8] *The National Board of Trade: Its Past and Future; Report of a Committee of the Executive Council* (Boston: James F. Cotter & Co., 1878), 5.

[9] Ibid., 3.

[10] *Proceedings of the Fifteenth Annual Meeting of the Board of Trade* (Boston: Tolman & White, 1885), 172.

[11] Sen. Rep. 2373, 50th Congress, 1st Session. *Operations of the Civil Service*, October 10, 1888.

has not yet become a law."[12] And they argued there is an "urgent necessity which exists for the passage of some such Bill ... in order to secure the highest degree of efficiency and purity in the administration of public affairs."[13] In a discussion of whether to push for federal control of telegraph lines, a board member noted that "there are fifty thousand appointees of the Executive of our Government, selected without reference to their qualifications, but simply as they are active partisan supporters of the members of our national legislature." There was a back-and-forth among members who lamented the lack of a civil service law. One went so far as to call patronage a "stench in the nostrils of the people of this country."[14] This sentiment continued and grew over the next decade and a half; in 1885, the proceedings noted that "our army of office-holders and Government departments is now a vast one ... I would not increase its patronage and power over the people."[15] They argued that administration of government needed to be "separated utterly from party politics, free from the usurped authority of party dictation, and controlled always and only by the consideration of what will promote the best good of the people as a whole."[16]

Federal Oversight and Regulation of Industry

One of the NBT's goals was the creation of a Department of Commerce. In the first meeting, the board adopted a proposal for a cabinet-level executive agency to oversee commercial matters. At the time, they speculated about what such an agency might look like, but insisted that only a federal agency could adequately represent business interests and provide consistent commercial policy. By 1878, the board was frustrated that despite many inroads into the policy-making process – they had already appeared before Congress and met with heads of departments, and "seldom failed to influence ... such executive or congressional action as may have followed" – they had not yet secured a Department of Commerce.

In addition to an executive agency, the board also advocated for federal regulation of industry. They lamented the overlapping jurisdiction over important areas like ports and harbors, calling instead for Congress to adopt legislation to give the federal government supervision.[17] The railways, in particular, were a scourge for traders suffering from price discrimination. The NBT began advocating for a National Board of Railway Commissioners, the form eventually adopted by the ICC, rather than an early bill that simply ended price discrimination. The board argued instead that prices could not be enforced without a commission, and therefore "it is our duty, as a sort of advisory board,

---

[12] *Proceedings of the First Annual Meeting of the National Board of Trade* (Boston: J. H. Eastburn's Press, 1868), v.
[13] Ibid.   [14] Ibid., 149.
[15] *Proceedings of the Fifteenth Annual Meeting of the Board of Trade*, 167.
[16] Hill 1885, 8, 12.   [17] Ibid., p. 172.

to formulate something practical ... I think we should go before the Committee on Commerce, or some other committee of Congress, and see if we could not arrive at a wise, proper, and just conclusion."[18]

At this point, businesses themselves had developed institutions to regulate corporate affairs. *Within* corporations, managers established centrally overseen, bureaucratic hierarchies based on technical and scientific values (Hays 1957; Walker 1991). Through principles of expertise and bureaucratic administration, businesses developed ideas for how to govern complex economic areas (Tarr 1984).

As a result, businesses became increasingly frustrated with the laissez-faire politics characteristic of the mid-century. Inconsistent regulation combined with patronage-appointed bureaucrats caused significant uncertainty for business leaders. Associations found that self-regulation alone could do very little, and they "looked as well to a variety of government bureaus and agencies that would provide the technical services their specialized needs demanded. In almost every case, these groups depended upon the government for the means of independence from all intruders, including the government itself" (Wiebe 1967, 129). There were diverse roots of business support for regulation, ranging from merchants who were actively disadvantaged by discriminatory rates to those who advocated a public interest approach (Purcell 1967).

The NBT helped to crystallize business preferences in favor of political reform. Although the activities of the organization were limited in its twenty or so years of meeting – in 1878, the Executive Council observed that there were sectional jealousies, suspicious motives, and an absence of a well-defined plan of activity – it laid an important groundwork for the political focus of business organizations in the twentieth century.[19] From its inception, the NBT advocated national economic policies, such as the expansion of infrastructure and uniformity in the legal code.

The board acknowledged, for example, that it could expend its energies securing state and federal funds for local public works projects, but decided to focus on general policies and principles. It condemned subsidies and land grants to railways, steamship lines, and private corporations as "favoritism and monopolies ... incompatible with the spirit of free institutions ... a fertile source of jobbery and corruption."[20] This was an explicit attack against distributive politics. In maintaining a distance from partisan politics, and in carefully selecting issues to lobby for, the board received "a cordial reception and respectful hearing" whenever it appeared before the congressional committees or government departments. While the board had not secured all the policies

---

[18] Ibid., 70.
[19] *The National Board of Trade: Its Past and Future; Report of a Committee of the Executive Council*, 2.
[20] *Proceedings of the Third Annual Meeting of the National Board of Trade*, 118.

it pushed for, its recommendations were nonetheless "entitled to weight, and they have seldom failed to influence ... such executive or congressional action."[21]

The growth of government and the growing scope of public policy made functional bureaucracies increasingly consequential for business profitability, and politicians came under growing pressure from business groups to provide government services more effectively (Johnson and Libecap 1994; Martin 2010). Regulation therefore helped companies monitor their own industries. To a lesser extent, regulation also served as a way to improve the industry's relations with the public as many sectors of society clamored for more stringent protection against monopolistic corporations (Higgens-Evenson 2003, 5). Business organizations wanted government agencies that operated not according to partisan politics but according to professional standards. Pushing for great service provision, they railed against patronage and partisanship with slogans such as "There is no Democratic or Republican method for paving a street!" (Walker 1991, 24).

New classes of merchants and manufacturers saw a need for federal oversight of an increasingly national economy. While many states created commissions and agencies to regulate the transportation and industrial sectors of the economy, corporations became fed up with arbitrary and conflicting state regulations, pushing the national parties – particularly the Republicans – to sponsor regulatory laws at the national level (Sylla 2000, 539). Experimentation at the local and state levels taught business groups how to voice their political demands, particularly in pursuit of expanded state capacities. Class formation among commercial elites led to high levels of engagement between business groups and local reformers, as businessmen sought to influence infrastructure development, mercantile policy, and labor relations as part and parcel of a sense of civic responsibility (Clemens 2010). Commercial elites also became leaders in local politics, helping to create independent commissions to mitigate corrupt politics and to reduce rigid partisanship (Formisano 1999, 112).

The NBT also took a long view of business relations with government. Acknowledging that the push for a Department of Commerce had failed, the Executive Council nonetheless noted that "it requires patient and protracted effort to carry important measures of reform, whether in legislation or administration."[22] Civil service reforms might be achieved only at the end of the century, but "the action of ten years ago, and later, was neither premature nor thrown away."[23]

---

[21] *The National Board of Trade: Its Past and Future; Report of a Committee of the Executive Council*, 5.
[22] Ibid., 5.   [23] Ibid.

Business Organization and the Legacy of the National Board of Trade

After two active decades, the NBT was supplanted by other trade organizations that still exist today – the National Association of Manufacturers (NAM) and the Chambers of Commerce of the United States. NAM was established in 1895 and brought together commercial interests who wanted expansion into foreign markets as well as labor-unfriendly policies. Chambers of Commerce were established in the states, along with a lobbying arm in Washington. Both the Republican and Democratic parties came under pressure to accommodate business, particularly by reforming the state to better facilitate economic growth and development. These organizations built on the successes and lessons of the NBT, deepening the presence of business in politics.

NAM became an important player in politics, calling for the creation of the Department of Commerce and establishing a commission on tariffs (Bonnett 1922). It created planks for political parties to add to their platforms, and in 1907 created the National Industrial Council, a department of NAM that focused exclusively on legislative and political activities. Through the council, NAM organized members at each stage of the legislative process – testifying before committees, forcing bills out of committee, and securing votes for bill passage. As of 1922, NAM had more than 5,000 members employing more than 6 million workers, producing 75–80 percent of the total output of manufactured goods in the United States (Bonnett 1922).

NAM took partial credit for the success of another peak association, the Chambers of Commerce of the United States. Politicians directly mobilized the business community to create the Chambers of Commerce of the United States in 1912. The Chambers of Commerce represents an interesting endpoint in the efforts of the business community to become a prominent voice in political decision making. The decade leading up to the Chambers' founding was one of increasing efforts on the part of the government to mobilize business interests (Martin and Swank 2012). Bureuacrats including Frederic Emory, chief of the commercial office of the State Department, and John Kasson, the US Minister to Austria and Germany in the 1870s and 1880s, began to advocate stronger relations between the federal government and commercial associations at the turn of the century (Werking 1978).

The Department of Commerce and Labor, one of the foremost demands of the NBT and NAM, was created in 1903. An official from the census bureau, S. N. D. North, recommended that the department's new secretary, George Cortelyou, study the British Board of Trade for examples of how to institutionalize a relationship between business and government. In 1904, the department sent its head of the Bureau of Statistics, Oscar P. Austin, to Europe to study government trade promotion. He later reported to the National Board of Trade that Europe's successful "centralized and government-sponsored commercial organizations" provided a model for the United States (Werking 1978, 325).

By 1907, the Commerce Secretary, Oscar Straus, worked "to enable the Department to enlist the cooperation of commercial interests" by inviting delegates from the chambers of commerce of forty different cities to sit on a National Council of Commerce.[24] Straus himself had been a member of the New York State Chamber of Commerce and served as president of the New York Board of Trade and Transportation (Werking 1978). At the Chamber of Commerce's first meeting of delegates, held in December 1907, Straus urged the business community to coordinate on matters of industrial policy. He praised the semi-official status of commercial organizations in France and Germany, noting that even the voluntary commercial groups of Britain "speak the voice and wish of commercial and industrial England, and the Government takes notice accordingly."[25] In gathering the American manufacturers, he hoped the department could "avail itself of their invaluable assistance, their wise counsel, and systematic cooperation."[26] He further promised that with the cooperation of business, the department could devote itself to the subjects "most desired" by commercial interests.

Elihu Root, the Secretary of State, also addressed the delegates at the national conference of 1907. He lamented the disaggregation of bureaus within the executive apparatus, which impeded efficient communication between business and the government. Instead, he argued for the adoption of business standards:

I think we have come to the point where we can apply to the work of the different Departments of government, of different bureaus, of different experts and governmental servants, and of the great number of local commercial organizations throughout the country those *principles of organization* which are transforming the business of the world today.[27]

The national Chambers of Commerce was not created for a few more years – not until the president called for its formation. In an address to Congress in December 1911, President Taft encouraged a central body for commercial organizations and trade associations. In April 1912, leaders from the business community met in Washington with Taft and the Secretary of Commerce and Labor and established the U.S. Chamber of Commerce (Table 3.2). In the first-ever bulletin that the Chambers promulgated across the country, they bemoaned that "the government is rendering a service of immense value to the commercial interests of the country, which is only partially availed of, mainly because the business men are not fully informed."[28]

---

[24] Sturges 1915, 60.
[25] National Council of Commerce, *Proceedings of a Meeting of Delegates from the Chambers of Commerce, Boards of Trade, and Trade Organizations of the Leading Cities of the United States in Conference with the Secretary of Commerce and Labor, December 5–6, 1907* (Washington, DC: Government Printing Office), 10.
[26] Ibid., 11.   [27] Ibid., 17.
[28] Chambers of Commerce of the United States of America, Bulletin No. 1, 1912, p. 1.

TABLE 3.2 *Expansion of the chambers of commerce of the United States*

Year	# of Chambers	States	Members
1913	326	43	
1914	549	47	1,954
1915	646	47	2,724
1916	737	48	3,490
1917	919	48	5,716
1918	1,041	48	7,447
1919 (Apr)	1,177	48	10,193
1919 (Dec)	1,256	48	11,900

From Bruce 1920, 181.

By 1920, Merle Thorpe, editor of the Chambers of Commerce industry publication *Nation's Business*, wrote that the rapid expansion of the chambers was due to the fact that "our collective problems have become our individual problems. Business men have felt the want for some central organization that would promote a broader understanding of business in its national phase, that would apply to the industry of the nation the same principles of cooperation that have done so much for their own business" (Bruce 1920, 181). And in an early publication about the Chambers of Commerce, Kenneth Sturges, secretary of the Cleveland Chamber of Commerce, argued that the "invasion of politics by the commercial organizations" was simply an effort to apply "sound business principles to a system of government ... to accomplish reform" (Sturges 1915, 172).

Regarding tariff activity, for example, rather than lobby for specific positions on tariff legislation, the Chambers instead advocated the establishment "on a permanent basis, [of] a non-partisan board of experts for the scientific investigation of all facts pertinent to the tariff schedules."[29] They also spoke out against patronage in the Consular Service, writing that business interests "could not stand for such a 'clean sweep' of the consular service as has taken place heretofore with each change of administration that involved a change of party control."[30] They note that legislation improving the foreign service had just been referred to a House committee.

In industry publications, leaders of the Chambers of Commerce discuss tactics for recruiting and retaining members of local business communities. Further, they discuss the important role of organization in contemporary politics. William Bruce, from the Milwaukee Merchants and Manufacturers' Association, wrote in 1920 that

[29] Ibid., 1.   [30] Ibid., 2.

Statesmanship must ... employ the judgment of business on problems of a purely economic character. The function of government is to protect and to regulate. It has no special promotional function. But government requires that stimulus which springs from a wholesome public sentiment. The commercial organization must radiate its influence over a wider circle. It must touch government as well as commerce; it must stimulate action, both promotional and corrective, in the direction of efficiency, higher standards and nobler ideals. (Bruce 1920, 27)

Members of Congress responded by praising the collective efforts of the US Chambers of Commerce. Regarding lobbying efforts on a railroad bill, Senator Curtis said that legislators "were impressed by the national Chambers' referendum ... a statement by folks with whom we are acquainted of a conclusion reached as the outgrowth of study for a period of days, or weeks, carries weight ... regardless of the outcome of the proposed legislation, the Chambers of Commerce of the United States has set an example of how to present helpful information to Congress which others engaged in similar work could follow with profit" (Bruce 1920, 183). He also noted that the principles and policies advocated by the Chambers made their way into legislation.

The Chambers of Commerce quickly institutionalized its relationships with Congress and policy making. It secured a legislative reference division in the congressional library and also pushed for a dedicated bureau for bill drafting for "more carefully considered and better prepared legislation."[31] In annual meetings, the Chambers of Commerce noted its success in helping to create institutions such as the Federal Trade Commission. A special committee composed of four businessmen, two economists, and one lawyer submitted drafts of legislation. And in testimony before the Senate Committee on Interstate Commerce, the Chambers recommended changes to the Interstate Trade Commission, which "were incorporated in the bill as enacted."[32] In a how-to guide to running trade associations, Emmett Hay Naylor, president of the Trade Association Executives, instructed businessmen to go directly to members of Congress with their preferences on pending legislation. He argued that "unrestricted competition is unnatural and fallacious" and that cooperation among different sectors of the business community was "essential to industrial welfare."[33]

The National Board of Trade, while relatively short lived, was critical to the development of national business organizations. It created a forum in which business leaders forged and nurtured a distinct class identity as capitalist merchants and manufacturers (Davis 2014). National organization cut across the sectoral lines of trade associations, which was critical to interest aggregation

---

[31] Annual Report of the Board of Directors of the Chambers of Commerce of the United States, Third Annual Meeting, February 1915, p. 6.

[32] Ibid., 9.

[33] Emmett Hay Naylor, *Trade Associations: Their Organization and Management* (New York, NY: Ronald Press Co., 1921), 28.

and prioritization. Further, the NBT showed how business leaders sought to apply principles that were revolutionizing corporations, such as management and oversight, to the work of governing. Finally, the political activities of business groups in the time of the NBT laid the groundwork for the later successes of NAM and the Chambers of Commerce.

Business Linkages to Parties

Business organization was critical not only to the formation of business preferences, but also to the politicization of business activity. From 1870 to 1890, business groups and leaders pioneered nascent techniques of political influence and lobbying. They testified before Congress, financed political campaigns, and served as advisors to new administrative agencies and committees of the federal government. Their demands and tactics undermined clientelistic business–party linkages, ushering in a new politics of pluralism.

The distributive nature of congressional politics through most of the nineteenth century created straightforward clientelistic relationships between parties and the nascent business community. Federal funds for local projects were used by local firms; as corporations became more important to the construction and management of transportation infrastructure, they would then seek further subsidies, land, and contracts from members of Congress. As the economic sector changed – as industry grew, manufacturing expanded, and the private sector overtook financing of infrastructure – business preferences for new kinds of governance also emerged.

As the previous section shows, business leaders debated the proper role of the federal government; they came to see clientelism and patronage as inimical to economic growth. Businesses advocated government solutions to complex economic problems. Their advocacy was based in part on successful adoption of institutional reforms and management practices within the business sector itself. They issued requests for the passage of specific pieces of legislation or the creation of regulatory boards. However, they also sought to establish long-term ties with political parties that would allow business influence in politics on a regular, routine basis. During the late nineteenth century, it was not just the preferences of business that evolved, but the politicization of those preferences and the translation of those preferences to direct political action. The politicization of business interests led to new forms of engagement between parties and interest groups that provided the foundation for programmatic competition.

Congressional Testimony

At meetings of the NBT, business leaders lamented that their knowledge of industry and policy often exceeded the knowledge of bureaucrats and politicians. They strategized how to develop relationships with politicians, and in particular how to help politicians craft more effective governing institutions.

One of the easiest ways to make their voices heard was to appear before Congress, which they did with increasing frequency in the late nineteenth century.

Business groups had occasionally testified before congressional committees during the nineteenth century, particularly on issues of local import. In 1861, the Boston Board of Trade sent a delegation of five members to advise on financial legislation pending before the Senate Finance Committee. The Boston Board of Trade also developed a simplified taxation scheme, working with the New York Chamber of Commerce and Philadelphia Board of Trade, and submitted it to the House Ways and Means Committee in 1862 (Davis 2014, 774). In 1865, the Treasury Secretary, Hugh McCulloch, appointed a three-person commission to examine federal revenue policy. He included two businessmen on the commission – David Wells, a textile manufacturer from Massachusetts, and Stephen Colwell, an iron manufacturer from Pennsylvania (Bensel 1990).

During the 1870s and 1880s, rates of business involvement in policy making increased. Not only did individual businesses appear more frequently before Congress, but also trade associations and peak organizations testified on behalf of the industries they represented. Trade associations therefore constituted the main interest group that appeared before Congress before the twentieth century, testifying on an array of policy issues.

Of the 250 organized interests that appeared at congressional hearings from 1870 to 1890, peak business organizations, large corporations, and trade associations made up over 70 percent of the testimonies (Loomis 2011, 31). Combined, these trade associations and private corporations tripled their appearances before Congress – from 800 to 3,000 appearances – between 1900 and 1909 alone (Tichenor and Harris 2002, 597). From 1899 to 1909, trade associations made up over 47 percent of appearances before Congress (Figure 3.1). These interests therefore became more intertwined with the policy-making community. In comparison, professional associations, trade unions, and agricultural interests testified before committees only on occasion.

In a study of all the groups that testified before Congress, Tichenor and Harris (2005) find that there has been no single decade from 1833 to 1968 in which citizen, labor, and professional groups rivaled the number of appearances from organized business interests. Over this century, business interests appeared in 54 percent of congressional hearings, while citizen and labor groups made up only 31 percent. Businesses were disproportionately active in the late nineteenth century, appearing before Congress to testify on programmatic issues such as civil service reform and national regulation.

Business testimony was crucial for passage of the Interstate Commerce Act of 1887, the first significant assertion of federal commerce power over the states. The act created a five-member commission to monitor and prevent rate discrimination and unfair practices. Although some large corporations were wary of what national regulation would entail, records of trade associations show widespread support for regulatory commissions among large and small firms across economic sectors. The legislative history of the act shows that it was

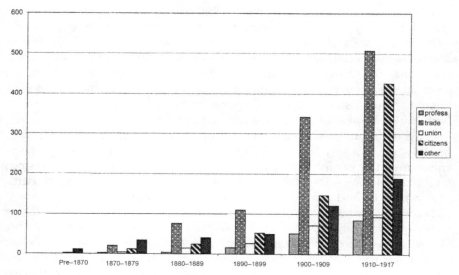

FIGURE 3.1 Interest group appearances before Congress. From Tichenor and Harris (2002).

created not to spite railways, but rather to foster productive relations between the federal government and the growing business community. Even the railways themselves were proponents of regulation; a full decade before the ICC, the trade publication *Railway World* argued that railways were now national, not state, affairs: "the Government must be placed, by law, in such a position as to protect, when necessary, the railways, or take control of them" (Kolko 1963, 17).

In 1882, appearing before the Committee on Commerce, Josiah White, a railway owner, testified in favor of the ICC on behalf of the Board of Trade and Transportation: "there must be, sooner or later, a department of this government to regulate it ... the problem is so complex in its minuteness and so extensive in its ramifications that nothing short of a governmental department of this kind can deal with it."[34] Delegates from the Pennsylvania Railroad testified against specific portions of drafts of the bill, while agreeing that the federal government nevertheless needed oversight of the industry. Testifying before the Senate Committee on Interstate Commerce, Simon Sterne, from the Board of Trade and Transportation of New York, also demanded "a national law upon this subject regulating interstate commerce ... and coupled with that

[34] H. Misc. Doc. 55, 47th Congress, 1st Session, "Arguments and Statements before the Commitee on Commerce in relation to certain bills referred to that committee proposing Congressional regulation of interstate commerce," February 22, 1882, p. 30.

law there should be a national commission, with judicial powers, for the purpose of giving that law its proper enforcement."[35]

In trying to win support from some of the reluctant railway owners, government officials assured them that there would be cooperative ties between business and politicians. Richard Olney, the Attorney General, wrote to the president of the Burlington Railroad that the ICC could be "of great use to the railroads ... the older such a commission gets to be, the more inclined it will be to take the business and railroad view of things" (McConnell 1966, 284). As Congress debated the ICC in its 1885–86 session, "businessmen throughout the nation supported the idea of regulation in overwhelming numbers ... petitions from business groups were almost unanimous in favoring federal action" (Purcell 1967, 575). The ICC created a precedent for federal regulation, and in the early twentieth century many commissions were established to oversee utilities and trade.

By the late nineteenth century, parties were becoming more responsive to groups in the electorate and were crafting ways to satisfy demands for national policies. The ties between businesses and parties established in the late nineteenth century created a model for political participation of other interest groups. First, the corporate sector helped legitimize government regulation and demonstrated how powerful an organized interest could be in seeing its policy demands met. Business was therefore on the vanguard of the nationalization of issues, and a transition away from federalist and laissez-faire principles. As "merchants, manufacturers, and bankers ... sought more dependable and rewarding relations with government," they laid the groundwork for future Progressive reformers to do the same (Wiebe 1967, 167).

Campaign Finance

Aside from direct influence of congressional testimony, businesses also sought to influence political parties themselves. They saw the parties of the nineteenth century as the "chief obstacles to the modernization of business ... in America" (Walker 1991, 24). The Grant campaigns of 1868 and 1872 cost roughly $200,000 – double what the Republican party had spent in 1860. The campaign's backers included John Jacob Astor II, the Vanderbilts, and corporations with Interior and War Department contracts. The Democratic party received $40,000 from H. T. Helmbold, an advertiser of patent medicines, and political figures like Samuel Tilden (Overacker 1932; Thayer 1973). Five of the six Democratic presidential nominees at the turn of the century were from New York – a concession to the party's need for Wall Street financing (diSalvo 2012).

---

[35] Sen. Rep. 46, 49th Congress, 1st Session, *Report of the Senate Select Committee on Interstate Commerce*, January 18, 1886, p. 81.

The Pendleton Act of 1883 enacted civil service reforms and banned assessments of federal employees. Parties were therefore deprived of their primary source of financing. The parties secured civil service reform only when "facing interest groups demands, and reliant on interest group contributions to finance campaigns." (Johnson and Libecap 1994, 93). Although both parties benefited from civil service reforms – by eliminating patronage, they freed up time for many other political duties – they also saw an opportunity to guarantee ongoing party resources through interest group politics. Business groups, through their pressure tactics before Congress, established integral links with parties that then led to "organizing ... around policies and not simply over spoils" (Silberman 1993, 283).

The Republican party in particular pioneered modern campaign financing techniques. In 1880, Mark Hanna, a Republican strategist from Ohio, founded the Business Men's League – an organization devoted to campaigning for James A. Garfield. By 1896, when he orchestrated William McKinley's victory, Hanna solicited funds from an array of deep-pocketed business leaders. By asking for donations to the party itself rather than to individual candidates, Hanna centralized party power and ensured coordinated campaign messages across Republican candidates. By creating a constant source of revenue from donors, parties could also fund activities to strategize between elections, rather than developing ad hoc policies only in election years.

Meanwhile, the Democrats included bankers and railway executives among their leaders – Senator Henry B. Payne was a railroad president, and his son was a treasurer of Standard Oil; the Clevelands and Tildens, powerful Democratic families, were corporate lawyers (diSalvo 2012). At the local level, parties developed ties to businesses as a way to build organization (Higgens-Evenson 2003; Shefter 1976).

Over the next few decades, companies across industrial sectors became wealthy backers of the national parties. By the interwar period, business was considered a privileged interest by the sheer fact of its necessity to campaign war chests (Summers 2002; Webber and Domhoff 1996). Campaign finance therefore created significant ties between the business sector and political parties. And through financing parties, industrialists such as manufacturers, financiers, and traders "place[d] the party leaders in a position in which they must hear, if not always heed, the wishes of business leaders" (Key 1964, 125). The cost of elections increased dramatically, as shown in Figure 3.2.

The period of 1870–1890 was one in which the preferences of the business community aligned with programmatic reforms. By pushing for more effective service delivery, less patronage, and more regulation, businesses and parties established lasting ties that fostered national public policy. Business organizations became increasingly important to government after the World War I. Corporations sought further regulation, and grew their lobbying arms in order to maintain a permanent presence in Congress and administrative agencies. Although there were debates about whether trade associations violated antitrust

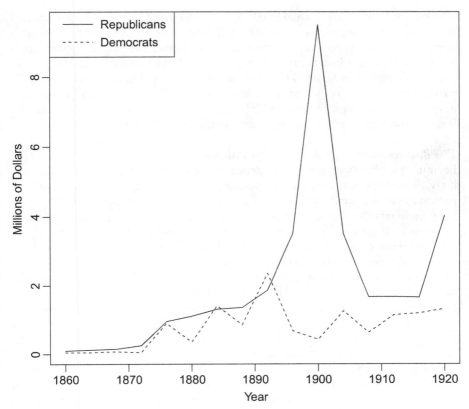

FIGURE 3.2 Campaign expenditures, 1860–1920. From Overacker (1932).

laws, by 1925, the Supreme Court ruled in favor of allowing them. Justices Stone, Brandeis, and Harlan argued that trade associations "prevented overproduction, led to a more scientific knowledge of business conditions, and avoided economic crises" (Carrott 1970, 335). In the 1920s, the heads of the antitrust division of the Department of Justice as well as the Federal Trade Commission both publicly acknowledged the utility of trade organizations. They argued that such associations blunted the hardships of competition, assisted small manufacturers, and improved economic laws.

BUSINESSES, PLURALISM, AND PROGRAMMATIC PARTIES

Although national parties were technically organized during the Second Party System in the mid-nineteenth century – the Democratic National Committee formed in 1848; the Republican National Committee in 1856 – they were beholden to local associations. After the Civil War, "the party system emerged strengthened rather than weakened" (Silberman 1993, 250). The parties had realigned along geographic lines, with the South solidly Democratic, and with Republican support concentrated in the North. Democrats enjoyed some measure of support in urban areas with high rates of immigration, such as cities in New York and New Jersey. However, neither party had programs to speak of, particularly programs that would address the needs of the new industrial economy and its groups of farmers, laborers, and industrialists (diSalvo 2012). Instead, the parties regarded patronage as the goal of governance.

The Business Template for Pluralist Politics

Beginning in the 1830s, political parties engaged with the electorate in increasingly clientelistic ways. The Jacksonian model of the party relied exclusively on patronage at the local and national levels, creating ties of material obligation between party leaders and voters. As suffrage expanded, parties mobilized voters with bribes and positions in government, and used the resources of the state to reward specific districts and individuals with benefits such as land grants and federal funds. Clientelistic politics impeded the development of more centralized administrative institutions, but were effective in facilitating the nascent industrial economy. These political strategies later became untenable to an emerging business elite. This chapter has shown that new forms of capitalist management and organization preceded political reforms and created a group of economic actors opposed to clientelism. Business leaders demanded programmatic politics to make democracy safe for capitalism and ensure sustained economic growth.

In the decades after the Civil War, a combination of the rise of managerial capitalism and government reliance on patronage led business interests to crystallize in favor of institutional reforms. Capitalist political identity was carefully constructed through the adaptation of the corporate form to government institutions, and through the creation of linkages to parties and to the political process. Commercial elites turned to the state to stabilize modern capitalism through improved government administration (Berk 1991; Hawley 1978). As businessmen became more involved in politics, it was not a "hostile attempt by capitalists to take over the parties," but instead a "confluence of interests" as parties themselves also sought to modernize their campaign methods and organizations (Klinghard 2010, 123).

Business was on the vanguard of nationalizing economic issues and expanding the administrative capacities of the federal government. Parties moved away from being vehicles of mass mobilization as they lessened reliance on patronage, since they could no longer build support through the disbursement of material benefits alone (Balogh 2003). This represented a rebuke of patronage and a turn toward a more pluralistic representative democracy that we see in modern politics. Congress and the bureaucracy, after the 1880s and 1890s, needed to mediate conflict among clashing interests through regulation and planning (Lowi 1964; McCormick 1981; Skowronek 1982).

A critical element of the shift to programmatic party strategies was that, in establishing new forms of political ties with business groups, parties reconfigured their relationships to other groups in society as well. Business organization and involvement in politics provided a framework for subsequent Progressive organization and success (Hays 1957; Hofstadter 1955; Lowi 1979; McCormick 1986; Wiebe 1967). While labor unions, women's groups, and farmers' and producers' organizations may not have been able to match the financial heft of business groups, they adopted the same repertoires of political engagement. The Progressive movement also built on the institutional successes of businesses at the state and federal levels by strengthening the commissions and agencies that business had advocated (McCormick 1981, 248). The rise of competing and distinct interests also forced parties to adopt coherent policy agendas that created different visions for society (Sklar 1988, 30). The groundwork for party linkages with Progressive organizations lay in the business groups that sought consistent policies from parties.

Citizens' groups adopted "business models" for organization and political activity (Clemens 1997, 11). The new administrative apparatus expanded opportunities for the involvement of other organized interests; "rather than denouncing large corporations, cooperative associations increasingly demanded to be treated on the same terms" (Clemens 1997, 166). Agrarian organizations, for example, adopted methods of corporate organization through "themes of efficiency and rationality." In 1915, a trade publication for an agricultural cooperative wrote that "there should be but little difference in the organization, control, and management of a co-operative business and a corporate business ... if a co-operative business is to succeed control must be lodged in a competent manager, just as it is in a corporation" (Clemens 1997, 201). Women's groups also "sought to appropriate the cultural cachet of business methods" through centralized hierarchies in clubs and temperance and labor groups. The progressive impulse of many of these groups was to apply scientific expertise to social problems through government commissions (Sanders 1999). Citizens' groups emulated the way businesses approached problem-solving and cooperation (Haber 1964).

The Gilded Age was a period of capitalist and democratic reconfiguration that served the interests of business and of political reformers. Assuming the structural power of business or monolithic position of the corporation in this period ignores the historical evidence that capitalists were invested in reducing patronage and erecting a stable, more effective regulatory apparatus that would serve the needs of the industrial economy. Regulation helped businesses shift the arena of political contestation from costly litigation battles to the legislature and bureaucracy. Rather than target business directly, citizens' and labor organizations "agitated for greater governmental role in support of their policy objectives" (Johnson 2009).

There is evidence that businessmen were instrumental in the origins of the Progressive movement itself, forming crucial alliances with middle-class, educated reformers in many states (Berk 1991; McCormick 1981). The organizational synthesis school argues that the Progressive movement was a culmination of organizational impulses epitomized by the corporation: While reformers may have decried the wealth and monopoly power of the industries, they nonetheless saw the corporation as a model for social organization (Galambos 1983). Further, while Progressives were able to constrain some of the activities of business through stronger regulation, the reforms of the 1880s forced Progressives to accept the corporation as a fact of American life: "more often than not, the achievement of what used to be called reform now appears to have benefited big business interests" (McCormick 1981, 248).

The impact of the expansion of the administrative state was a transition in economic policy away from one in which the government distributed resources on the basis of patronage. Regulation was a new and permanent feature of government, which then led associations to make demands on government agencies to meet their specialized needs. Federal regulation then spread to the states: From 1905 to 1907, fifteen states created railroad commissions; they also expanded commissions to oversee public utilities such as electricity, telegraphy, and gas (McCormick 1981). As Zunz notes, "big business ... not government invented American bureaucracy" (Zunz 1990). Newly organized interest groups needed to orient their political demands to the federal government, rather than the states, where administrative capacities were still "sporadic and uneven" (Johnson 2009, 98).

It might seem paradoxical that Progressive reformers both rallied against corporate influence and were also, in many ways, indebted to it. Corporations were rightfully seen as villainous dating to the 1870s, when the scandals of the Grant administration revealed just how far some robber barons went in securing economic advantage and political favors. In 1873, the founder of *The Nation*, E. L. Godkin, wrote that "the government must get out of the 'protective' business and the 'subsidy' business and the 'improvement' and the 'development' business. It must let trade, and commerce, and manufactures, and steamboats, and railroads, and telegraphs alone. It cannot touch them without breeding corruption."[36] What is notable is that businesses *themselves* had made the same determination – that the government's distributive role in facilitating economic development was no longer sufficient in a period of industrialization.

Programmatic Party Organization
As parties accommodated the demands of new organized interests in society through policy, they "reconfigured the key medium for influencing elections" (Balogh 2003, 226). The parties nationalized their offices and organizations,

---

[36] *The Nation*, January 30, 1873, p. 68.

developing modern forms of campaigning. The Democratic National Committee, in 1892, expanded the role of its executive and advisory committees. One committee supervised fund raising, while another conducted activities such as "the distribution of literature, the arrangements for speakers, the securing of reports from the several States, and the outlining of plans of battle in the various sections of the country" (Klinghard 2010, 113).

The Republican National Committee made similar changes to its organization. As the Republicans built their national organizations, their efforts were hamstrung by powerful state parties in New York and Pennsylvania. The national party therefore brought in John Wanamaker, the owner of a department store chain, to serve as chairman in 1888. Wanamaker created an advisory board of businessmen to supervise party funds, which "played into the business community's growing sense of its own role as a reforming element of American politics" (Klinghard 2010, 119).

The ties between business leaders and parties became formalized not only through campaign financing, but also through adoption of management techniques to the formal party organizations. A Minnesota Republican in 1887 advised his party to adopt the strategy of the American Iron and Steel Association by disseminating pamphlets and educational literature to help voters "read, think, and understand for themselves" (Klinghard 2010, 103). The national committees began to raise funds outside state parties, and used these funds for direct presidential campaigns and printed materials. Policy was central to party nationalization, with parties engaged in calibrating their public appeals in response to the demands of interest groups. Party leaders also pioneered education campaigns that sought to replace local interests with informed views on national policies.

As parties became more programmatic in orientation, they sought to build coalitions across different interests and to cater to those interests in and across elections. Pluralist demands from organized associations were integral to new programmatic parties. By 1890, "business, farmers and workers ... found that as organized groups they could wield far more power ... Industrialism had shifted the context of economic decisions from personal relationships among individuals to competition among well-organized groups" (Hays 1957). Progressive reformers were hostile to special interests, but they nonetheless used the framework of interest group politics to mobilize public support and to reach national markets (Balogh 2003). The Progressives therefore followed federal regulation and antitrust policies and "brought further centralization of regulatory, social welfare, and resource conservation functions at the federal level" (Sylla 2000, 539). Business provided the organizational repertoires that other interest groups adopted; as Clemens argues, only after learning from the engrained "business methods" established by the private sector did many farmers', women's, and labor groups succeed (Clemens 1997). These methods included bureaucratic organization, competent management, nonpartisan ties to political officials, and ongoing relationships with state institutions.

The national party organizations became more attuned to national issues such as currency policy, tariffs, and railway regulation as they crafted party platforms and developed policy agendas. Although Republican presidents were successively elected from 1860 to 1884, capitalizing on victory in war as well as a Democratic failure to develop "issues of national scope that could tie the party together and attract uncommitted voters," there were high levels of competition for congressional office (Friedman 1973, 887). The national parties, staffed with professionals and utilizing increasing financial and communications resources, developed issue-oriented campaigns with which to attract voters.

The issues that distinguished Republicans and Democrats first centered around tariffs. Republicans supported tariffs to benefit Northeast manufacturers and laborers. They argued that Democrats were insensitive to working-class laborers who were hurt by the import of goods manufactured with cheap labor, just as Democrats were insensitive to a host of moral issues, such as the freed slaves of the South. Democrats, on the other hand, argued that Republican tariffs were onerous, outweighed by personal liberty and limited government (Shefter 1976, 465).

After the 1890s, presidents began to commit themselves to specific legislative proposals. President McKinley delivered a speech to the National Association of Manufacturers on January 28, 1898, in which he addressed currency policy and pending congressional legislation. By the early twentieth century, it was commonplace when Teddy Roosevelt and Woodrow Wilson addressed policy issues. The clientelistic tactics parties had successfully employed as the party system evolved slowly gave way, after 1870, to issue-oriented programmatic competition.

The meteoric rise of the managerial corporation, and of its political influence, made the 1870s and 1880s a time of profound change. Political parties reconfigured their relationship with citizens by building institutions that allowed more uniformity and coherence in policy, with more attention to long-term policy consequences. The associational model of politics provided a "corrective to traditional party methods" by replacing reliance on local patronage with political organization and partisan loyalties (Klinghard 2010, 68).

By the late nineteenth century, business organizations created an efficient lobbying industry that replaced previous forms of haphazard distributive politics. In 1874 a special House investigating committee found that "this country is fast becoming filled with gigantic corporations wielding and controlling immense aggregations of money and thereby commanding great influence and power."[37] For the next half-century, business became synonymous with wealth and power. The lobbying industry became well established and was seen as a

---

[37] US House of Representatives, Report of the Select Committee to Investigate the Alleged Credit Mobilier Bribery, 42d Congress, 3rd Session, 1873, Report No. 77.

way for corporations to dominate policy, with many governors and public officials calling for control of lobbying and campaign finance (McCormick 1981, 264). In 1925, President Coolidge famously remarked that "the chief business of the American people is business." And by 1928, the historian W. B. Munro declared that "from the first to the last in the history of government, this money power, the interest of vested wealth, has been the best organized, the most inherently cohesive, and on the whole the most enlightened determinant of public policy" (Munro 1928, 115).

It is important to note that businesses indeed exerted undue influence in politics. The argument here is not necessarily that business demands somehow aligned with the public good, or that businesses' political activities were not self-serving. Indeed, business interests became so inextricably intertwined with regulatory politics that by the New Deal, commissions were controversial. In 1937 the President's Committee on Administrative Management called them a "headless fourth branch of the Government, responsible to no one, and impossible of coordination with the general policies and work of the Government"[38] Twentieth-century observers have accused even early commissions of regulatory capture: "The outstanding political fact about the independent regulatory commissions is that they have in general become promoters and protectors of the industries they have been established to regulate" (McConnell 1966, 287). Heilbroner also observed in the 1970s that "if nearly a century of regulatory history tells us anything, it's that the rules-making agencies of government are almost invariably captured by the industries which they are established to control" (Heilbroner 1972, 239).

Business groups nonetheless provided an impetus for parties to open the political process to various interests and to accommodate their demands through national policies. Interest group politics in itself was critical to programmatic party organization. It represented an explicit turn from the clientelism of the nineteenth century, since instead of just focusing on "distinct privileges to enterprising individuals and corporations ... the government now began to take explicit account of clashing interests and to assume the responsibility for mitigating their conflicts through regulation, administration, and planning" (McCormick 1981, 251). Herbert Hoover, who had been Secretary of Commerce before becoming president, mobilized organized interests in order to bolster electoral support. He appealed to specific constituencies by creating advisory committees with representatives drawn from the business community (Balogh 2003). While after the Civil War there were only around 50 interest groups in the District of Columbia; by 1930, there were more than 500 (Walker 1991).

[38] *Report of the President's Commission on Administrative Management*, 74th Congress, 2nd Session, 1937, p. 32.

This chapter has shown that changes in the economic sector led businesses to create new forms of political organization and to pressure parties to rethink their governing strategies. Business activities ushered in a new era of democratic representation, with parties responding to pressure to strengthen programmatic institutions and to create opportunities for influence in the political process.

4

Clientelism and Governance in Britain, 1850–1880

In the United States, clientelism and patronage evolved as democracy expanded in the nineteenth century. As more voters became enfranchised, parties courted them with promises of cash and jobs. In Britain, the timing of clientelism was relatively similar. Vote buying and bribery also rose throughout the nineteenth century as suffrage expanded. Parliament was concerned primarily with matters that emerged not from average British citizens, but rather from the king – such as taxation and foreign wars – while also using private bill procedure to enact minor development policy and personal favors. An established system of "Old Corruption" in the eighteenth century allowed aristocrats to use their status as parliamentarians to deliver favors to friends and family; state offices and sinecures were often passed down within families.

This chapter describes the way clientelism evolved in Britain over a series of three extensions of the suffrage in 1832, 1867, and 1885. Vote buying was widespread in this period, growing out of a tradition of "treating" electors with transportation, lodging, food, and similar gifts of appreciation. Despite concerns over vote buying, efforts to curb these practices, such as a Corrupt Practices Act in 1854, did little to stop elected officials from engaging in bribery. Further, Britain's central government lacked authority to address increasingly national issues brought on by industrialization. Longstanding practices of patronage and parliamentary distributive policy made it difficult for parties to devise issue-oriented campaigns. Similarly to the United States, clientelism in Britain was used across multiple arenas of politics, constituting an overarching strategy that parties used both to win elections and to govern. Unlike in the United States, however, British parties began to pursue a strategy of programmatic linkage in conjunction with British business activity, which will be detailed in Chapter 5. As a result, the British reformed the state in accordance with business demands, while also establishing methods of interest representation that allowed them to integrate the concerns of organized segments of voters.

CLIENTELISM AND VOTE BUYING IN BRITISH ELECTIONS

In Britain, although the electorate was much more restricted than that of the United States through the nineteenth century, elections were conducted in a similar manner: with raucous fanfare and little policy substance. Although full suffrage would not be achieved until the twentieth century, the electoral politics of the nineteenth century were turbulent, with many unsuccessful efforts to root out clientelism.

Prior to 1832, limited suffrage in Britain had established longstanding electoral traditions. Elections were multiday (if not multiweek) affairs in which candidates plied voters with food and drink and provided housing to voters traveling long distances. Aristocratic landowners provided favors – blankets in winter, leisure outings – in exchange for unwavering electoral support. Aristocratic influence was considered natural, and citizens were expected to defer to ranks and titles (Heesom 1988; Moore 1976). Poll books from the years before 1832 document voters' choices, since voting was conducted *viva voce*, and show that landowners enjoyed near-unanimous support. The most egregious forms of aristocratic influence, however, were considered illegitimate. Some constituencies became known as "rotten boroughs," in which landlords possessed so much influence so as to render electoral competition nonexistent. In Parliament, representatives from these constituencies wielded disproportionate power, while growing urban areas such as Manchester, Birmingham, and Sheffield were unrepresented in the House of Commons.

Malapportionment between rural and urban areas, combined with popular discontent against limited suffrage, led to passage of the 1832 Representation of the People Act. Also known as the Great Reform Act, this legislation expanded the electorate by changing the requirements to vote, and created a new system of election registration whereby election agents would have to document the qualified voters in each constituency (Table 4.1). The electorate expanded to between 650,000 and 800,000 voters (Phillips and Wetherell 1995, 414). More than eighty small boroughs, most of which were rotten or pocket boroughs – so termed because voters were completely indebted to individual aristocrats – were stripped of representation. Other small boroughs had representation reduced from multiple members to single members. Forty towns and cities were given representation, and more MPs were allocated to urban areas (Phillips and Wetherell 1995; Porritt 1909). Both Liberal and Conservative party leaders supported political reform, although specific legislation was extensively negotiated. The franchise, for example, had created a system in which some electors were given multiple votes depending on their professions or where they lived. Clergymen and university dons were eligible for multiple votes, and in districts with multiple members in the House of Commons, electors were given more

TABLE 4.1 *Changes in the British electorate, 1801–1911*

Year	Estimated No. of Voters	% Enfranchised Males	No. of Constituencies
1801	503,640	16	380
1831	497,197	11	379
1833	811,443	18	401
1866	1,364,000	20	401
1868	2,477,713	33	420
1883	3,152,000	34	416
1885	5,708,000	62	643
1911	7,904,000		643

From Salmon 2009b, 262.

votes. Other qualifications for voting were related to occupation, lodging, freemen status, and university employment. The Great Reform Act tried to create more uniformity by introducing requirements for the franchise, usually in the form of property ownership. While historians acknowledge a minor role that "average" citizens played in passage of the first Reform Act, they find very little role for the working class in the politics of the 1867 and 1884 reform acts (Salmon 2009a).[1] The main purpose of the Reform Acts was to overhaul an antiquated and inefficient voting system.

The Great Reform Act led to more popular participation in elections, and parties responded to new levels of competition by amplifying the corrupt strategies to which they were accustomed. Even into the Victorian period, "some 'influence' was considered natural and proper" (Pugh 2002, 10). Election agents, typically local solicitors, "grew fat" by using elections "for their financial rather than their political significance" (Gash 1977, xi). Similarly, Nossiter describes an "instrumental rationality" in which "the floating voter in Victorian England was often the 'quoting voter' polling when and where the price was right" (Nossiter 1975, 7). There were also examples of threats being used to influence voters, rather than positive inducements. Landlords could threaten termination of tenancy; employers could threaten to dismiss employees. In some districts, election agents also threatened voters with violence, "cooping" (imprisonment), or military conscription (Gash 1977).

Landlords exerted influence in Conservative counties, and much of the clientelism that took place in British elections was a result of established traditions in these areas: "[T]he political character of a county was decided almost entirely by its landlords" (Hanham 1978, 6). There was a culture of deference

---

[1] See also the debate between Rueschemeyer, Stephens, and Stephens (1992) and Collier (1999).

that pervaded elections, with adherence to tradition paramount (Moore 1976). It was not necessarily considered nefarious for landlords to influence tenants – rather, being part of the landlord's party was "often a tacit condition of tenancy" (Pollock 1883, 151). Given that counties were dominated by landholding elites, they tended to align with conservative interests; by 1874, Conservatives won five times as many county seats as their opponents (Hanham 1978, 25).

While many industrial towns of the boroughs, such as Leeds, Manchester, and Birmingham, were strongholds for Liberal politics, elections were no less predetermined. Influence of a similar nature flourished; "the pattern in new industrial boroughs often repeated in certain respects that of county or medieval borough seats," except with factories acting as the rural estate (Pugh 2002, 13). Manufacturers' factories or mills were "the main source of income and employment" (Hanham 1978, 41). Sometimes there was little need even for electoral pressure – knowledge of an employer's party preference alone could determine the district's persuasion. Voters were not simply deferential, but also viewed employers' interests as aligned with their own (Hanham 1978, 77).

Practices of bribery and treating therefore emerged from traditional landlord–tenant relationships that were then adapted by candidates vying for electoral support. But even as attitudes about these practices evolved, politicians continued to use bribes to win votes. Gifts to constituencies grew from mere cash handouts: A wealthy MP in Westminster, for example, was expected to provide dinners and donations continuously throughout the year (Hanham 1978, 254). Some MPs provided ongoing donations for specific purposes, such as to maintain local clubs or museums. MPs also erected libraries, hosted weddings and banquets, and dispensed coal and bedding to the poor during winter. Election agents and solicitors hired to assist with electioneering also acted as negotiators for blocs of voters seeking the highest payout from candidates (Hanham 1978; Pugh 2002; Stokes 2013).

Just as the US Congress had procedures to evaluate claims of election corruption, Parliament also investigated the conduct of elections. An 1835 Royal Commission established to look into bribery in elections found flagrant abuses by at least eighteen MPs. Claims of bribery were difficult to prosecute because they needed to be explicitly linked to election agents working for parliamentary candidates. Nonetheless, in 1844, the town of Sudbury was disenfranchised because there was evidence of bribery that could not be tied to a specific agent. Parliament then passed the Corrupt Practices Act of 1853, which banned treating and bribery in elections, and also instituted procedures for the filing of campaign expenditures. However, the bill was widely considered an abject failure (Rix 2008; Seymour 1915). The act only penalized election candidates if they were directly involved in bribes, and MPs became adept at deflecting blame. Local election agents and temporary party workers became the vehicle of much electoral corruption, and candidates, for the most part, were able to evade punishment. Bribery continued through this period, sustained by cooperation between both parties to divide electoral constituencies between one another (Kam 2011).

The Royal Commissions continued to investigate bribery through the nineteenth century. Commission reports show that voters were offered treats such as hot breakfasts, jugs of ale, and "dinner money" (Gash 1977, 119). Money also went directly to publicans for allowing voters unlimited access to liquor and beer; voters sometimes received tickets for free alcohol at partisan-aligned pubs (Gash 1977, 120). Many pubs themselves served as polling sites (Clark 1983; Harrison 1971). Election agents, together with local publicans, "united to force a system of treating on the candidates."[2] Not only did politicians use bribes to win votes, but they also employed violence and intimidation. Rival parties hired gangs, and radical mobs often threatened or harmed voters and party agents (Gash 1977; Richter 1971).

Election petitions were also filed in this period, allowing losing candidates to bring suit when corrupt tactics were employed. The number of petitions peaked in the 1850s, but at least sixty-four districts in England experienced corruption in parliamentary elections between 1865 and 1884 as well (Figure 4.1).

In Britain, election petitions also show that vote buying was widespread throughout the nineteenth century. In the House of Commons, anticorruption legislation in the 1850s did almost nothing to curb the use of bribery and treating in parliamentary elections; by the 1880s, elections had become "unparalleled orgies of extravagance" (O'Gorman 1984, 157).

The House of Commons assigned Royal Commissions to investigate bribery in elections, resulting in lengthy reports documenting systematic use not only of money but also alcohol and food in campaigns. In 1870, Lord Hartington's Select Committee on Parliamentary and Municipal Elections found that "a considerable number of voters will not vote unless they are paid ... in some instances the bribery takes the form of payment by drink tickets instead of money; and more frequently the election is accompanied by an amount of drinking which is described as demoralising to the town."[3]

These petitions may understate the extent of clientelism because they were often negotiated behind the scenes. Since both parties engaged in vote buying, candidates were often reluctant to accuse opponents of bribery if they, too, could be found guilty. The worst scenario was that a constituency could be stripped of representation in the next election, further deterring a petition (Emanuel 1881). The costs of petitioning were also very high, requiring legal expenses and time to take testimonies (Gwyn 1962; Hanham 1978). In one case, J. A. Coppock, a Liberal party organizer, asked an opponent not to file a petition if the Liberals promised not to field a candidate at the next election (Burn 1950).

---

[2] *Report from the Select Committee on Bribery at Elections*, PP 1835 VIII, p. 34.
[3] *Report from the Select Committee on Parliamentary and Municipal Elections*, PP 1870 VI, p. 133.

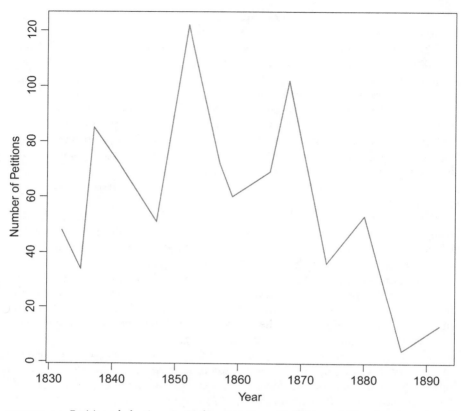

FIGURE 4.1 Petitioned elections in Parliament. From Rallings and Thrasher (2009).

From 1830 to 1880, electoral politics in Britain were very similar to that of the Second Party System in the United States. By creating a system of partisan voter registration, the 1832 Reform Act led candidates to adopt party labels in campaigns. Election registration therefore ensured local-level partisanship, although these parties were more akin to local networks than they were to organizations with distinct policy agendas (Ostrogorski 1903). General patterns did emerge – large rural areas dominated by aristocratic landlords voted for Conservatives and larger towns with industrial economies voted for Liberals (Cox 1987; Phillips and Wetherell 1995). As Prime Minister Robert Peel predicted, "registration will govern the disposal of offices, and determine the policy of party attack; and the power of this new element will go on increasing as its secret strength becomes better known and is more fully developed."[4] Registration societies sprang up across the country to monitor levels of electoral

---

[4] Quoted in Bulmer-Thomas (1953, 14).

support for each party and created lists of dues-paying party members who would also help with election-day activities. While the registration societies were later integrated into national party organizations, they initially served as conduits of clientelism. Society agents would bargain with railways or carriage proprietors to help transport voters to the polls, for example. They also helped connect potential local candidates for office with the party whip in Parliament, who would ask candidates for money before nominating them to office (Ostrogorski 1903). On election day, agents of registration societies stationed themselves at polling booths and in pubs to monitor voters and then reward them, with food and drink, after they cast their ballots.

The party in power alternated frequently over the nineteenth century, the result of local party organizing (Figure 4.2). Elections were dominated by local concerns, rather than national ones; they were run by local bosses; and MPs used office to dole out favors to themselves and their close supporters (Hanham 1978).

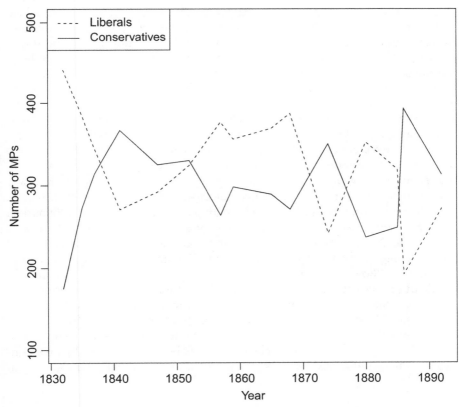

FIGURE 4.2 Party seat shares in House of Commons, 1832–1892. From Rallings and Thrasher (2009).

In 1867, the Second Reform Act further expanded the franchise. It also created new parliamentary constituencies (in urban areas), introducing new blocs of voters to the electorate. But this act did "nothing to check bribery and treating, which reached massive levels in the general election of 1880" (Hanham 1978, xii). Over the period 1832–1870, ideas about representation were more functional than direct; members of Parliament were not to follow the precise dictates of their constituents, but rather to act as natural leaders of the people (Beer 1982). By 1870, elections were evolving from contests shaped by local idiosyncrasies to races in which party control of the Parliament was at stake. Elections were rather uncompetitive through the mid-twentieth century, with the number of unopposed seats averaging around 50 percent. Low levels of electoral competition were attributed to Whigs and Tories "frequently agree [ing] ... to avoiding the trouble and expense of a contest" by letting certain seats go uncontested (Pugh 2002, 14). Further, there were so many elements of influence at work – landlords, municipal corporations, industrialists, parsons – that parties could not simply appeal to impartial choices of electors. At this point, parties were well served by patronage and vote buying, both of which helped them to secure support and also strengthened the party in Westminster (Gash 1977). As the historian Asa Briggs described elections, "if Westminster was a palace, the constituency at election times was often a pigsty ... bribery, intimidation, and treating were still commonplace" (Briggs 1959, 358). Electoral competition rose after the mid-nineteenth century, when parties stopped colluding on districts.

In 1872, Parliament passed the Ballot Act, establishing secrecy in elections. Although designed to curb excessive vote buying and intimidation, implementation of the secret ballot led some voters to demand higher bribes from parties. An early twentieth-century historian wrote that the "evil rather increased" in the 1870s as bribe prices rose (Seymour 1915, 435). The election of 1880 was so expensive and corrupt that eighteen members of Parliament were unseated. A British solicitor, in an address to a local affiliate of the Liberal party, remarked that the money spent on the 1880 election "went to enrich the agents, the publicans, and the sinners of the electoral body ... [such bribery is] debasing and demoralising" (Emanuel 1881, 16). A Royal Commission investigating corruption in the 1880 election in Sandwich lamented that "it did not appear that the mode of taking votes by ballot had the slightest effect in checking bribery ... [and] the engagement of committee-rooms at public-houses afforded a method by which ... clientele were very easily bribed."[5] In North Durham from 1868 to 1885, more than £90,000 was spent in parliamentary elections (Hanham 1978).

By the early 1900s, electoral clientelism was being supplanted by programmatic strategies and new ideas about representation. National campaigns began

---

[5] *Report of the Commissioners to Inquire into the Existence of Corrupt Practices in the Borough of Sandwich*, PP 1881 XLV, p. 15.

to focus on issues such as defense, taxation, and trade. Ideas about treating and bribery were also changing. A judge presiding over a contested election in Britain in 1886 wrote that treating was not corrupt per se, but "at the same time, the gifts of honest and sincere friendship may be perverted for corrupt purposes" (Seager 1909).

Clientleism in Britain therefore emerged from practices of patron–client benevolence and dependence. Voters did not have much power over legislators, so they used whatever bargaining power they had to exact benefits from MPs and to retain some measure of independence. Empirically, there was little correlation between constituency demographics and the voting records of parliamentarians – constituents did not hold politicians accountable "by rejecting, at the next general election, those who did not behave in the desired fashion" (Aydelotte 1976, 245). Bribery in the form of monetary payments, helping electors pay off debts, or providing compensation for injury was universal (O'Gorman 1984, 411).

The rise of programmatic competition after the Second Reform Act was evidenced by a delegitimization of clientelistic tactics, on the one hand, and adoption of new forms of party organization and voter mobilization, on the other. After 1870, political parties put into place an election machinery to oversee all candidates for office. Electoral competition increased, and parties contested seats in nonstronghold districts (Figure 4.3). Individual MPs could use state resources and party funds to build campaign war chests, and reached out to networks of social and extraparliamentary political organizations to expand their base of support. After the 1880s, "very few candidates would stand for election without the support of an agent, a constituency association and a number of local clubs" (Ingle 2008, 12). Elections became more competitive as parties organized new ways to shape election contests – previously, party ideologies were blurry enough that the Whigs and Tories would fight more *within* themselves to nominate candidates in single-party districts than they would *between* themselves (Pugh 2002).

The 1880 election represented a turning point in electoral clientelism in Britain. Levels of bribery reached unprecedented levels. Lewis Emanuel, a judge investigating bribery in elections, noted that Parliament had opened many inquiries into the 1880 election and "we find ... gross and unblushing bribery and corruption have prevailed ... more much was spent throughout the country by the Conservative than by Liberal candidates ... [but] both parties are pretty well tarred with the same brush, and the question of their relative turpitude is merely a question of degree" (Emanuel 1881, 16). He further noted that the election cost around 2 million pounds, "double the amount of any previous contest. How was all that money spent? The amount of the bribe ranged from a few shillings to 30 or 40 pounds, according to the rank of the elector and the severity of the fight" (Emanuel 1881, 16). The average cost of a campaign from 1832 to 1880 was £3,000 for a county, and these costs included not only registering voters but also financially supporting local activities,

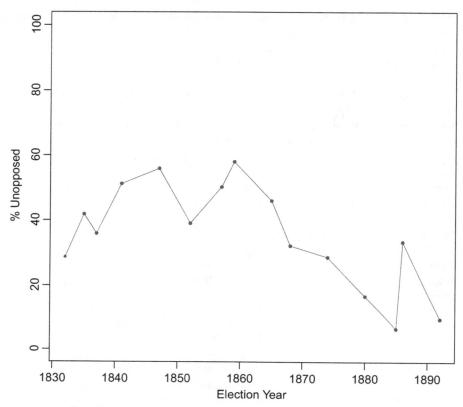

FIGURE 4.3 Unopposed seats in nineteenth-century parliamentary elections. From Rallings and Thrasher (2009).

paying local election agents and publicans, and hiring cabdrivers, canvassers, clerks, and messengers (Pinto-Duschkinsky 1981, 17).

The *Daily Telegraph* "noted the 'feeling of shame and humiliation which is experienced by all those who value the purity of national life'" (Rix 2008, 67). The election prompted 39 petitions, of which 25 went to trial, and ultimately 15 succeeded, unseating 18 MPs.[6] Parliament appointed a record eight Royal Commissions for the most egregious bribery cases, which far surpassed the number of Royal commissions previously appointed to investigate electoral corruption.

But in many ways, 1880 also heralded the first *modern* election: William Gladstone, leader of the Liberal party, conducted a whistle-stop national tour and made speeches to the public and to the press. This became standard fare for

---

[6] Single-member districts were not established until the Redistribution of Seats Act of 1885, so some constituencies elected multiple members to Parliament.

party leaders, with Lord Salisbury complaining to Queen Victoria in 1887 that "this duty of making political speeches is an aggravation of the labours of your Majesty's servant which we owe entirely to Mr. Gladstone" (Pugh 2002, 4). Furthermore, a full 83 percent of seats were contested, the highest number yet since the 1832 Reform Act. The elections of 1880 "produced a national campaign as distinct from the sporadic, localized contests typical of mid-Victorian elections" (Pugh 2002, 3). Programmatic issues included Gladstone's promise to reverse the foreign policy of the Tory leader Benjamin Disraeli, particularly regarding imperialism in Afghanistan and the Balkans, if elected. Gladstone used "active mobilization of public opinion behind a clearly articulated set of proposals" in the election, and as a result, the Liberals under Gladstone trounced Disraeli and the Conservatives (Hoppen 1998, 592). Lord Salisbury bemoaned this loss as partly the Conservatives' fault for fielding too many candidates instead of concentrating resources in key districts (Lloyd 1965, 265).

Election handy sheets from the 1880 election also emphasize war, particularly Conservatives blaming Liberals for wars in the colonies from the 1830s through the 1870s.[7] These campaign materials also highlight election issues such as religion, the Corn Laws, suffrage reform, and wine and liquor policies. In particular, parties do seem to try to claim credit; one example is the Conservatives blaming the Liberals for opposing the secret ballot.[8] With Gladstone as Prime Minister, the Liberal majority of 110 seats in Parliament allowed him to "embark upon an unprecedented programme of legislation designed to confirm the voters' faith" (Hoppen 1998, 592). This was a watershed development: No Prime Ministers had previously considered legislation as the main function of government. By 1885, the Liberal MP Joseph Chamberlain was following suit with a set of proposals including abolishment of plural voting, paying MPs, and establishing graduated taxes.

Although bribery continued into the twentieth century, Parliament strengthened anticorruption statutes with the 1883 Corrupt and Illegal Practices Act. This legislation was more stringent than its 1853 counterpart: It set maximum expenditure limits in campaigns, required candidates to submit election expenses, and granted the Director of Public Prosecutions power to bring legal cases about corruption. By 1885, "corruption of the more blatant sort steadily decreased" (Hanham 1978, 281).

CLIENTELISM AND DISTRIBUTIVE POLICY IN BRITAIN

As the Liberal and Conservative parties increasingly used party labels as meaningful signifiers of policy, they also strengthened their policy-making responsibilities in Parliament. For the better part of the nineteenth century, MPs in the

---

[7] Election materials in London School of Economics (LSE) Archives, Coll. Misc. 653.
[8] Coll Misc 653, LSE archives.

House of Commons had very limited responsibilities. They provided patronage to supporters and family, and occasionally legislated on matters of defense, finance, and local development. Attendance in Parliament was "fitful," and MPs took long breaks between August and February for the shooting season (Pugh 2002). Even after the Great Reform Act of 1832, party discipline was low, and the Commons in particular was composed of moderates – there was little evidence of partisan factions in roll call voting (Berrington 1968; Pugh 2002). The period between the First and Second Reform Acts, or 1832–1867, has been described instead as a golden age of backbenchers, when MPs with no party affiliation wielded political power (Pares 1963). In the final decades of the nineteenth century, however, parties – which had relied on distributive policies – began to expand ministerial and administrative control. This section describes how the activities of Parliament developed in the nineteenth century, and shows that Parliament concerned itself with local, distributive policies rather than programmatic goods.

Parliamentary legislation served little function before the eighteenth century except the expansion of the fiscal-military state. After that point, legislation began to address transportation, such as turnpikes, bridges, and canals. Private act procedure also allowed Parliament to legislate on personal matters dealing with estates, inheritances, and wills. The government was primarily responsible for maintaining order, fighting wars, and overseeing foreign affairs. Parliament was not the locus of public policy, nor did it regulate domestic affairs.

Examining the distinct types of legislation enacted by Parliament provides insight into distributive politics and clientelism. Entering the nineteenth century, Parliament could pass three types of legislation: public and general acts, which were acts of national import; local and personal acts; and private bills, which concerned personal matters. Local acts emerged from the tradition of petitioning the king for redress. In the eighteenth century, landowners petitioned Parliament for enclosures of the commons and privatization of land. After this, local landowners and corporations increasingly turned to Parliament to assist with economic enterprise and local development. Individuals and corporations would propose local acts, and proposals had to "contain allegations of some sort of affairs which could not be remedied" through private activity alone (Williams 1948, 28). As Table 4.2 shows, by the early nineteenth

TABLE 4.2 *The growth of private bills in the eighteenth century*

Years	Turnpike Acts	Years	Enclosure Acts
1760–1774	452	1719–1743	87
1785–1800	643	1770–1794	1058
1800–1809	419	1800+	1100+

From Williams (1948).

century, Parliament had passed many acts dealing with turnpikes and enclosures. These laid a foundation for local and private interests to seek distributive policies from Parliament in the nineteenth century.

Although Britain had developed a strong fiscal-military state before the eighteenth century, the role of the state in effecting economic activity was seen as developmental and passive. Government could assist only in funding projects, developing resources, and creating schemes from which private enterprise could later benefit. Legislation was "private, local, and facultative" to help erect turnpikes, enclosures, or town improvements where local interests called for them (Pares 1963, 3). Occasionally, local acts assisted with nascent social policy (Silberman 1993, 344). For example, thousands of local acts passed during the eighteenth century created more than 300 improvement commissions. These commissions had power over lighting, paving, and sewage (Gutchen 1961).

The government therefore facilitated the shift to an industrial economy through distributive policy, rather than national coordinated policies. Local acts represented a "vivid example of the ways commercial groups utilized political authority for essentially narrow financial ends. Frequently monopoly rights were granted and, additionally, businessmen and investors well knew that parliament could provide exemplary security for their speculations" (Hoppit 1996, 121). Similarly to members of the U.S. Congress, in the absence of overarching principles guiding policy creation, MPs used their office for personal and local ends (Namier 1963). And this went hand in hand with electoral bribery. Candidates for office not only paid voters for their votes, but also "bestow [ed] their largess on boroughs as a whole and on electors individually" by building bridges and expanding harbors (Porritt 1909, 7).

Debates in the nineteenth century centered on the proper role of government, with most members of Parliament showing a strong preference for laissez-faire policies. However, local interests increasingly turned to Parliament for favorable resources as problems became national in scope (Nossiter 1975). Parties became even more reliant on distributive policy, since government "failed to provide an adequate nexus between Ministers, Members of Parliament, and leaders of the significant groups or communities" throughout the country (Porritt 1909, 309).

Some 21,000 local acts were passed in the nineteenth century, many of which concerned the railways. These acts allowed parties in Parliament to allocate resources to their constituencies and local supporters. These acts also disbursed funds to local and municipal corporations established with the limited purpose of building bridges and quays or deepening harbors and rivers (Porritt 1909). But interestingly, they also created a foundation for programmatic legislation in the 1900s. This is because, after decades of passing local legislation, politicians became motivated to seek general solutions for national problems:

The most important fact is ... that the expansion of railways for the first time brought more clearly than ever before into the consciousness of Parliament the conception that in private legislation there was an aspect of public, as well as one of private interest, to which no government could be indifferent; and that the function of Parliament was not merely to act justly as between parties, but also to consider and promote the interests of the public as a whole. (Williams 1948, 67)

The glut of railway legislation required procedural changes to expedite committee activity and bill passage, for example. From 1844 to 1847 alone, 600 private acts granted benefits to railways companies (Lindblom 1977). By the 1860s, "practically all the major changes made ... flowed, directly or indirectly, from the further development of railways ... and from the various problems that it raised – the protection of the public, the time spent on committees, on hearing contentious issues, and the expenses to parties" (Williams 1948, 127).

As Tilly (1998, 53) put it, "concentration of capital and the expansion of the estate pushed popular struggles from the local arena and from significant reliance on patronage toward claim-making in national arenas." The mid-Victorian period fundamentally shaped legislation; Parliament used local acts both to ameliorate the effects of industrialization and to develop public utilities such as railways, roads, canals, and gas and water. MPs developed political expertise in dealing with private acts – they could "modify and correct local provisions upon proof of their failure, and at last found on them a safe basis for general legislation" (Clifford 1885, 1: 266). Between 1858 and 1871, Parliament allocated £7.5 million to local areas; by 1871–1888, Parliament loaned £31.5 million (Williams 1948, 125). Between 1868 and 1896 expenditures at the local level rose by 150 percent, far outpacing population growth (Palmowski 2002, 381).

But local legislation grew onerous, and by the late nineteenth century, economists wondered if slavish adherence to laissez-faire ideas was really sustainable. Nassau Senior, a lawyer and political economist, argued that it was foolhardy to see no right for government interference, for "such an admission would prevent our profiting by experience." Similarly, the economist J. R. McCullouch called laissez-faire ideas "more the policy of a parrot than of a statesman," and even the classical economist J. E. Cairnes said that a rule of nonintervention was "liable to numerous exceptions" (Hoppen 1998, 93). Writing in the *Fortnightly Review*, Edmund Wilson, an advocate of national legislation, argued that laissez-faire "may be philosophical, but it may also be the result of cowardice, selfishness, and stupidity" (Wilson 1866).

In 1848, reformers in Parliament began to criticize the power of private bills:

The party bringing in the public bill is aiming at some public advantage – he is proposing to amend a law for the general good. The party promoting the private good, on the contrary, is aiming at some private advantage, and this often at the expense of the public.[9]

___

[9] Hume Tracts, 1848, Private Business in Parliament: Consolidation Acts, University College London Library.

Meanwhile, public business increased drastically, doubling from 1801 to 1813 alone. In the parliamentary session of 1831–32, public acts averaged 237 pages. By the 1868–74 period, public acts in each parliamentary session had increased to 514 pages.[10] Local acts still outnumbered public acts through the nineteenth century, with more than 2,000 passed each decade (Salmon 2009b, 255). In 1810, the House of Commons established a private bill office to oversee the preparation of private acts, after which many were simply rubber-stamped (Salmon 2009b, 256). The fact-finding ability of Parliament also increased. By 1820, select committee inquiry with a printed report was a "standard precursor to each public bill," and royal commissions "appointed by ministers and staffed by up-and-coming lawyers" also increased, eclipsing the select committees by the 1830s (Salmon 2009b, 256). Parliament's investigatory instruments quickly developed in this period, which assisted Parliament with the growing volume and subject matter of legislation (MacDonagh 1958, 58).

The late Victorian period reshaped private legislation even further, as economic and social changes led to "a large amount of domestic legislation on the public side, of an ameliorative or regulative nature, and, on the private side, by way of [a] still further developing public" (Williams 1948, 12). An early example of general legislation was the model clauses act, a series of which, beginning in 1847, created statutes for local emulation. They applied to public utilities such as gas and water. They became particularly important as early interventionist schemes failed. The creation of a central Board of Health in the 1830s led to repudiation of centralization; the former Secretary of the Board, Tom Taylor, argued that "the central authority, which should attempt to supersede the fulfillment of local duty by local agency, instead of aiding ... would be following a mischievous and mistaken course." In mid-century most extensions of government occurred only at the local level and were "never directly administered by agents and servants of the central government" (Gutchen 1961, 86). But the model clauses were a successful attempt to standardize parliamentary legislation across localities.

Although social legislation of the mid-nineteenth century increased inspections in mines, food adulteration, and factory administration, the expansion of government was both limited and contested. Parliament still preferred delegation to centralization, and specific legislation to general legislation. Most general legislation served to curtail abuses, rather than to provide or to create positive goods (Hoppen 1998, 99). In 1847, the *Economist* warned against "engrossing centralisation, which is in truth absorbing all things into itself, and dwarfing down the whole nation to the poor standard of ministerial capacity." That same year, Disraeli declared that "the enervating system of centralisation ... if left unchecked will prove fatal to the national character" (Hoppen 1998, 104).

---

[10] It is important to note that this was not simply due to bills being longer in length: The sheer quantity of public bills doubled from 1832 to 1874; see Salmon (2009b, 256).

The British bureaucracy therefore developed in an ad hoc manner. Although Britain was not a federal state, local control grew exponentially in the nineteenth century. By 1870, England had 65 counties (each with their own magistrates), 224 municipal borough councils, 852 turnpike trusts, 637 local boards of health, and 404 highway authorities (Chester 1981, 347). Parliament still tended toward specific local legislation or private bills to create these authorities rather than pass general legislation. Efforts to centralize were so reviled that by 1870, most civil servants still worked in the Post Office; "as a direct operator, the state was doing little more in 1865 than in 1790" (Hoppen 1998, 108).

It was not until very end of the nineteenth century that Parliament began to focus on public and general legislation. In the early twentieth century, local authorities and public departments became the "predominant parties in private legislation, while their powers and responsibilities were being concurrently increased by public legislation, progressively widening in scope" (Williams 1948, 177). The sheer quantity of Public Acts doubled between 1832 and 1874.

As Figure 4.4 indicates, the gap between the number of local acts and public acts decreased significantly in the early twentieth century. Many fewer local acts were passed; further, public acts increased in length and covered new areas for regulation. Clientelism therefore declined as public legislation supplanted the ad hoc, highly distributive nature of local legislation.

Further, in the late nineteenth century, the Ministry became more powerful and acquired more control over legislation (Cox 1987). William Gladstone, who was prime minister immediately after passage of the Second Reform Act, lengthened the parliamentary year and reduced the time afforded to backbencher legislation. A series of reforms decreased the power of private members, including in 1811 giving precedence to public bills on Monday and Friday, and in 1835 adding Wednesday – thus decreasing the time allotted to private acts proposed by each MP and targeted toward constituencies (Salmon 2009b). In 1882, standing committees were established for specific issue areas. Further, party voting rose after 1860 in Britain, with backbenchers increasingly marginalized. While governments in the 1850s had faced defections from 10 to 15 percent of MPs who broke with party-line voting, by the 1890s, there averaged only one defection per year (Lowell 1908; Pugh 2002).

By 1900, the system of private bill committees was destroyed, and railroads, canals, and health and sanitation were overseen by civil servants (Pinto-Duschkinsky 1981, 30). Due not only to industrialization but also to the rise of utilitarian ideas, there was an "increasing sensitivity of politics to public pressures, and the extraordinary growth in both the volume of legislation and the degree to which its introduction became the responsibility of governments" (MacDonagh 1958, 58). The state also created institutions to strengthen local enforcement (Cronin 1991, 19). And by the early twentieth century, there was a decline in private bills. After the parliamentary election of 1906, parties and national issues were stronger than ever given that there was an "absence of national grants for local improvements" (Lowell 1908, 1: 499).

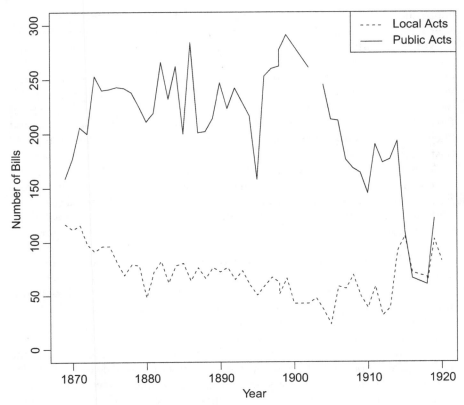

FIGURE 4.4 Public and local acts in Parliament, 1870–1920. From the Index to the Statutes, London.

The administrative power of the state in the mid-nineteenth century extended only to regulation of the textile industry, and expanded to other trades in subsequent decades (Bartrip 1983). Regulation of railways and canals only began with legislation in the 1880s. In the mid-nineteenth century, administration grew in a patchwork manner – "the continuous creation of special bodies for particular functions parceled out the growth of government into pockets exceedingly small" (Hoppen 1998, 107). Counties, municipal borough councils, poor law unions, boards of improvement, and local boards of health were all examples of local institutions created to oversee delegated policy matters. But after 1890, British industrialists forced the state to expand its administrative capacities.

PATRONAGE IN BRITAIN

Practices of patronage dated to the eighteenth century – indeed, one of the foremost reasons to become an MP had been to use the office to grant favors, contracts, and sinecures. "Old corruption," which dated from the English Civil War and was particularly rampant in the late eighteenth century, involved the provision of patronage, staffing bureaucracies and offices with friends and family of members. In 1714, the First Lord of the Treasury created the office of the Patronage Secretary as part of the Treasury. The Patronage Secretary, which William Wilberforce, an independent MP, described as a "rather roguish office," was responsible for dispensing appointments to the Customs House, Post Office, and Excise. The party secretary also sold constituencies and would "negotiate with corporations or private individuals who had seats to sell" (Ostrogorski 1903).

As parties expanded their use of patronage, even electoral constituencies were considered up for grabs. Through the eighteenth and nineteenth centuries, candidates could pay tens of thousands of pounds to bribe electors and continue constituency services. The Patronage Secretary was responsible for keeping track of constituencies in which wealthy landowners could purchase influence. MPs used their office less to advance partisan agendas than to advance their own personal agendas through sporadic cooperation with other MPs (McKenzie 1966; Sack 1980). Patronage functioned through "social networks of allocating power and resources," including offices in church positions and military offices (Porritt 1909, 312). Offices were considered private property and highly valuable. Parliamentary offices came with opportunities to appoint a variety of civil offices, so "it was asked what an office was worth; not what services were to be rendered" (May 1863, 548). MPs devoted time and resources not only to buying votes and favors in their districts, but also to currying favor with ministers and the king's retinue. They could provide charitable donations to aristocrats and gifts to friends of the king, and they could also supplement ministerial salaries (Namier 1963).

In a study of the Parliament of 1761, Namier found that fifty-one MPs could exert influence in the election of more than sixty members and that at least ninety seats were determined by some sort of patronage. At least 19 of 20 boroughs experienced some sort of gentry influence (Namier 1963, 73). In 1844, one of the patronage secretaries wrote to Gladstone explaining how useful patronage was as a political tool. After Gladstone recommended a candidate for a civil service position, Sir Thomas Fremantle replied that "at the Treasury we must look first to the claims of our political supporters ... the son of a good voter at Newark would stand a better chance under your recommendation than the son of a poor clergyman who probably made it a point of duty not to interfere with politics" (Hughes 1949, 67).

Historically, British patronage took the form of nomination of parliamentary candidates (or influence in their elections), appointment to civil list offices and church positions, and nomination for service commissions. Employment in lower-level positions in postal service and customs alone rose from 17,640 in 1797 to 22,367 in 1822 (Chester 1981, 167). Additional patronage offices included stamp distributors, museum attendants, housemaids at the National

Galleries, and office typists (Hanham 1960b).The Reform Act of 1832, which expanded and reconfigured suffrage, led to more patronage appointments as MPs needed to cement support from their local constituencies. Therefore, patronage "became an increasing burden, spreading disappointment and disaffection among incumbents' constituencies and, therefore, among the backbenchers themselves" (Silberman 1993, 349).

Patronage became increasingly inefficient in the nineteenth century, and MPs sought ways to reduce it. Patronage practices first changed with the publication of the Northcote–Trevelyan report, which served as the charter for the modern civil service. It recommended that civil servants be hired through competitive examination. Further, it recommended a hierarchical division between routine work, which could be done by nonexperts, and top-ranked positions that would be reserved for first-rate university graduates. Promotion would be based on merit, rather than on politics. The report was controversial, and while a Civil Service Commission was established in 1855 to draft a preliminary examination, no provisions of the report were immediately implemented.

The reforms advocated by the Northcote–Trevelyan Report were finally enacted through an Order of Council in 1870, which made open competition obligatory throughout the Home Service (McMurtry 1976, 326). But adoption of open competition was discretionary, so the Foreign Office and many Home departments took more than forty years to adopt meritocratic hiring procedures. The Patronage Secretary, for example, still had access to Treasury Secret Service funds with which it could reward supporters. In 1885, the Patronage Secretary gifted over 17,000 spots in the Post Office, many of which were low-level offices such as customshouse boatmen and messengers in the Revenue office (Hanham 1960a, 80). By the turn of the century, however, patronage was less widely distributed. In 1912, the prime minister discontinued access to Secret Service Funds by the Patronage Secretary, and recategorized many administrative offices as merit based.

THE EMERGENCE OF PROGRAMMATIC PARTIES, 1870–1900

In Britain, as suffrage expanded over the course of the nineteenth century, the Conservative and Liberal parties expanded their use of clientelistic strategies to win elections, staff state offices, and enact legislation. Clientelism was a governing strategy in the United States that parties used to win and maintain support both in and across elections. In Britain, clientelism was also a governing strategy that grew out of longstanding patron–client ties between landlords who provided safety and resources to tenants and laborers in exchange for deference.

In the first half of the nineteenth century, clientelistic strategies in different arenas of politics were dependent on each other, in that elected officials' use of vote buying was related to the limited British state. Parliamentary activity was highly distributive, with MPs devoting more attention to private bills and incremental developmental policy than to policies of national scope and import. Further, British patronage weakened the administrative capacity of various departments within the civil service. Wickwire (1965) shows how the absence of constraints on bureaucrats led some departments to become politicized, with bureaucrats explicitly serving politicians and their individual goals; it also led other bureaucrats to serve the king's goals at the expense of the state. Finally, patronage and nepotism led to problems similar to those in the American civil service, whereby bureaucrats exploited their positions through graft and corruption.

After the Second Reform Act of 1867, parties began to change the way they engaged with the electorate. While parties had been established at the state level in the United States beginning in the 1830s, the British were somewhat slower to develop party machinery (Hanham 1978). Similar to the Second Party System, however, nascent parties grew through the development of networks and intermediary organizations rather than through ideologies and policies. The relationship of state administration, particularly the development of greater administrative capacity and new regulatory agencies, to programmatic parties will be developed in Chapter 5.

In Britain, there were legislative factions but not yet strong national, societally embedded parties in 1870. MPs tended to be monied landowners from aristocratic families, and "membership was widely regarded less as a career than as a part-time activity undertaken along with other unpaid duties towards the community" (Pugh 2002, 17). Instead, "for those who could afford it, membership of the House was a sign of social eminence and members were generally wealthy and independent minded" (Ingle 2008, 7). Membership in Parliament was costly, so through the first half of the nineteenth century, parliamentarians were drawn almost exclusively from the landholding classes. Once in office, they spent little time legislating, but did spend a great deal of time serving their constituencies through contributions of charity (such as sick and burial societies and cooperative societies), leisure activities, and material provisions of food and drink. These activities helped to maintain ties of dependence and support between MPs and their electorates.

After the Great Reform Act, party labels, rather than individual largesse, became increasingly important to candidates for parliamentary elections. Registration societies were established at the local level in order to nominate candidates, maintain control of the party list, and canvass voters. By 1868, "almost everywhere the election was fought on an *ad hoc* basis by an organisation specially formed or adapted for the purpose" (Hanham 1978, 93). Registration societies served as the basic unit on which national party organization was constructed.

In addition to registration societies, local clubs combining social activity with political engagement were established, particularly in larger towns. Conservatives established the Carlton Club in London in 1831; it served as a place for gentlemen not only to convene, but also to discuss the needs and goals of the Conservative party. Liberals founded the Reform Club a few years later, in 1836 (Ostrogorski 1903). These clubs provided a model for a way parties could combine political activity with social engagement.

How did partisan organization take place? Particularly among the Conservatives, elites developed a two-fold strategy (Ziblatt 2017). First, they created a consistent party message by connecting all local Conservative party associations into one central party. Second, they adopted a grassroots strategy of establishing local social organizations for voters. The Conservative clubs established included the Primrose League and Carlton Club, while Liberal clubs included Brooks's Club and the Reform Club. While these clubs were particularly well attended in large cities like London, both parties also created regional associations. Foremost among them were conservative-leaning Working Men's Associations, temperance societies, and friendly societies. Many clubs were also held in local pubs. Some clubs were explicitly political: Parties established political debating societies or even local Houses of Commons. By 1883, more than 100 towns had these local houses, in which citizens would participate in parliamentary debates and assume the roles of government and opposition (Jerrold 1883).

After the Second Reform Act (1867), the Conservative party, led by Benjamin Disraeli, lost in the general election of 1868. Disraeli then spearheaded an effort to modernize the Tories. Disraeli famously described the working classes as "angels in marble," envisioning the Conservative party as a mass organization with popular support. In 1867, the Conservatives created the National Union of Conservative Constitutional Associations (NUCCA). Its first meeting was held on November 12, 1867, at a Freemasons Tavern and chaired by John Gorst, an MP from Cambridge, who became the first party secretary. The meeting, attended by delegates from fifty-six towns, was "to consider by what particular organization we may make those Conservative principles effective among the masses."[11] A few principles were set from the beginning: "There is, of course, no intention to interfere in any way with local action; the object of the union is to strengthen the hands of the associations ... and to encourage the establishment of associations in districts where they are wanting, and further, to organize associations by the holding of meetings for the general expression and diffusion of constitutional principles, and the dissemination of sound information upon topics of general political interest, and to secure the combined action of all constitutional associations."[12]

Together, the delegates determined that an annual conference would be held in London each year and that an executive council should be established with the election of a new president and vice president each year. Other goals included the advancement of conservative candidates in elections, the expansion of the Conservative Party, and the denunciation of Radical press and associations.

---

[11] *Archives of the British Conservative Party, Annual Conference Reports, 1867*, microfiche (Brighton, UK: Harvester, 1982).
[12] Ibid.

In a subsequent meeting in 1872, delegates discussed the pending Ballot Act, which established voting secrecy. They worried it might lead to "secret political societies," and the Conservative Party therefore "must still recognise the duty of stimulating, and fostering organization which afford the most efficient means of counteracting revolutionary opinions."[13] This was an early signal of the move toward issue-oriented campaigns, beyond appeals to tradition and virtue. The Conservatives also noted that since beginning their organization in 1867, they had gained seats in Parliament; they attributed this to the consistency of campaign messages and dissemination of pamphlets and periodicals to local party associations. In 1870, Gorst established the Conservative Central Office to work with the party whip and tie constituency developments to national legislative activity (Ball 1987).

By 1875, 472 local Conservative associations were affiliated with the National Union. The party's integration of registration societies allowed central management of the infrastructure of elections, and also professionalization of the party's agents. Formal constituency associations kept membership rosters, and these members served as volunteers who took on election-related activities such as canvassing, transporting, and providing information to voters. The displacement of election agents by professional staff and volunteer activists was a critical step away from clientelism. Stokes (2013) has argued that brokers were expensive and unreliable, creating information asymmetries for parties and candidates. When party agents paid brokers rather than directly paying voters, they were not sure if brokers would turn out enough votes in support. As a result, parties professionalized the office of the party agent and tasked agents with maintaining electoral registers and engaging party loyalists in constituencies between elections.

The Liberal party followed the Conservative party's lead in modernizing its party apparatus, although it enjoyed more regional success than national success in its first years. After the 1867 Reform Act, the Liberal party created four three-member constituencies in urban areas of Leeds, Manchester, Liverpool, and Birmingham. Under the leadership of Joseph Chamberlain, the Birmingham Liberal Association secured Liberal victories in municipal elections, and Chamberlain was elected mayor of Birmingham in 1873. When Conservatives won the 1874 general elections, the Liberals turned instead to national organization. Chamberlain became president of the National Liberal Federation, which united Liberal associations. The Liberal Federation operated like a parliament, debating the policies of the Liberal Party. Disraeli, leader of the Conservative party, therefore termed the Liberal organization the "caucus" and attributed the Liberal victory in the election of 1880 to its style of association.

Frank Schnadhorst, secretary of the National Liberal Federation, said in a letter to the *Times* in 1878 – describing why the Liberals lacked party leaders

---

[13] Ibid.

but instead had a representative committee – "We object to self-elected leaders ... to constituencies being made the instruments of personal ambition or the victims of crotchet mongers. We are anxious to promote the unity and strength of the Liberal party. We think without organization this is impossible" (Hanham 1978, 133). The Tories were excellent organizers, but the "caucus" system of party organization was "pioneered by Radical Liberals ... who gave it central institutional form in the National Liberal Federation (NLF) of 1877" (Pugh 2002, 10). Although the parties chose different methods of decision making, they nonetheless adopted democratic means of deliberating and creating national party agendas in the 1870s. Like the Conservatives, Liberals became more and more reliant on central funds for campaigning (Ingle 2008, 14). While central funds provided only 4 percent of party expenses in 1880, by 1906, almost a third of party funds were centralized (Pinto-Duschkinsky 1981).

Prior to 1870, MPs provided an array of services for their districts through their own personal funds. Not only did they act as employers, they also invested in community projects, acted as charities, and provided leisure activities such as sport and tea parties (Pugh 2002, 13). Many of these activities, however, became the purview of social clubs in Victorian England. These clubs therefore served to promote "central machinery for the supervision of the register and the conduct of elections" (Gash 1977, 394). Party-sponsored clubs might offer a few rooms for lectures and billiards, picnics, and train excursions to an MP's country home, and occasionally had bands and football clubs in urban areas. This was intended to "foster a habitual loyalty on the part of those who were uninterested in or ignorant of politics" (Pugh 2002, 17). Local clubs "fulfilled a number of social functions, providing reading rooms and educational facilities, sickness benefits, seaside excursions ... they helped to integrate into politics a body of men most of whom, until 1867, did not possess the vote" (Ingle 2008, 12).

In Britain, the expansion of suffrage led both to the expansion of clientelism and to the development of new party strategies. Vote buying was still rampant, but MPs sought to replace outright material dependence with a party loyalty based on social identity. Party integration in the social lives of electors was a critical component of party organization, in that it provided parties with professional agents, volunteers, and funds, all of which were vital resources for winning elections. The following chapter details how parties created the next components of programmatic competition – stronger administrative capacity, interest mediation, and policy-oriented campaigns – as they faced pressure from capitalist interests.

5

Administrative Reform and Programmatic Parties in Britain

In Britain, the gradual expansion of suffrage in 1832 and 1867 led parties to increase their use of vote buying. By the 1870s, parties were also establishing components of modern party organization through the creation of national associations linked to local registration societies and social clubs. However, as Chapter 4 has shown, the establishment of party organization was not itself an indication of programmatic competition. This chapter therefore examines the way parties reconfigured their bases of support and, more importantly, the way they conducted the business of government, from 1870 to 1900. These final decades of the nineteenth century led Parliament to change the legislative process so as to serve collective, rather than individual, interests. Further, parties also expanded the state's administrative capacity and regulatory oversight, particularly of industry, as an accommodation of demands from capitalists.

The transition to programmatic politics in Britain involved more than simply the establishment of party organization. It also involved a reconfiguration of traditional relationships between elected officials as patrons and electors as clients. Vote buying and patronage endured out of custom: Voters used elections to receive rewards they felt they were owed, and friends and family of those serving in government also expected favorable positions in state, clergy, or military offices. Unlike in the United States, where clientelistic strategies were part of an effort to wrest control of government from elites, British clientelism rested on a system of class and hierarchy. Instead, parties needed to develop new methods of interest representation – they needed to serve new and emerging interests in society. They could accomplish some of this through party organization, but more importantly, they needed to widen the scope of government to accommodate rising demands.

After the Second Reform Act of 1867, British political elites saw it necessary to reach out to newly enfranchised voters. They did so in traditional ways, such as using bribery and material inducements in campaigns. Parties also tried to coordinate activities across local registration societies through national meetings and promulgation of a partisan press. These efforts served to make party labels meaningful in the constituencies, but did not entail the adoption of policy-oriented campaigns. Government still served limited interests, primarily those of the landowning elite.

This chapter details how the rise of industrial elites was critical to how political parties engaged with, and responded to, new interests in society. It will argue that British capitalism evolved in ways similar to the United States: Family firms adopted the corporate form, businesses consolidated through mergers and combinations, and trade associations at the sectoral and national level were created to advance business interests. As capitalist interests pushed for greater state intervention in various aspects of social and economic life, Parliament expanded the central government's role in the industrial economy.

The difference between the United States and Britain lay in the power of organized business interests relative to party organizations. In the United States, capitalists came to constitute a powerful force in politics in relatively short order. Although capital was heterogeneous, the combination of large corporations in railroads, steel, and oil and medium-sized corporations in manufacturing, raw materials, machinery, and chemical processing (to name but a few), not to mention banking and finance led "big business" to wield enormous financial and political influence with the parties. Party organizations, once deprived of patronage as a source of party revenue, became increasingly dependent on financing from businesses. Business was also provided access to politics in the form of lobbying – of articulating their interests at every stage of the policy-making process. By the early twentieth century, modern-day interest group politics had become enmeshed in Washington, particularly after the government's active involvement in establishing the Chambers of Commerce of the United States.

In Britain, on the other hand, the timing of business organization to party organization differed. Although parties responded to capitalist pressures over policy, parties established mechanisms of integrating business opinions without catering exclusively to them. The successes of party organization from the 1870s meant that parties did not need to cultivate dependent ties with business in order to grow the party. Further, the fact that the corporate form was still limited in England meant the power of the business lobby did not come close to its counterpart in the United States.

TIES BETWEEN PARLIAMENT AND BUSINESS BEFORE 1870

Similar to the United States, British democracy and industrialization expanded together over the nineteenth century. While British industrialization occurred prior to that of the United States, the increase in the scale of manufacturing was slower. Between 1870 and 1914, agriculture comprised the largest sector of the British economy, while 40 percent of the labor force worked in manufacturing.

In the mid-nineteenth century, the vast majority of the 677 engineering firms in the 1851 census reported employing fewer than 10 workers, and only 14 employed more than 350 workers. Although the scale of manufacturing operations was less impressive than in the United States, British manufacturing was nonetheless a significant driver of growth in the nineteenth century. It was export oriented and regionally concentrated as a result of its production base. And despite the slower growth of managerial capitalism, British business still used coordination – and ultimately national organization – to seek programmatic changes to government.

Just as the history of corporate development in the United States was linked to the activities of Congress, with Congress subsidizing land and granting usage rights to nascent industries, the rise of British corporations was similarly tied to the activities of Parliament. Prior to the mid-nineteenth century, the corporate form was rare in Britain. Corporate charters were granted by Parliament or by royal charter for specific, narrow purposes. In the seventeenth century, for example, as colonialism and foreign trade expanded, merchants formed companies and received royal charters that granted exclusive rights of trade over various foreign territories. Perhaps the most famous was the East India Company, a joint-stock company that received a royal charter in 1600 to trade with, and also to govern, India and parts of China. Similar corporations were established to govern and trade with the American colonies.

By the eighteenth century, Parliament used private bill procedure to privatize common lands through the enclosure acts, as detailed in Chapter 4. Landowners were therefore given exclusive rights to land use. Through the eighteenth century, canals and roads were built through a succession of parliamentary acts. In the 1830s, the development of local railways began. Rail companies often sold stock to local aristocrats, and they relied on special charters granted through private bill procedure to build out railway networks. Private act procedures were necessary to confer the benefits of incorporation, granting compulsory powers to acquire land, allowing capital to be raised publicly, and giving monopoly powers over use of capital (Mathias 1983, 106). As industrialization proceeded, however, the lack of statutory clarity over the corporate form created uncertainty for businesses. Because it was difficult to obtain corporate charters, many businesses operated like trade associations, with a voluntary nature and little distinction between ownership and management (Chandler 1984; Shannon 1931).

Parliament became increasingly burdened by private bill procedure in the nineteenth century and investigated ways to streamline the process of incorporation. In the 1840s, Parliament loosened restrictions on the formation of corporations through a series of general incorporation laws (Butler 1986). The Joint Stock Act of 1844 allowed for companies to register as corporations by simply filling out a form. In 1855, the Limited Liability Act ensured that these corporations were granted limited liability. By the 1860s, limited companies constituted 10 percent of business organizations (Melling 1992). Corporations adopted bureaucratic organization and professional management in multiple sectors, including banking, transport, and other forms of industrial manufacturing, by the 1890s (Clapham 1926).

Particularly for the railways, the shift from parliamentary private bill procedure to general incorporation changed the relationship between business and government. Through the 1830s and 1840s, railway owners had gone not only to MPs but also to the Board of Trade, a group under the privy council of the British government.

The ties between British MPs and the private sector were more pronounced than in the United States, which the scandals of the Gilded Age obscure. In Britain, the ties between corporations and government were quite direct; by 1852, ninety-nine MPs were railway directors, in addition to many more who were subscribers to new railway companies (Mathias 1983). And in the Victorian period, 26 percent of the largest firms had an MP on their boards, whereas only 0.08 percent of the largest firms in the United States had members of Congress on their boards (Braggion and Moore 2012). Private enterprise was important to economic development since the state played such a small role in planning or executing industrial and infrastructure policy. The railways, for example, were built entirely through private enterprise. Railway policy exemplified the relationship between business and politics. Railway companies began to lobby Parliament, especially when Gladstone was head of the Board of Trade. Business successfully defeated a provision in the Railways Act of 1844 to allow state purchasing of railways. By 1871, twenty-eight companies owned 80 percent of the railway tracks. Traders whose interests were hurt by monopolistic railway activity petitioned the House of Commons in 1839, calling for greater control "in the hands of the Executive Government" (Parris 1965). Control over the railways shifted between Select Committees of Parliament and the Board of Trade for the next few decades.

The proximity between business and landed interests had to do with private bill procedure. Early in the Industrial Revolution, businessmen sought to prove to their local MPs that development projects such as roads and canals could be beneficial. This resulted in many private bills being allocated to localities through the eighteenth and nineteenth century; landed agricultural interests did not block the preferences of the manufacturing class. Therefore, the composition of Parliament did not begin to change until the 1870s. In 1874, the House was composed of 24 percent merchants and bankers, the same percentage as 1832.

Until the 1870s, "there was an exceptionally high correlation between wealth, status, and power, for the simple reason that they were all territorially determined and defined" (Cannadine 1990, 16). This basis of this correlation shifted as the economy became more industrial and wealth creation became a process independent of aristocratic landholding. Until 1870, Conservative and Liberal MPs tended to come from landowning, aristocratic families; they advanced the interests of their economic peers through patronage and private

TABLE 5.1　*Changes in occupational shares of Conservative and Liberal Party MPs*

	Conservative 1868 (%)	Conservative 1910 (%)	Liberal 1868 (%)	Liberal 1910 (%)
Landowners	46	26	26	7
Industry and trade	31	51	50	66
Legal and professional	9	12	17	23

From Guttsman (1965, 104).

bills that directed funds to local corporations. Candidates themselves funded most campaigns. But ongoing expansion of the franchise led parties to search for regular sources of campaign contributions. Further, industrialists were becoming powerful political actors in themselves (Table 5.1). In Northeast England, a stronghold of the landed gentry as well as the rising coal industry, agricultural interests lost ground to industrialists in elections after 1867. More local constituencies were contested, and in 1868, there were sixteen industrialist candidates for office and only twelve landowners. Industrialists won more seats, reflecting changes to the long-established social structure of British towns (Nossiter 1975). Whereas aristocratic landowners had perpetuated patron–client hierarchies, the new industrialists heralded a differentiated society and the rise of new commercial interests requiring development policy and the integration of individual opinions in politics.

　　The process of lobbying Parliament to secure contracts over specific lands or infrastructure projects gave individuals from manufacturing, mining, and ship building, and construction many ties to their MPs. And business was highly influential at the local level; provincial businessmen could "exercise influence over government without devising powerful central organizations" (Melling 1992, 468). When passing a Limited Liability Act in 1867, for example, the Select Committee working on the bill was composed of 17 MPs, 10 of whom were directly involved in finance and trade. Through the 1870s, Parliament called "expert witnesses" who came from business or accounting (Robb 1992). Employers were still disorganized; efforts to block the Factory Acts in the 1850s were unsuccessful despite the fact that various employers' associations sent 85 delegates from 42 towns to the Home Office to protest.

　　This changed as employers' associations grew after 1870, particularly given the exigencies of labor politics: Employers wanted to clarify their contractual obligations to employees. Trade associations initially formed to exchange information about specific industries. In Britain, which had a longer and more deeply rooted history of craft industry, many associations developed from guilds. Skills-intensive industries, such as the manufacture of textiles, boots, and brewing, grew alongside heavy industry such as cotton, mining, and ship building. As early as the 1745, cotton-growers had created a trade association, followed by colliery owners and bookbinders in 1786. In 1824, with the repeal of the combination laws, associations of all kinds flourished. Many employers' associations organized against the labor threat, so the number of associations tends to wax and wane with labor activity.

New associations formed as economic competition led to rising competition within various industries, including ship building, brewing, glass, coal mining, and iron. Just as in the United States, associations were formed to fix prices and regulate output. As technology became more specialized, these associations also brought together firms that used similar machines and processes to share technical expertise. By the 1880s, most industrial sectors had created associations at the local level, if not nationally (Mathias 1983, 355). Economic depressions and severe competition spurred cooperation among reluctant producers. National associations were particularly likely where a few firms were on the brink of breaking through to the national market.

Further, cartels and mergers also led to agglomeration within industries. While the turn of the century was an active period of cartelization in the United States, the Sherman Anti-Trust Act of 1888 banned many of the most widespread forms of pooling. There were no proscriptions on mergers in Britain, so cartelization became even more widespread in Britain (Blackford 2008). Trade associations were "intimately connected with the rise of economic concentration" (Beer 1982, 294). As firms increasingly consolidated, there was a greater need to regulate output and fix prices. Regional trade associations came together to advocate their national interests before Parliament. Early examples of national associations included the United Kingdom Soap Manufacturers' Association, a voluntary and informal group of regional associations formed in 1867. Throughout the 1880s and 1890s, these trade associations also helped businesses consolidate into cartels or trust. The Bleachers' Association, which formed in 1900, was a cartel of fifty-three firms. Shippers also united to limit tonnage in competing trade routes (Mathias 1983).

Laissez-faire government policies toward industry led to the flourishing of combinations and mergers. There were also outright amalgamations of separate companies into combines, and use of holding companies to control smaller firms. Many of these combinations went undocumented. To the extent that business was regulated, it was only to stop the grossest fraudulent or violent relations caused by competition. So investors and creditors were protected against fraud, while corporate combinations flourished, taking the form of syndicates, cartels, and mergers.

TRADE ASSOCIATIONS AND POLITICAL ENGAGEMENT

Not only were corporations engaging in mergers and cartels in order to reduce market competition, but they also created trade associations to help fix prices, regulate output, and advocate business interests before Parliament (Clapham 1926). By the 1870s, peak associations such as the Chamber of Commerce also laid a new foundation for business to make collective demands in public policy

(Beer 1957). National associations facilitated the creation of trusts between larger firms, and provided an even better way to reduce competition. Their tactics included applying pressure in the House of Commons in addition to propaganda campaigns, deputations, and petitions. In response to strikes, employers' associations created shared insurance funds and blacklists of union leaders. Many employers' and trades associations were unofficial and undocumented – for example, an 1867 Royal Commission parliamentary report seeking to understand organizations in Britain received overwhelming responses from unions but few from employers. This masks, however, the extent to which business interests were represented in Parliament and integrated into legislative processes.

In the eighteenth century, trade associations used private bill procedure to promote their interests to local parliamentarians (Beer 1982; Mathias 1983). There was minimal administrative oversight of trade associations, and few rules governing day-to-day industrial policy (Blank 1973). Britain's history of industrial association is considered much weaker than that of the United States – the first truly national organization, the Federation of British Industries, did not form until after World War I – but Britain actually had a rich and deeply rooted history of local business groups. The Chamber of Commerce, which first organized in French cities in the eighteenth century, and the Board of Trade were two economic groups that brought together merchants and organized local markets.

From 1870 onward, the Association of British Chambers of Commerce began to lobby for greater programmatic oversight of the economy and for uniform regulation rather than ad hoc distributional policies.

In a U.S. Department of Commerce investigation of commercial groups in other nations, Wolfe (1915, 8) found that the British Chambers of Commerce, "in spite of their unofficial character, are frequently consulted by governmental authorities in regard to the commercial interests of local character or matters affecting industries strongly represented in certain localities." But for the most part, these associations were secretive; they had "hitherto concealed their activities. There does not exist any publication in the United Kingdom from which data covering the association of British Manufacturers can be gained. In many instances even the reports of the associations are not accessible" (Wolfe 1915, 37).

There was widespread episodic trade associationism as a result of labor union activity; in 1873 the National Federation of Associated Employers of Labor was created to oppose repealing the Criminal Law Amendment Act; strikes among engineers and miners led to the creation of the Employers' Parliamentary Council in 1898. But neither was long-lived. In the years 1880–1914, employers wavered between cooperation and independence. While most British industrialists preferred independence to trade organization, larger firms that were at less risk during strikes (since they could ride out periods of nonproductivity or lockouts) saw the benefits of organizing (Blank 1973;

Yarmie 1980). It was not until the Federation of British Industry was created after World War I, in 1917, that national trade organization became an established part of British political life.

However, given that markets were integrating and government was providing more services, industrialists "relied on political authorities to provide an infrastructure of institutions which would enable markets to function, exchanges to be made and contracts to be legally executed" (Melling 1992, 458).

Therefore, new employers' federations took on activities similar to those in the United States: They testified before Royal Commissions, and by 1914 had moved their secretariats to London. The state was growing in infrastructural power – civil servants at the Board of Trade, for example, were known for their autonomy as well as statistical expertise. As a result, employers became more involved in the political process so as to express their preferences over social policy. There were many more employers' associations than trade associations, so business associations were more concerned with industrial relations and labor policy than defending their other economic interests.

By 1890, new relations had been forged between British industry and British government; industrialists "were forced to come to terms with the shift in the balance of both services and politics to national level, and the need to participate in a new kind of organizational politics" (Melling 1992, 454). And "capitalist firms relied on the political authorities to provide an infrastructure of institutions which would enable markets to function, exchanges to be made and contracts to be legally executed" (Melling 1992, 458).

The ship-building, engineering, coal-mining, and shipping trades established offices in London around the turn of the century and testified before Royal Commissions. Some associations even had permanent parliamentary committees – the Cotton Employers Parliamentary Association, the Coal Owners' Associations of England, and the Mining Association of Great Britain (Wolfe 1915, 38). By 1920 there were more than 2,500 employers' associations representing capital against trade unions (McIvor 2002, 14).

THE ASSOCIATION OF BRITISH CHAMBERS OF COMMERCE

The business community, by coming together in national organizations, pushed for a change to laissez-faire politics. The earliest chambers of commerce in the United Kingdom were established in Glasgow in 1783, and in Jersey in 1786. Manchester followed shortly with the creation of a chamber in 1794. The chambers were incorporated through royal charters and had the standing of corporate bodies. However, local associations were inadequate to fix the problems of large-scale industrial development. The "legal system was unsuited to the needs of the new commercial world ... [and] were singularly ill-equipped to deal with these new problems" (Ilersic and Liddle 1960, 6).

In 1786, Josiah Wedgwood, the famed potter, created a General Chamber of Manufactures of Great Britain, but the organization failed due to disagreements on tariff policy. By the 1860s, the need for national organization had become more pressing. Therefore, the Association of British Chambers of Commerce (ABCC) was founded in 1860 and incorporated in 1875. This began an annual meeting of business leaders with 30–100 MPs each month. By 1900, there were 93 chambers across Britain; London's chamber of commerce alone had 3,744 members. The ABCC also became, in its own words, a "little commercial Parliament" (Yarmie 1980, 224).

Records of the ABCC show that businessmen adopted new techniques to pressure politicians and influence general legislation. Further, the organization pushed for national institutional improvements to regulate the economy – similar to their American counterparts, they sought a minister dedicated to commercial and manufacturing concerns. The ABCC also created organizational procedures to increase their frequency of interaction with parliamentarians. It helped to draft legislation, for example, since MPs were generalists with no special knowledge of commerce and manufacturing. As early as 1866, the ABCC began to meet with MPs to further manufacturing and merchant interests.

From 1860 onward the ABCC lobbied Parliament for a number of regulatory measures, including a commercial code, commercial courts, bankruptcy legislation, trademark protection, and uniform weights and measures. In 1879, at the Nineteenth Annual Meeting of the ABCC, the executive council lamented that many of these policies had not been passed: "There have been few Sessions in which less commercial legislation has been accomplished."[1] That same year, the ABCC appointed committees to give recommendations directly to the Railway Commission and the president of the Board of Trade. One such recommendation was that "the opinions of the commercial community should be numerously and influentially expressed in favour of the continuance of the Railway Commission, from which the traders of this country have derived invaluable protection and assistance."[2]

Therefore, just as in the United States, the unified business interests under the ABCC pushed for railway regulation. A railway commission was established in 1873 to ensure that the management of railway companies obeyed the law. In 1888, this law was expanded to allow the government to constrain railway price fixing. Sometimes the Chambers of Commerce went up against transportation interests; they demanded regulation of the railways as early as 1867, while the Railway Companies' Association actively opposed it. A few years later, the Bristol Chamber of Commerce testified before a Select Committee against special fares on the Great Western Railway Company, and successfully convinced Parliament to abolish the railway's policies.[3] By 1920, the ABCC felt

---

[1] Nineteenth Annual Meeting of the Association of British Chambers of Commerce Archives, 1879, p. 2.
[2] Ibid., p. 12.
[3] Twentieth Annual Meeting of the Association of British Chambers of Commerce Archives, 1883, p. 12.

that it deserved a spot as a permanent member of the commission. At their annual meeting, they noted that since the commission's creation in 1873, there had always been a commercial representative until recently, when that representative was replaced by a lawyer – which the ABCC found unfair.[4]

A second issue that the ABCC fought for was a cabinet-level minister. The Board of Trade had been established as a department of the Privy Council, a group of advisors to the sovereign, in the eighteenth century. The board was given administrative duties over harbors, railways, shipping, and patents. The ABCC and others considered this position inadequate, arguing that the lack of a minister was a "direct reflection of the relative importance which governments of the day attached to commercial matters" (Ilersic and Liddle 1960, 30).

At the annual meeting of the ABCC in 1879, the executive council remarked:

The fact that in this, the greatest commercial State of the world, no department of the Executive Government exists charged with protecting and promoting the general interests of its Commerce, is a striking anomaly, unique, or nearly so, as compared with the Governments of other important commercial countries ... the Council believe that, sooner or later, enlightened public opinion will support the contention of the Association in favour of establishing a distinct department of the Executive Government, charge with watching over the interests and extension of British Commerce, and presided over by a Cabinet Minister of adequate ability and experience.[5]

The Chambers lobbied for a minister by sending deputies to Parliament and asking MPs to pass motions supporting the cabinet. The House of Commons never did, and the ABCC therefore adjusted their strategy to push for reorganization of the Board of Trade itself. They therefore worked to become familiar with the individual presidents of the Board of Trade. While originally the Chambers felt that the Board of Trade served as a poor intermediary between business interests and the government, "the appointment ... of men of outstanding ability with an understanding of the business community's views diminished the urgency and need for administrative reform" (Ilersic and Liddle 1960, 37). Further, in 1897, the Board of Trade established a Commercial Intelligence Branch that disseminated and collected information from the commercial community. This office consisted of four official members, four administrators from other departments, and fifteen commercial representatives. The Commercial Intelligence Branch also sent confidential information to the ABCC; by 1907, individual firms could be entered into a special register to gain access to this information. The Branch also responded to written inquiries – in 1912 alone, it received 16,488 inquiries about commercial matters (Wolfe 1915, 31).

---

[4] Sixty-First Annual Meeting of the Association of British Chambers of Commerce, 1921.
[5] Association of British Chambers of Commerce, 1879 Nineteenth Annual Proceedings, Executive Council Report, p. 6.

In pushing for specific policy changes, such as guaranteed interest on capital for building railways and shipping lines or guarantees against losses in war, businesses actually legitimated and expanded state activity. This provided parties with areas in which they could claim credit and downplayed the significance of private bill procedure. As Ridings notes, "the pursuit of economic efficiency by the commercial associations and Chambers of Commerce not only contravened laissez-faire but also tended to undermine it" (Ridings 2001).

The ABCC also sought to hold MPs accountable for their policy promises. The Chambers noted the necessity of constant engagement with MPs; when strategizing about the lack of adequate parliamentary representation on commercial matters, they also remarked that "the blame is partly due to the Chambers and constituencies, in consequence of their not keeping up a more active and influential communication, on commercial subjects, with their Members of Parliament, such as inviting them whenever important public meetings of Chambers take place."[6] The ABCC also praised the beneficial effect of cooperation, noting that while Parliament used to disregard commercial questions, "the Chambers of Commerce, by banding themselves together in one central association, [have] found a means of making their wishes heard, and [have] obtained the influence which they were able to bring to bear ... to take their part in the counsels of the nation."[7] The council of the ABCC encouraged local associations to keep track of their MPs' policy promises – "the only pressure MPs could understand was, if you will not vote for the measure we are supporting, we will not vote for you" (Ilersic and Liddle 1960, 141). ABCC members were encouraged to maintain active communication with their MPs, to call up MPs who missed important discussion in the House of Commons concerning commercial policy, and to provide MPs with resolutions that they might adopt. Similar to the United States, the ABCC expressed disdain for partisan matters, lamenting that even when commercial men were elected to Parliament, they were whipped into voting against business concerns (Ilersic and Liddle 1960, 143).

In this period, the Central Office of the Parliament began sending to the ABCC the public bills introduced in the House of Commons each week. The ABCC became a crucial arbiter between businesses and Parliament. The association collected, synthesized, and then disseminated information about legislation to all the local branches. They also reported their opinions back to Parliament through meetings with, and petitions of, political officials. Finally, the ABCC prepared bills for parliamentary consideration on a range of topics such as trade, commerce, manufacture, and shipping (Wolfe 1915, 10).

---

[6] Nineteenth Annual Meeting of the Association of British Chambers of Commerce Archives, 1879, p. 21.
[7] Twentieth Annual Meeting of the Association of British Chambers of Commerce Archives, 1883, p. 121.

Their efforts paid off. In the 1883 meeting of the ABCC, the executive council happily remarked that while prior parliamentary session was concerned primarily with questions relating to Ireland, "three important measures drafted at the insistence of the Association have become law."[8]

The ABCC also began to argue for *locus standi* in Parliament, which would certify that it had the right to testify on business matters. As early as 1883, the ABCC archives show the Select Committee of the ABCC recommending that the Chambers of Commerce be given *locus standi* before the Railway Commission and Board of Trade.[9] They won the legal right to testify before committees in 1896, although they long had the right to testify on private committee hearings over transport bills.

MPs acknowledged the role that the Chambers played, praising their "varied and ample experience" in helping the House of Commons "point out the needs of the commercial legislation of the day, and the direction which that legislation should take."[10] By 1901, even King George V publicly remarked that "We live in an age of competition ... it is to Chambers of Commerce, the eyes and ears of our national commercial system, that we turn for help and guidance" (Musgrave 1914).

The records of the ABCC are replete with requests for state intervention – its former president noted, in 1883, that "people who are jealous of state interference, and who say that the state should not aid private individuals ... may consistently ask the State fairly and justly to do for inhabitants of the community what those inhabitants cannot do individually."[11] Various members of the Chambers acknowledged that "there were certain functions pertaining to commerce and agriculture, which only government could discharge with efficiency."[12]

After World War I, the membership of the British Chambers of Commerce grew from 25,018 in 1914 to 45,568 by 1921.[13] Similar to the active mobilization of business interests by the federal government in the United States, the Minister for Reconstruction after World War I wrote in 1917 that all trades should be organized (Blank 1973). By the 1920s, the ABCC had institutionalized ties between the business community and Parliament. Records from the meetings in the 1920s show daily correspondence between the Chambers and various ministers on matters pertaining to labor, transport, and employment. When the General Post Office established a permanent committee of users of

---

[8] Twentieth Annual Meeting of the Association of British Chambers of Commerce Archives, 1883.
[9] Ibid.   [10] Ibid., p. 127.
[11] Twentieth Annual Meeting of the Association of British Chambers of Commerce Archives, 1883, p. 50.
[12] Ibid., p. 74.
[13] Report of a Meeting of the Executive Council of the Association of British Chambers of Commerce, April 5, 1921, p. 12.

cable services, it created a permanent seat for both the ABCC and the London Chamber of Commerce.[14]

PARTIES, ADMINISTRATIVE POLICY, AND PROGRAMMATIC REPRESENTATION AFTER 1880

The ties between politicians and manufacturers had already been well established in Victorian Britain. Unlike the United States, many aspects of lobbying were built into parliamentary procedure – MPs had long been inviting the say of commercial and manufacturing interests in matters of policy. Although industrial interests threatened the power of the landholding elites, by the mid-nineteenth century, many landowners themselves had a stake in industry. The railways had recruited many aristocrats to serve on their boards of directors, and manufacturing interests followed suit.

Similar to the United States, manufacturing and commercial interests in Britain successfully lobbied for more services from the ministry. In 1873, Parliament created the Railway and Canal Commission; in 1875, the Registry of Trade. Between 1851 and 1891 the British central government tripled in size due to institutions serving the interests of business (Ridings 2001). By then, the "the rise of nation-wide associations of manufacturers and traders was introducing a new element into the politics of this country" (Beer 1982, 68). In 1888, when the Railway and Canal Traffic Act made the commissions permanent, British businesses were fixtures in the policy-making process of new administrative institutions. That same year, Parliament passed the Local Government Act, which bureaucratized local government and wrested control of local administration from the influence of landed gentry (Cannadine 1990).

The expansion of British administrative institutions furthered the ties between political parties, which were themselves becoming more hierarchically organized and managed, and businesses, which sought national policies. National regulatory schemes began in the 1840s and 1850s with initiatives such as the Factory Acts (governing children and women's labor in textiles and mines), Poor Laws, and public education. Parliament also adopted model clauses in 1847 about town police, waterworks, and gasworks; these were designed for localities to adopt and implement (Hoppen 1998). On occasion, ministries were also involved in the inspection of mines, shipping, and factories.

As the century progressed, opponents of centralization lost ground as the inefficiencies of patchwork administration became more apparent. By 1870, policy was administered by 65 counties, 224 municipal borough councils, 117 boards of improvement commissioners, 637 local boards of health, and 15,414 parishes and townships (Chester 1981). Parliamentary

---

[14] Report of a Meeting of the Executive Council of the Association of British Chambers of Commerce, March 2, 1921, p. 201.

dependence on local policy administration led to frustration on the part of industrialists and merchants. By working directly with parliamentary commissions, party leaders began to craft legislative programs designed to accommodate the demands of newly organized business groups. In 1880, the first active manufacturer, Joseph Chamberlain, became a cabinet minister; a partner in a firm making metal screws, Chamberlain had also been elected mayor of Birmingham and was appointed by Gladstone to head the Board of Trade.

From the period 1870–1890, a new relationship evolved between businesses and parties. Businesses successfully secured spots on special commissions and used formal associations to socialize with and integrate politicians into trade activities. They recognized that politics was becoming increasingly national, and configured their political activities to influence the national "infrastructure of institutions which would enable markets to function, exchanges to be made, and contracts to be legally executed" (Melling 1992, 458). Employers' associations also testified before Royal Commissions and moved their central offices to London as they demanded consolidation of social legislation, particularly governing industrial relations.

As the parties moved away from patronage and distributive politics, they expanded the functions of the central government and thereby changed the policy-making process. Bureaucrats developed expertise in statistical analysis and data collection to inform reform proposals and became intermediaries between MPs and "executives in the field" (Checkland 1989; MacDonagh 1958). Parties created a nexus of policy making between Parliament and the bureaucracy, allowing politicians to hold bureaucrats accountable for implementation. Unlike the United States, where managerial capitalism led corporations to perfect these practices prior to the state, British industry had less experience with managerial hierarchy (Zeitlin 1987).

Businesses tried to solidify their ties with parties through campaign donations. By centralizing their campaign funds, the two parties were able to coordinate campaign messages among candidates for office. They turned to national issues in campaigns, rather than vote buying or distribution of incremental resources through local parliamentary acts.

The Liberals and Conservatives increasingly relied on their central offices for campaign activities and funding. The National Union of Conservative Constitutional Associations (NUCCA), the organization of the Conservative party, first convened in 1867. By the 1870s, the Liberals had organized as the National Liberal Federation. As competition between the two parties grew, candidates spent increasingly lavish amounts on campaigns. From 1868 to 1880, an election could cost between £30,000 and £50,000 (Hanham 1978, 372). Whichever party was in government also had access to some £10,000 in secret service funds annually, which the party whips used to coordinate campaign activities. The chief whip of the party, usually appointed by the party leader, was responsible for party discipline in the House of Commons as well as distributing party funds. Central campaign funds grew rapidly, from £20,000–£30,000 in the 1880s to £60,000–£80,000 a decade later (Gwyn 1962). Liberal candidates received only about 4 percent of their campaign funds from the central party in 1880, three decades later, the party provided a third of campaign finances. (Pugh 2002). In 1880, the total amount of election expenditures filed by the Home Office to Parliament was more than £1.7 million. These numbers mask the true costs of elections, since many of the discretionary costs associated with administering a campaign – printing and distributing pamphlets, registering voters, paying poll watchers and agents, buying print space in newspapers – were covered by constituents or local elites (Pinto-Duschkinsky 1981).

Parliament responded to this rise in election costs by passing the Corrupt and Illegal Practices Act (CIPA) of 1883. This was a follow-up to a similar piece of legislation from 1854, which banned bribery and treating in elections. The CIPA led to a swift curtailment of election expenses – while the election of 1885 still cost more than £1 million, that of 1886 was only £624,086 (Pollock 1932). But while the amounts used by individual candidates had declined, parties were seeking greater sources of revenue to fund organizational and administrative activities. And by the election of 1906, election expenses were back up to £1,166,858. Both parties began to rely on donations from wealthy individuals, with funds "hidden by a fog, only the fog which obscures the party war-chests is even more impenetrable and of longer duration" than fog induced by London weather (Pollock 1932, 53). The Conservative Central Office received £10,000 from at least ten men in the 1920s, but none of the checks was traceable. And in 1920, the president of the National Liberal Federation remarked that the party had for too long relied on "the generous gifts of a few public-spirited wealthy men."[15]

One of the more effective ways for parties to raise revenue was through the selling of honors and peerages. These honors included hereditary titles ("Lord") and baronetcies ("Sir"), as well as nonhereditary knighthoods. In 1868, Gladstone, the prime minister, ennobled a few businessmen and manufacturers. It was not until 1886, however, that parties began ennobling industrialists in earnest. From 1876 to 1886, only four members of the commercial community received seats in the House of Lords; from 1886 to 1896, that number grew to eighteen. The number of baronetcies and knighthoods was even greater (Hanham 1960b). Even Sir Stafford Northcote, the famous architect of the Northcote–Trevelyan report, recommended that the Conservative party use the promise of baronetcies to recruit candidates for office.

The chief whip of the party in government typically sold a peerage as an explicit quid pro quo; he would receive a contribution from a businessman, and then send that businessman's name to the prime minister, who would then

---

[15] Proceedings of the National Liberal Federation, 1920, p. 44.

await approval of the peerage from the monarch. By the beginning of the twentieth century, "titles were being marketed by the party whips like merchandise" (Pugh 2002, 32). Of the 200 people receiving the hereditary peerage for the first time between 1886 and 1914, only a quarter came from patrician families; most were from industry and business (Cannadine 1990, 196). And between 1911 and 1940, of the 312 newly ennobled, a third were from finance, industry, and commerce. Many of these men were involved with businesses, representing companies such as the Southern Railway, the Foreign and Colonial Investment Trust, Ogilvy Gilland, and P&O. As of 1922, 272 of the 680 peers were company directors, while 242 were major landowners (Cannadine 1990, 204). Corporations could also contribute money to subsidize members of Parliament or to fund party activities (Pollock 1932).

Clientelism also became untenable as agricultural profitability fell relative to industrial profitability after 1875. Landed gentry began to rent out estates to families with few local or traditional connections, and landowners even sold off unprofitable estates. Although employers also had been able to exert influence over electors in their districts, these practices became less effective as norms against clientelism evolved and party labels became more important. In medium-sized towns, industrial magnates such as Joseph Pease at Darlington (ironmaster), Charles Mark Palmer in Jarrow (ship building), and Arthus Markham in Nottinghamshire (coal) had wielded immense influence over voters. However, by the turn of the century, "entrepreneurs with political ambitions were migrating away from the seats of their businesses ... [instead,] allegiance to a political party furnished the safest guide to a constituency's representation" (Pugh 2002, 14).

Both parties even turned to American businessmen for funds. In 1887, Gladstone, leader of the Liberal party, complained to Andrew Carnegie that the party was cash-strapped. In response, Carnegie sent a check for $25,000. A few years later, the chief agent of the Conservative party elicited funds from Indian rajahs and foreign business owners. He received £20,000 from William Waldorf Astor, who was awarded a peerage in 1916. The 1870s and 1880s were therefore a period of plutocracy in elections to the Commons, with parties becoming more dependent on financing from industrial and business leaders (Pinto-Duschkinsky 1981).

Programmatic Parties: The Adoption of Policies and Programs

The demands of business ushered in new practices on the part of parties. Not only was business a group with electoral and market power, but also industrialists and entrepreneurs constituted a legitimate threat to the landed establishment's foothold on state power.

In the 1840s, urban and nascent industrial forces organized the Anti-Corn Law League to oppose restrictive tariffs on corn imports that increased the price of food throughout Britain. The Conservative government, led by Robert Peel, acquiesced to their demands and reduced the tariffs in 1846 over the opposition of other Tories, as well as Whigs. Schonhardt-Bailey (2006) described this as a shift from trustee to delegate representation, indicating that MPs felt a duty to vote according to their constituents' interests.

Election administration also became regularized through professional party agents, rather than voluntary election agents. In 1882 and 1891 the Liberal and Conservative party agents, respectively, created professional associations. They adopted examinations for membership, published and disseminated journals, and lobbied for better salaries. Party organization, the professionalization of party staff, and the creation of social organizations to promote partisan ideas all fostered programmatic competition and delegitimized clientelistic tactics (Pugh 2002; Rix 2008).

The timing of party organization relative to business organization in Britain shows that British parties had already created methods of interest representation that prevented business interests from dominating those of others. In the last two decades of the nineteenth century, the members of the British Chambers of Commerce asked for a party devoted exclusively to business interests in the House of Commons, since "matters of a party political character" made MPs "indifferent" to commercial concerns (Ilersic and Liddle 1960, 143).

The timing of the organization of parties, the organization of business interests, and state building influenced the extent to which parties accommodated economic elites. In Britain, businesses benefited from distributive policy and clientelism in the mid-nineteenth century. But the Conservative and Liberal parties then replaced patronage with party organization and expansion of state regulation, while business interests were less organized. By the time businesses were in a position to make concentrated demands, parties had developed ways to balance the demands of capital against the needs of other interests.

Conclusion

Capitalist Interests, Programmatic Parties, and Elusive Reforms

In the nineteenth century, political parties in the United States and Britain developed a set of strategies to win elected office and retain power. These strategies involved piecemeal rewards to voters in exchange for their support, as parties pioneered the use of clientelism. Clientelism was not simply a cynical tactic to undermine democratic accountability; in both countries, clientelism was rooted in a tradition of mutual obligation between representatives and citizens. In the United States, Jacksonian politics and the spoils system ensured that average citizens would have access to government, rather than simply elites. In Britain, deeply engrained patronage relations provided ways for members of Parliament to serve their local constituents and to dole out sinecures to local elites and supporters.

Over the course of the nineteenth century, clientelism became a way not only to provide material rewards of cash or food to voters, but also to expand the state itself. Given the limited administrative capacities of the state, clientelism as a form of distributive politics provided political officials with a rationale for distributing state resources. Targeted and discretionary funds to infrastructure development, such as land grants and property rights to railway developers or subsidies to local corporations building roads, canals, and bridges, were a way to foster the nascent industrial economy while also strengthening relationships of dependency between politicians and economic interests.

In the long run, however, clientelism hampered the ability of the state to effectively facilitate economic growth. First, reliance on patronage weakened the civil service; bureaucrats were simply political appointees with no training and high rates of turnover. This impacted the state's ability to carry out routine functions at post offices and customs houses, and all but guaranteed that national laws would be poorly implemented. Second, the state's reliance on ad hoc clientelistic policy created unpredictability for emerging economic actors who relied on services provided by the state.

This book has shown how the development of capitalism, particularly the emergence of the modern corporation and its techniques of management and organization, profoundly shaped the political landscape. The rise of managerial capitalism, particularly in the United States, led businesses to adopt hierarchical, meritocratic organizational management structures and to develop management as a profession in itself. Managers were used to overseeing complex production, manufacturing, and distribution processes and were critical to the transition from small-scale to mass production.

Corporations fostered a national consumer market, fueled by technological change and the railway revolution. While the business community was fractured and disaggregated during long phases of industrialization, the end of the nineteenth century led to the emergence of a business community with distinct interests and preferences. By developing political strategies to press their demands on parties, and by providing parties with informational and monetary resources, businesses became instrumental in the development of both new state institutions and new forms of party organization.

The book makes three contributions to the study of clientelistic politics: examining clientelism as a governing strategy, integrating capitalist interests into the study of programmatic politics, and better articulating how business interests affect periods of democratic reform.

CLIENTELISM AS A GOVERNING STRATEGY

This book has shown that in the nineteenth century, clientelism and patronage were critical to the development and organization of political parties. Not only did clientelism allow parties to win votes, finance campaigns, and ensure voter loyalty, but it also dovetailed with politicians' view of the state as a vehicle for resource distribution rather than public policy. By explicating how clientelism worked in three distinct arenas of politics – in elections, in staffing the civil service, and in legislative politics – I show how these strategies complement and reinforce one another.

Current research into clientelistic politics often focuses on clientelism in one arena of politics, such as bribery in elections or manipulation and politicization of service distribution. While many theories explain why politicians are more likely to target certain segments of the population with clientelism, such as low-income voters, these theories do a poor job explaining change over time, particularly the adoption of programmatic party strategies. In order to understand how parties change their strategies over time, this analysis has tried to show that we need to understand the *relationship* of clientelistic strategies, and how they enable and constrain politicians' abilities to offer programmatic goods. For example, reliance on patronage can hollow out the administrative capacities of the state. As a result, politicians may not be able to commit credibly to policy goals in campaigns. Alternatively, politicians may pass policies in the legislature that require regulation and oversight, while the state itself lacks the institutions to effectively carry out regulatory schemes.

One major contribution of this book is therefore to show how programmatic policy takes different forms in the electoral, legislative, and bureaucratic arenas, and how parties become dependent on them as a way to govern industrializing democracies. Clientelism can actually serve as an effective way to inculcate voter loyalty, staff a growing state, and support the expansion of political parties. Many clientelistic arrangements require that voters serve as party volunteers or donate campaign funds back to the party; clientelistic parties also work through party brokers who serve as intermediaries to communities. This analysis shows the connections between clientelistic politics by using archival data to measure the growth and extent of clientelism in nineteenth-century Britain and the United States. By triangulating data on disputed elections, on patronage appointments, and on different types of legislation passed by Congress and Parliament, I show that clientelism was not isolated to one arena of politics. Instead, parties used clientelism as an overarching strategy to govern as democracy expanded.

The shift to programmatic strategies involved parties adopting both new governing strategies in office and new linkage strategies with voters between elections. First, parties needed to expand the institutional capacities of the state, particularly to allow for regulatory and administrative policies. While clientelistic distributive policy entails targeted benefits with diffuse costs, regulatory and administrative policies allow widely shared benefits with concentrated costs. Enhancing the capacity of the state by reducing reliance on patronage allowed trained and qualified bureaucrats to oversee implementation of new forms of policy that parties could then tout as successes in election campaigns.

Second, programmatic politics also necessitated new forms of party organization itself. Parties became more professionalized, hiring full-time staff rather than relying on volunteers and brokers. They developed systematic linkages with newly organized groups, such as labor unions, farmers' associations, community interests, and, of course, businesses. These linkages allowed parties to aggregate and mediate diverging interests and to get critical input on policies and priorities. Business groups in particular served as essential sources of technical and professional information and statistics. In developing programmatic linkages, parties reconfigured their relationships with voters and took on new representative functions that focused on interest articulation and mediation rather than ad hoc distribution of material rewards.

CAPITALISM AND CLIENTELISM

This book has argued that under certain conditions, capitalists can serve to undermine clientelistic politics and to usher in new forms of representative politics. These include expanding the state's administrative capacities so that politicians and bureaucrats can credibly implement stated policy objectives. They also include a shift in how parties develop and maintain linkages with voters. Clientelistic arrangements allow parties to cultivate narrow relationships at the expense of the public interest and to develop policy in an ad hoc and piecemeal way according to the exigencies of politics. Programmatic party organization, on the other hand, forces parties to negotiate among competing demands from society and to mediate and accommodate these demands by crafting policies that satisfy the needs of voters.

In the United States and Britain, the emergence of new classes of capitalist actors in the late nineteenth century led to a reconfiguration of party politics. These new actors – primarily merchants and industrialists who relied on state services, including infrastructure development, revenue collection at points of entry, and postal delivery – felt that clientelism undermined not only their material interests but also national long-term economic prospects.

By disaggregating "capitalist actors," the theory advanced here distinguishes between industries with high levels of concentration and monopoly power and industries with greater levels of competition that might be at a disadvantage relative to more concentrated economic interests. In the United States, the railway industry assumed a great deal of economic and political power after the Civil War. It was not the primary driver of programmatic politics at the national level. Instead, railways were often the beneficiaries of clientelism; railway companies regularly engaged in corrupt transactions with members of Congress and countless state legislators (White 2012). This does not mean, however, that all capitalists were corrupt in the late nineteenth century.

Business organization also changed. Managerial capitalism led to new forms of organization within firms, while trade associations led to cooperation across firms. As a result, a variety of manufacturing and commercial interests developed a distinct political identity aligned with reforming the state and securing more effective policies and services from political officials. They saw the state as a *complement*, rather than impediment, to capitalist goals. Further, the successful managerial and bureaucratic practices adopted within firms provided business leaders with a template for reforming the state. The National Board of Trade, for example, and the Association of British Chambers of Commerce both advocated the creation of state institutions that would create policy according to scientific principles and implement policy through skilled, trained bureaucrats.

BUSINESS INTERESTS AND DEMOCRATIC REFORMS

Using the cases of the United States and Great Britain, I illustrate two possibilities for transitions to programmatic politics. In both cases, political parties were organized to serve clientelistic outcomes as they mobilized voters for most of the nineteenth century. In both cases, business interests coalesced against reliance on patronage and demanded that parties reform the state to serve economic interests by improving bureaucratic quality and regulatory oversight. And in both cases, parties engaged in a period of state building that ultimately provided a foundation on which they could build programmatic messages and policies. Where they differ is in the level and timing of party organization, which then determined how parties responded to capitalist pressure.

In Britain, the Conservative and Liberal parties began to build hierarchical organizations that connected parliamentary party leaders to party offices in the districts. The parties actively sought to mobilize specific interests, such as those of labor, as they built modern parties from the 1870s onward. Further, since business input had been routine in parliamentary policy for many decades, parties were able to integrate business input while centralizing state institutions and developing administrative capacities. They did not become beholden to business interests, which were relatively less organized than the parties. As parties replaced patronage with policy appeals, business became one of many organized interests with which parties developed programmatic linkages.

The development of programmatic parties in the United States was somewhat different. As the Republican and Democratic parties expanded their organizations in the 1880s and 1890s, they faced a much better organized business community and turned to capitalists for campaign financing and assistance with policy. As businesses and parties developed systematic linkages, parties accommodated the needs of business when creating new institutions such as the Interstate Commerce Commission. The commissions and regulatory agencies were nascent attempts to create federal capacity, and politicians needed the input and support of business leaders. Although Progressive reformers, farmers, and laborers later took on the mantle of demanding state reform, businesses had already established an advantaged position in policy making. While both parties developed issue-oriented campaigns and linkages with emerging interest groups, the needs of these groups were often in tension with those of business.

However, the overarching trajectory of programmatic politics in the United States and Great Britain in the nineteenth century was similar. After decades of reliance on clientelistic tactics, including vote buying and patronage, the two parties in both countries began to distinguish themselves on the basis of distinct policies. The effects of patronage were to weaken the capacities of the federal government, which already lacked strong central institutions. Patronage was the primary way to finance the activities of local party organizations and campaigns. Civil servants "were expected to contribute their votes and a portion, often substantial, of their time, energy, and income to the political party to which they were indebted for their employment" (van Riper 1958, 46).

While parties relied increasingly on patronage (and, in elections, vote buying and bribery), businesses – particularly merchants and manufacturers – were coordinating through trade associations and chambers of commerce. The foremost national association was the National Board of Trade, which preceded its successors, the National Association of Manufacturers and the Chambers of Commerce of the United States, by many decades. Proceedings and debates from the board reveal how business interests coalesced around political reforms, including regulation and civil service reform, in the 1870s and 1880s.

The transition to programmatic politics followed two developments: first, the expansion of state capacity, and second, the growth of party organization and the development of programmatic linkages. Britain and the United States adopted meritocratic civil service reforms (in 1870 in Britain, in 1883 in the United States) and expanded the scope of state activity to include regulation and oversight of the industrial economy. While the U.S. federal government might have been weak relative to the centralized government of Britain, neither performed many regulatory functions prior to the 1870s.

These commissions and executive agencies were critical to the transition to programmatic politics because they provided parties with a means to enact national economic programs. Whereas parties previously used their legislative authority for distributive goals, and therefore used state resources as a vehicle for patronage, a reformed civil service and new federal powers gave parties the ability to craft and implement public policy.

This shift to programmatic politics was not just evidenced by less clientelism in elections, but instead shows how parties reconfigured the role of the state and the political arena to mediate competing interests. Whereas parties used to assemble electoral majorities without concern for interests or ideology, the turn of the century ushered in a new form of democratic accountability whereby parties sought out systematic linkages with different groups. This was a period in which pluralistic representative democracy supplanted distributive policy.

Importantly, parties strengthened both their own organizations and state institutions because of new demands from business interests in society. In both the American and British case, businesses were influential in many aspects of politics. However, I have tried to demonstrate here that the timing of the organization of parties, the organization of business interests, and state building influenced the extent to which parties accommodated economic elites. In Britain, businesses benefited from distributive policy and clientelism in the mid-nineteenth century. The Conservative and Liberal parties then replaced patronage with party organization and expansion of state regulation, while business interests were less organized. By the time businesses were in a position to make concentrated demands, parties had developed ways to balance the demands of capital against the needs of other interests.

In the United States, on the other hand, businesses organized prior to the organization of parties. Therefore, as parties embarked to expand programmatic politics through reducing patronage, they turned to businesses to assist with party building and state building. Business was able to finance parties and to have a significant say in how the federal government would regulate the industrial economy. While parties did shift to programmatic competition, businesses were able to influence agency politics in ways that shifted the arena of clientelism.

Finally, it is worth noting that in both the United States and Britain, clientelism was a governing strategy that helped both parties develop bases of loyalty and hone nascent ties to communities and organizations at the local level. Through networks of brokers, election agents, ward bosses, and local firms, clientelistic linkages nonetheless provided parties with ways to build parties over the course of the nineteenth century. As a result, even when businesses became politically active and vocal, parties still served to mediate and integrate the needs of business in the broader context of pluralistic interest group demands.

FUTURE RESEARCH

State building and party building are essential to the transition to programmatic politics. While this book does not offer a general theory of programmatic transition, it shows that the ways parties accommodate demands for programmatic reform influence the way clientelistic and programmatic politics develop over time. I offer an explanation that relies on capitalist interests, which are poorly served by distributive politics and clientelistic governance. This research adds to the body of work by Mares (2003a) and Swenson (2002) on capitalist interests in promoting social policy, as well as work by Arriola (2012) showing that autonomous business interests are critical to opposition parties in single-party democracies. Where capital is well organized and ill-served by a clientelistic regime, it can serve as a powerful constituency in favor of programmatic reforms.

Future research can and should refine modernization hypotheses by examining how economic factors shape political party organization and state building. The historical cases of the United States and Britain are relevant to politics in the developing world, where capitalist institutions and states are likely to be weak. A better understanding of the relationship of programmatic politics to capitalism and state building can therefore help to answer central questions in comparative politics.

The United States and Britain in the nineteenth century were both laissez-faire market economies with little direct government intervention in the industrialization process. They look very different from economies of the twentieth century, where there is much more government involvement in promoting economic growth. In Latin American countries that pursued strategies of import-substitution industrialization, in East Asian countries pursuing export-oriented industrialization, or in states with communist legacies of centralized economies, the relationship between the state and the capitalist sector is much closer than it was in the cases used in this book.

While this theory may not travel directly to contemporary industrializing societies, it nonetheless makes important predictions about clientelistic politics. Where capital continues to be organized in family firms or in deeply entrenched networks with politicians, it is unlikely that capitalists will organize in opposition to clientelism. The argument in this book is premised on capitalists adopting their own internal bureaucratic management practices that reduce personalistic ownership with technocratic management. Further, the argument also requires that businesses organize across sectors and industries in order to develop unified, collective interests about the need for parties and states to clean up their institutions.

The argument of this book does not apply to countries without competitive market economies. This does not mean, however, that agricultural economies or countries with only one or two dominant industrial sectors are necessarily clientelistic. This theory instead shows that parties will not always take the lead in developing avenues of interest articulation and aggregation in the context of clientelistic politics – instead, powerful interest groups can spur parties to reconfigure their bases of representation. Future areas of study can delineate the conditions under which nonstate actors serve as the drivers of programmatic reform, rather than focusing simply on economic development alone.

There are certain conditions that might make parties more receptive to programmatic demands. When an emerging class of capitalists is disadvantaged by clientelism, it can organize in favor of reforms that strengthen regulation and dismantle patronage. Further, when business is sufficiently organized, it can provide parties with campaign financing and informational resources that then can help parties create stronger bases of organization and representation. Of course, business financing of parties and input into politics can also undermine the public interest when business is able to extract concessions from the state. Future research therefore needs to examine the conditions under which capitalists can serve the public interest, even if only unwittingly, and distinguish these conditions from those of pure rent seeking and corruption.

Clientelism is a pervasive system of democratic accountability in which politicians privilege electoral expediency and the piecemeal allocation of resources over the development of representative parties and programmatic policies. Empirically, clientelism is associated with poverty, electoral monopoly and less electoral competition, and weak states. Further, clientelism is not just a symptom of underdevelopment; in advanced industrialized democracies, the influence of powerful interest groups is also considered clientelistic. Therefore, it is important to understand the historical origins of programmatic competition and to develop contingent, process-based theories of how parties transition away from clientelism. By better understanding how the evolution of capitalism changes the demands and political preferences of business actors, this book shows that the relationship between capitalism, clientelism, and democracy is critical to understanding the rise of programmatic politics.

References

Acemoglu, Daron, and James Robinson. 2012. *Why Nations Fail: The Origins of Power, Prosperity and Poverty*. New York, NY: Crown Publishers.

Aldrich, Howard E. 1979. *A Study of Public Works Investment in the United States, 1789–1970*. Washington, DC: CONSAD Research Corporation.

Aldrich, John. 1995. *Why Parties? The Origins and Transformation of Party Politics in America*. Chicago, IL: University of Chicago Press.

Alesina, Alberto, Edward Glaeser, and Bruce Sacerdote. 2001. "Why Doesn't the US Have a European-Style Welfare State?" *Brookings Paper on Economics Activity* (Fall): 187–278.

Allen, Howard W., and Kay Warren Allen. 1981. "Vote Fraud and Data Validity." In *Analyzing Electoral History: A Guide to the Study of American Voting Behavior*, edited by Jerome M. Clubb, William H. Flanigan, and Nancy H. Zingale 153–94. Beverly Hills, CA: Sage Publications.

Altschuler, Glenn, and Stuart Blumin. 2000. *Rude Republic: Americans and Their Politics in the Nineteenth Century*. Princeton, NJ: Princeton University Press.

Anderson, Margaret. 2000. *Practicing Democracy: Elections and Political Culture in Imperial Germany*. Princeton, NJ: Princeton University Press.

Argersinger, Peter. 1985. "New Perspectives on Election Fraud in the Gilded Age." *Political Science Quarterly* 100 (4): 669–87.

Arriola, Leonard. 2012. *Multiethnic Coalitions in Africa: Business Financing of Opposition Election Campaigns*. New York, NY: Cambridge University Press.

Atack, Jeremy, and Fred Bateman. 2006. "Manufacturing." In *Historical Statistics of the United States, Earliest Times to Present: Millenial Edition*, edited by Susan B. Carter, Scott Sigmund Gartner, Michael R. Haines, Alan L. Olmstead, Richard Sutch, and Gavin Wright. New York, NY: Cambridge University Press.

Aydelotte, William. 1976. "Constituency Influence in the British House of Commons, 1841–1847." In *The History of Parliamentary Behavior* 225–46. Princeton, NJ: Princeton University Press.

Ball, Alan. 1987. *British Political Parties: The Emergence of a Modern Party System*. 2nd ed. London: Macmillan.

Balogh, Brian. 2003. "Mirrors of Desires: Interest Groups, Election, and the Targeted Style in Twentieth-Century America." In *The Democratic Experiment*, edited by Meg Jacobs, William Novak, and Julian Zelizer, 222–49. Princeton, NJ: Princeton University Press.

2009. *A Government Out of Sight: The Mystery of National Authority in Nineteenth-Century America*. New York, NY: Cambridge University Press.

Banfield, Edward C., and James Q. Wilson. 1963. *City Politics*. Cambridge, MA: Harvard University Press.

Bartrip, P. W. J. 1983. "State Intervention in Mid-Nineteenth Century Britain: Fact or Fiction?" *Journal of British Studies* 23 (1): 63–83.

Beer, Samuel. 1957. "The Representation of Interests in British Government: Historical Background." *The American Political Science Review* 51 (3): 613–50.

1982. *Modern British Politics: Parties and Pressure Groups in the Collectivist Age*. New York, NY: W. W. Norton.

Bensel, Richard. 1990. *Yankee Leviathan: The Origins of Central State Authority in America, 1859–1877*. New York, NY: Cambridge University Press.

2004. *The American Ballot Box in the Mid-Nineteenth Century*. New York, NY: Cambridge University Press.

Benson, Lee. 1955. *Merchants, Farmers, and Railroads: Railroad Regulation and New York Politics, 1850–1887*. Cambridge, MA: Harvard University Press.

Berk, Gerald. 1991. "Corporate Liberalism Reconsidered: A Review Essay." *Journal of Policy History* 3 (1): 70.

Berrington, Hugh. 1968. "Partisanship and Dissidence in the Nineteenth-Century House of Commons." *Parliamentary Affairs* 21: 338–74.

Blackford, Mansel G. 2008. *The Rise of Modern Business: Great Britain, the United States, Germany, Japan, and China*. 3rd ed. Chapel Hill, NC: University of North Carolina Press.

Blank, Stephen. 1973. *Industry and Government in Britain: The Federation of British Industries in Politics, 1945–65*. Lexington, MA: Lexington Books.

Bonnett, Clarence. 1922. *Employers' Associations in the United States: A Study of Typical Associations*. New York, NY: Macmillan.

Braggion, Fabio, and Lyndon Moore. 2013. "The Economic Benefits of Political Connections in Late Victorian Britain." *The Journal of Economic History* 73 (1): 142–76.

Bratton, Michael, and Nicholas van de Walle, eds. 1997. *Democratic Experiments in Africa*. New York, NY: Cambridge University Press.

Briggs, Asa. 1959. *Chartist Studies*. London: Macmillan.

Bruce, William George. 1920. *Commercial Organizations: Their Function, Operation, and Service*. Milwaukee, WI: Bruce Publishing Company.

Bulmer-Thomas, Ivor. 1953. *The Party System in Great Britain*. London: Phoenix House.

Burke, Albie. 1970. "Federal Regulation of Congressional Elections in Northern Cities, 1871–1894." *The American Journal of Legal History* 14 (1): 17–34.

Burn, W. L. 1950. "Electoral Corruption in the Nineteenth Century." *Parliamentary Affairs* IV (4): 437–42.

Bustikova, Lenka, and Cristina Corduneanu-Huci. 2017. "Patronage, Trust, and State Capacity: The Historical Trajectories of Clientelism." *World Politics* 69 (2): 277–326.

Butler, Henry N. 1986. "General Incorporation in Nineteenth Century England: Interaction of Common Law and Legislative Processes." *International Review of Law and Economics* 6: 169–87.

Butler, Jon. 2000. *Becoming America: The Revolution before 1776*. Cambridge, MA: Harvard University Press.

Calvo, Ernesto, and Maria Victoria Murillo. 2004. "Who Delivers? Partisan Clients in the Argentine Electoral Market." *American Journal of Political Science* 48 (4): 742–57.

Cannadine, David. 1990. *Decline and Fall of British Aristocracy*. Avon, UK: Bath Press.

Capoccia, Giovanni, and Daniel Ziblatt. 2010. "The Historical Turn in Democratization Studies: A New Research Agenda for Europe and Beyond." *Comparative Political Studies* 43 (8–9): 931–68.

Carpenter, Daniel P. 2001. *The Forging of Bureaucratic Autonomy: Reputation, Networks, and Policy Innovation in Executive Agencies, 1862–1928*. Princeton, NJ: Princeton University Press.

2005. "The Evolution of National Bureaucracy in the United States." In *The Executive Branch*, edited by Joel D. Aberbach and Mark A. Peterson, 41–71. New York, NY: Oxford University Press.

Carrott, M. Browning. 1970. "The Supreme Court and American Trade Associations 1921–1925." *The Business History Review* 44 (3): 320–38.

Cassis, Youssef. 2007. "Big Business." In *Oxford Handbook of Business History*, edited by Geoffrey Jones and Jonathan Zeitlin, 171–93. New York, NY: Oxford University Press.

Chambers, William, and Paul Davis. 1978. "Party, Competition and Mass Participation: The Case of the Democratizing Party System, 1824–1852." In *The History of American Electoral Behavior*, edited by Joel Sibley, Allan Bogue, and William Flanigan, 174–97. Princeton, NJ: Princeton University Press.

Chandler, Alfred D. 1977. *The Visible Hand: The Managerial Revolution in American Business*. Cambridge, MA: Belknap Press.

1984. "The Emergence of Managerial Capitalism." *The Business History Review* 58 (4): 473–503.

Checkland, Sydney. 1989. "British Public Policy 1776–1939." In *The Cambridge Economic History of Europe*, vol. 8, edited by P. Mathias and S. Pollard, 607–40. Cambridge: Cambridge University Press.

Chester, Daniel. 1981. *The English Administrative System 1780–1870*. Oxford, UK: Clarendon Press.

Chubb, Judith. 1982. *Patronage, Power, and Poverty in Southern Italy: A Tale of Two Cities*. New York, NY: Cambridge University Press.

Clapham, Christopher. 1982. *Private Patronage and Public Power: Political Clientelism in the Modern State*. New York, NY: St. Martin's.

Clapham, J. H. 1926. *An Economic History of Modern Britain*. Cambridge: Cambridge University Press.

Clark, P. 1983. *The English Alehouse: A Social History, 1200–1830*. London: Longman.

Clemens, Elisabeth. 1997. *The People's Lobby: Organizational Innovation and the Rise of Interest Group Politics in the United States, 1890–1925*. Chicago, IL: University of Chicago Press.

2010. "From City Club to Nation State: Business Networks in American Political Development." *Theory and Society* 39 (3/4): 377–96.

Clifford, Frederick. 1885. *A History of Private Bill Legislation*. Vol. 1. London: Butterworths.

Collier, Ruth. 1999. *Paths toward Democracy: The Working Class and Elites in Western Europe and South America*. Cambridge, UK: Cambridge University Press.

Cox, Gary. 1987. *The Efficient Secret*. New York, NY: Cambridge University Press.

Cox, Gary W. 2009. "Swing Voters, Core Voters and Distributive Politics." In *Political Representation*, edited by Ian Shapiro, Susan Stokes, Elisabeth Wood, and Alexander S. Kirshner 342–57. New York, NY: Cambridge University Press.

Cox, Gary W., and J. Morgan Kousser. 1981. "Turnout and Rural Corruption: New York as a Test Case." *American Journal of Political Science* 25 (4): 646–63.

Cox, Gary W., and Mathew D. McCubbins. 1986. "Electoral Politics as a Redistributive Game." *The Journal of Politics* 48 (2): 370–89.

Cronin, James E. 1991. *The Politics of State Expansion: War, State, and Society in Twentieth-Century Britain*. New York, NY: Routledge.

Crowley, Jocelyn, and Theda Skocpol. 2001. "The Rush to Organize: Explaining Associational Formation in the United States, 1860s–1920s." *American Journal of Political Science* 45 (4): 813–29.

Cruz, Cesi, and Philip Keefer. 2015. "Political Parties, Clientelism, and Bureaucratic Reform." *Comparative Political Studies* 46 (14): 1942–73.

Culpepper, Pepper. 2015. "Structural Power and Political Science in the Post-Crisis Era." *Business and Politics* 17(3): 391–409.

Dahlberg, Matz, and Eva Johansson. 2002. "On the Vote-Purchasing Behavior of Incumbent Governments." *American Political Science Review* 96 (1): 27–40.

Davis, Cory. 2014. "The Political Economy of Commercial Associations: Building the National Board of Trade, 1840–1868." *Business History Review* 88 (Winter): 761–83.

De La O, Ana. 2015. *Crafting Policies to End Poverty in Latin America: The Quiet Transformation*. New York, NY: Cambridge University Press.

Dempsey, John. 1956. "Control by Congress over the Seating and Disciplining of Members." PhD thesis, University of Michigan.

Diaz-Cayeros, Alberto, Federico Estévez, and Beatriz Magaloni. 2016. *The Political Logic of Poverty Relief: Electoral Strategies and Social Policy in Mexico*. New York, NY: Cambridge University Press.

diSalvo, Daniel. 2012. *Engines of Change: Party Factions in American Politics, 1868–2010*. New York, NY: Oxford University Press.

Dixit, Avinash, and John Londregan. 1996. "The Determinants of Success of Special Interests in Redistributive Politics." *The Journal of Politics* 58 (4): 1132–55.

Eisenstadt, S. N., and Rene Lemarchand, eds. 1981. *Political Clientelism, Patronage, and Development*. Beverly Hills, CA: Sage Publishers.

Emanuel, Lewis. 1881. *Corrupt Practices at Parliamentary Elections: An Address Delivered to the Lewisham and Lee Liberal Club*. London: Chapman and Hall.

Erie, Stephen. 1988. *Rainbow's End: Irish-Americans and the Dilemma of Urban Machine Politics, 1840–1985*. Berkeley, CA: University of California Press.

Fligstein, Neil. 1990. *The Transformation of Corporate Control*. Cambridge, MA: Harvard University Press.

Foner, Eric. 2002. *Reconstruction: America's Unfinished Revolution, 1863–1877.* New York, NY: Harper.

Formisano, Ronald P. 1999. "The 'Party Period' Revisited." *The Journal of American History* 86 (1): 93–120.

Foth, Joseph Henry. 1930. *Trade Associations: Their Services to Industry.* New York, NY: Ronald Press Company.

Fox, Jonathan. 1994. "The Difficult Transition from Clientelism to Citizenship: Lessons from Mexico." *World Politics* 46: 151–84.

Friedman, Leon. 1973. "The Democratic Party 1860–1884." In *History of U.S. Political Parties*, edited by Arthur M. Schlesinger, Jr., 2: 885–908. New York, NY: Chelsea House Publishers.

Frye, Timothy, Ora John Reuter, and David Szakonyi. 2014. "Political Machines at Work: Voter Mobilization and Electoral Subversion in the Workplace." *World Politics* 66 (2): 195–228.

Fukuyama, Francis. 2014. *Political Order: From the Industrial Revolution to the Globalization of Democracy.* New York, NY: Farrar, Straus, Giroux.

Galambos, Louis. 1970. "The Emerging Organizational Synthesis in Modern American History." *The Business History Review* 44 (3): 279–90.

1983. "Technology, Political Economy, and Professionalization: Central Themes of the Organizational Synthesis." *Business History Review* 57 (4): 471–93.

Gans-Morse, Jordan, Sebastian Mazzuca, and Simeon Nichter. 2014. "Varieties of Clientelism: Machine Politics during Elections." *American Journal of Political Science* 58 (2): 415–32.

Gash, Norman. 1977. *Politics in the Age of Peel: A Study in the Technique of Parliamentary Representation, 1830–50.* 2nd ed. Atlantic Highlands, NJ: Humanities Press.

Geddes, Barbara. 1996. *Politician's Dilemma: Building State Capacity in Latin America.* Berkeley, CA: University of California Press.

Gellner, Ernest, and John Waterbury. 1977. *Patrons and Clients in Mediterranean Societies.* London: Duckworth.

Gienapp, William E. 1982. "Politics Seem to Enter into Everything: Political Culture in the North, 1840–1860." In *Essays on American Antebellum Politics, 1840–1860*, edited by Stephen E. Maizlish and John J. Kushma 14–69. College Station, TX: Texas A&M Press.

Glaeser, Edward L., and Andrei Shleifer. 2003. "The Rise of the Regulatory State." *Journal of Economic Literature* 41: 401–25.

Golden, Miriam. 2003. "Electoral Connections: The Effects of the Personal Vote on Political Patronage, Bureaucracy, and Legislation in Postwar Italy." *British Journal of Political Science* 33: 189–212.

Golden, Miriam, and Brian Min. 2013. "Distributive Politics around the World." *Annual Review of Political Science* 16: 73–99.

Goldin, Claudia, and Gary Libecap. 1994. *The Regulated Economy: A Historical Approach to Political Economy.* Chicago, IL: University of Chicago Press.

Goodrich, Carter. 1960. *Government Promotion of American Canals and Railroads, 1800–1890.* New York, NY: Columbia University Press.

Gordon, Colin. 1994. *New Deals: Business, Labor, and Politics in America, 1920–1935.* New York, NY: Cambridge University Press.

Green, Matthew. 2007. "Race, Party, and Contested Elections to the U.S. House of Representatives." *Polity* 39 (2): 155–78.

Grzymala-Busse, Anna. 2007. *Rebuilding Leviathan: Party Competition and State Exploitation in Post-Communist Democracies*. New York, NY: Cambridge University Press.

2008. "Beyond Clientelism: Incumbent State Capture and State Formation." *Comparative Political Studies* 41 (4/5): 638–73.

Gutchen, Robert. 1961. "Local Improvements and Centralization in Nineteenth-Century England." *The Historical Journal* 4 (1): 85–96.

Guttsman, W. L. 1965. *The British Political Elite*. London: MacGibbon & Kee.

Gwyn, William B. 1962. *Democracy and the Cost of Politics in Britain*. London: Athlone Press.

Haber, Samuel. 1964. *Efficiency and Uplift: Scientific Management in the Progressive Era*. Chicago, IL: University of Chicago Press.

Hagopian, Frances. 2007. "Parties and Voters in Emerging Democracies." In *Oxford Handbook of Comparative Politics*, edited by Carles Boix and Susan Stokes, 582–603. New York, NY: Oxford University Press.

Reorganizing Representation in Latin America: Parties, Program, and Patronage in Argentina, Brazil, Chile, and Mexico. Forthcoming, Cambridge University Press.

Hagopian, Frances, Carlos Gervasoni, and Juan Andres Moraes. 2009. "From Patronage to Program: The Emergence of Party-Oriented Legislators in Brazil." *Comparative Political Studies* 42 (3): 360–391.

Hanham, H. J. 1960a. "Political Patronage at the Treasury, 1870–1912." *The Historical Journal* 3 (1): 75–84.

1960b. "The Sale of Honours in Late Victorian England." *Victorian Studies* 3 (3): 277–89.

1978. *Elections and Party Management: Politics in the Time of Disraeli and Gladstone*. 2nd ed. Hamden, CT: Archon Book.

Hansen, John Mark. 1991. *Gaining Access: Congress and the Farm Lobby, 1919–1981*. Chicago, IL: University of Chicago Press.

Harrison, B. H. 1971. *Drink and the Victorians: The Temperance Question in England, 1815–1872*. Pittsburgh, PA: University of Pittsburgh Press.

Hart, David. 2004. "'Business' Is Not an Interest Group: On the Study of Companies in American Politics." *Annual Review of Political Science* 7: 47–69.

Hartz, Louis. 1955. *The Liberal Tradition in America*. New York, NY: Harcourt, Brace.

Hawley, Ellis. 1978. "The Discovery and Study of a Corporate Liberalism." *Business History Review* 52 (3): 309–20.

Hay, Roy. 1977. "Employers and Social Policy in Britain: The Evolution of Welfare Legislation, 1905–14." *Social History* 2 (4): 435–55.

Hays, Samuel P. 1957. *The Response to Industrialism, 1885–1914*. Chicago, IL: University of Chicago Press.

Heesom, Alan. 1988. "'Legitimtate' versus 'Illegitimate' Influences: Aristocratic Electioneering in Mid-Victorian Britain." *Parliamentary History* 7 (2): 282–305.

Heilbroner, Robert. 1972. *In the Name of Profit*. Garden City, NY: Doubleday.

Hellman, Joel. 1998. "Winners Take All: The Politics of Partial Reform in Postcommunist Transitions." *World Politics* 50 (January): 203–34.

Hicken, Allen. 2011. "Clientelism." *Annual Review of Political Science* 14: 289–310.

Higgens-Evenson, R. Rudy. 2003. *The Price of Progress: Public Services, Taxation and the American Corporate State, 1877–1929*. Baltimore, MD: Johns Hopkins University Press.

Hill, Hamilton Andrew. 1885. *Commercial Conventions and the National Board of Trade*. Boston, MA: Tolman & White Printers.

Hofstadter, Richard. 1955. *The Age of Reform*. New York, NY: Knopf.

Hoppen, K. Theodore. 1998. *The Mid-Victorian Generation*. New York, NY: Oxford University Press.

Hoppit, Julian. 1996. "Patterns of Parliamentary Legislation, 1660–1800." *The Historical Journal* 39 (1): 109–31.

Horwitz, Morton. 1992. *The Transformation of American Law, 1870–1960: The Crisis of Legal Orthodoxy*. New York, NY: Oxford University Press.

Hughes, Edward. 1949. "Sir Charles Trevelyan and Civil Service Reform." *English Historical Review* 64 (250): 53–88.

Huntington, Samuel. 1968. *Political Order in Changing Societies*. New Haven, CT: Yale University Press.

Ilersic, A. R., and P. F. B. Liddle. 1960. *Parliament of Commerce: The Story of the Association of British Chambers of Commerce, 1860–1960*. London: Millbrook Press.

Ingle, Stephen. 2008. *The British Party System*. 4th ed. New York, NY: Routledge.

Iversen, Torben, and David Soskice. 2009. "Distribution and Redistribution: The Shadow from the Nineteenth Century." *World Politics* 61 (3): 438–86.

James, Scott. 2006. "Patronage Regimes and American Party Development from the Age of Jackson to the Progressive Era." *British Journal of Political Science* 36 (1): 39–60.

Jenkins, Jeffrey. 2004. "Partisanship and Contested Election Cases in the House of Representatives, 1789–2002." *Studies in American Political Development* 18: 112–35.

Jerrold, Blanchard. 1883. "On the Manufacture of Public Opinion." *Nineteenth Century* 13: 1080–92.

John, Richard. 1995. *Spreading the News: The American Postal System from Franklin to Morse*. Cambridge, MA: Harvard University Press.

Johnson, Kimberly S. 2009. "The First New Federalism and the Development of the Modern American State." In *The Unsustainable American State*, edited by Lawrence Jacobs and Desmond King, 88–115. New York, NY: Oxford University Press.

Johnson, Ronald, and Gary Libecap. 1994. "Patronage to Merit and Control of the Federal Government Labor Force." *Explorations in Economic History* 31: 91–119.

Kam, Christopher. 2011. "Partisanship, Enfranchisement, and the Political Economy of Electioneering in the United Kingdom, 1826–1906." Working Paper.

Katznelson, Ira, and John Lapinski. 2006. "The Substance of Representation: Studying Policy Content and Legislative Behavior." In *The Macropolitics of Congress*, edited by E. Scott Adler and John Lapinski, 96–128. Princeton, NJ: Princeton University Press.

Keefer, Philip. 2006. "Programmatic Parties: Where Do They Come from and Do They Matter?" Working Paper.

——— 2007. "Clientelism, Credibility, and the Policy Choices of Young Democracies." *American Journal of Political Science* 51 (4): 804–21.

Keefer, Philip, and Razvan Vlaicu. 2007. "Democracy, Credibility, and Clientelism." *The Journal of Law, Economics, and Organization* 24 (2): 371–406.

Kernell, Samuel, and Michael McDonald. 1999. "Congress and America's Political Development: The Transformation of the Post Office from Patronage to Service." *American Journal of Political Science* 43 (3): 792–811.

Key, V. O. 1964. *Politics, Parties, and Pressure Groups*. 5th ed. New York, NY: Crowell.

Khan, Mushtaq H. 2005. "Markets, States and Democracy: Patron–Client Networks and the Case for Democracy in Developing Countries." *Democratization* 12 (5): 704–24.

Kitschelt, Herbert. 2000. "Linkages between Citizens and Politicians in Democratic Polities." *Comparative Political Studies* 33 (6): 845–79.

Kitschelt, Herbert, and Daniel M. Kselman. 2013. "Economic Development, Democratic Experience, and Political Parties' Linkage Strategies." *Comparative Political Studies* 20 (10): 1–32.

Kitschelt, Herbert and Kent Freeze. 2010. "Programmatic Party Structuration: Developing and Comparing Cross-National and Cross-Party Measures with a New Global Data Set." Paper presented at the Annual Meeting of the American Political Science Association, Washington, DC.

Kitschelt, Herbert, and Melina Altamirano. 2015. "Clientelism in Latin America: Effort and Effectiveness." In *The Latin American Voter*, edited by Ryan E. Carlin, Matthew M. Singer, and Elizabeth J. Zechmeister, 259–87. Ann Arbor, MI: University of Michigan Press.

Kitschelt, Herbert, and Steven Wilkinson, eds. 2007. *Patrons, Clients, and Policies: Patterns of Democratic Accountability and Political Competition*. New York, NY: Cambridge University Press.

Klinghard, Daniel. 2010. *The Nationalization of American Political Parties, 1880–1896*. New York, NY: Cambridge University Press.

Kolko, Gabriel. 1963. *The Triumph of Conservatism: A Reinterpretation of American History, 1900–1916*. New York, NY: Free Press.

Kornbluh, Mark Lawrence. 2000. *Why America Stopped Voting: The Decline of Participatory Democracy and the Emergence of Modern American Politics*. New York, NY: New York University Press.

Kuo, Didi, and Jan Teorell. 2017. "Illicit Tactics as Substitutes: Election Fraud, Ballot Reform, and Contested Congressional Elections in the United States, 1860–1930." *Comparative Political Studies* 50 (5): 665–96.

Larson, John. 2001. *Internal Improvement: National Public Works and the Promise of Popular Government in the Early United Stats*. Chapel Hill, NC: University of North Carolina Press.

Lehoucq, Fabrice. 2003. "Electoral Fraud: Causes, Types, and Consequences." *Annual Review of Political Science* 6: 233–56.

Lehoucq, Fabrice, and Ivan Molina. 2002. *Stuffing the Ballot Box: Fraud, Electoral Reform, and Democratization in Costa Rica*. New York, NY: Cambridge University Press.

Lerner, Daniel. 1958. *The Passing of Traditional Society: Modernizing the Middle East*. Glencoe, IL: Free Press.

Levitsky, Steven. 2007. "From Populism to Clientelism? The Transformation of Labor-Based Party Linkages in Latin America." In *Patrons, Clients, and Policies*, edited by Herbert Kitschelt and Steven Wilkinson, 335–80. New York, NY: Cambridge University Press.

Lindbeck, Assar, and Jorgen Weibull. 1987. "Balanced-Budget Redistribution as the Outcome of Political Competition." *Public Choice* 52 (3): 273–97.

Lindblom, Charles E. 1977. *Politics and Markets*. New York, NY: Basic Books.

Lipset, Seymour Martin. 1996. *American Exceptionalism: A Double-Edged Sword*. New York, NY: W. W. Norton.

Lizzeri, Alessandro, and Nicola Persico. 2004. "Why Did Elites Extend the Suffrage? Democracy and the Scope of Government, with an Application to Britain's 'Age of Reform.'" *Quarterly Journal of Economics* 119 (2): 705–63.

Lloyd, Trevor. 1965. "Uncontested Seats in British General Elections 1852–1910." *The Historical Journal* 8 (2): 260–65.

Loomis, Burdett A. 2011. *Guide to Interest Groups and Lobbying in the United States*. Washington, DC: CQ Press.

Lowell, A. Lawrence. 1908. *The Government of England*. Vol. 1. New York, NY: Macmillan.

Lowi, Theodore J. 1964. "American Business, Public Policy, Case-Studies, and Political Theory." *World Politics* 16 (4): 677–715.

1972. "Four Systems of Policy, Politics, and Choice." *Public Administration Review* 32 (4): 298–310.

1979. *The End of Liberalism: The Second Republic of the United States*. 2nd ed. New York, NY: W. W. Norton.

Lyne, Mona. 2008. *The Voter's Dilemma and Democratic Accountability: Latin America and Beyond*. University Park, PA: Penn State University Press.

MacDonagh, Oliver. 1958. "The Nineteenth-Century Revolution in Government: A Reappraisal." *The Historical Journal* 1 (1): 52–67.

Magaloni, Beatriz, Alberto Diaz-Cayeros, and Federico Estvez. 2007. "Clientelism and Portfolio Diversification: A Model of Electoral Investment with Applications to Mexico." In *Patrons, Clients, and Policies*, edited by Herbert Kitschelt and Steven Wilkinson, 182–205. New York, NY: Cambridge University Press.

Mares, Isabela. 2003a. *The Politics of Social Risk: Business and Welfare State Development*. New York, NY: Cambridge University Press.

2003b. "The Sources of Business Interest in Social Insurance: Sectoral vs. National Differences." *World Politics* 55 (2): 229–58.

2015. *From Open Secrets to Secret Ballots: Democratic Electoral Reforms and Voter Autonomy*. New York, NY: Cambridge University Press.

Mares, Isabela, and Lauren Young. 2016. "Buying, Expropriating, and Stealing Votes." *Annual Review of Political Science* 19: 267–88.

Martin, Cathie Jo. 2000. *Stuck in Neutral: Business and the Politics of Human Capital Investment Policy*. Princeton, NJ: Princeton University Press.

2010. "Social Policy and Business." In *Oxford Handbook of Business and Government*, edited by Graham Wilson, Wyn Grant, and David Coen 565–84. Oxford University Press.

Martin, Cathie Jo, and Duane Swank. 2008. "The Political Origins of Coordinated Capitalism: Business Organizations, Party Systems, and State Structure in the Age of Innocence." *American Political Science Review* 102 (2): 181–98.

2012. *The Political Construction of Business Interests: Coordination, Growth, and Equality*. New York, NY: Cambridge University Press.

Martis, Kenneth. 1989. *The Historical Atlas of Political Parties in the United States Congress 1789–1989*. New York, NY: Macmillan.

Mathias, Peter. 1983. *The First Industrial Nation*. 2nd ed. London: Methuen.

May, Thomas Erskine. 1863. *The Constitutional History of England: Since the Accession of George the Third, 1760–1860*. New York, NY: A. C. Armstrong.

McChesney, Fred S. 1987. "Rent Extraction and Rent Creation in the Economic Theory of Regulation." *The Journal of Legal Studies* 16 (1): 101–18.

McConnell, Grant. 1966. *Private Power and American Democracy*. New York, NY: Knopf.

McCormick, Richard L. 1981. "The Discovery That Business Corrupts Politics: A Reappraisal of the Origins of Progressivism." *American History Review* 86 (2): 247–74.

——— 1986. *The Party Period and Public Policy: American Politics from the Age of Jackson to the Progressive Era*. New York, NY: Oxford University Press.

McCormick, Richard P. 1966. *The Second American Party System: Party Formation in the Jacksonian Era*. Chapel Hill, NC: University of North Carolina Press.

McCraw, Thomas K. 1975. "Regulation in America: A Review Article." *The Business History Review* 49 (2): 159–83.

McIvor, Arthur. 2002. *Organised Capital: Employers' Associations and Industrial Relations in Northern England, 1880–1939*. New York, NY: Cambridge University Press.

McIvor, John P. 2006. "Congressional Bills and Resolutions: 1789–2000." In *Historical Statistics of the United States, Earliest Times to Present: Millennial Edition*, edited by Susan Carter, Scott Sigmunt Gartner, Michael R. Haines, Alan L. Olmstead, Richard Sutch, and Gavin Wright, table Eb268–278. New York, NY: Cambridge University Press.

McKenzie, Robert. 1966. *British Political Parties*. New York, NY: Praeger.

McMenamin, Iain. 2012. "If Money Talks, What Does It Say? Varieties of Capitalism and Business Financing of Parties." *World Politics* 64 (1): 1–38.

McMurtry, Virginia, et al. 1976. *History of Civil Service Merit Systems of the United States and Select Foreign Countries*. Congressional Research Service. Washington, DC: Government Printing Office.

Melling, Joseph. 1992. "Welfare Capitalism and the Origins of Welfare States: British Industry, Workplace Welfare and Social Reform c. 1870–1914." *Social History* 17 (3): 453–78.

Merton, Robert. 1968. *Social Theory and Social Structure*. New York, NY: Free Press.

Minicucci, Stephen. 2004. "Internal Improvements and the Union, 1790–1860." *Studies in American Political Development* 18 (Fall): 160–85.

Mizruchi, Mark S. 2013. *The Fracturing of the American Corporate Elite*. Cambridge, MA: Harvard University Press.

Montinola, Gabriella, and Robert Jackman. 2002. "Sources of Corruption: A Cross-Country Case Study." *British Journal of Political Science* 32: 147–70.

Moore, D. C. 1976. *The Politics of Deference*. New York, NY: Harvester Press.

Moynihan, Daniel Patrick. 1963. "The Irish." In *Behind the Melting Pot*, edited by Nathan Glazer and Daniel Moynihan, 217–87. Cambridge, MA: MIT Press.

Munro, W. B. 1928. *The Invisible Government*. New York, NY: Macmillan.

Musgrave, Charles. 1914. *The London Chamber of Commerce from 1881–1914*. London: Effingham Wilson.

Namier, L. B. 1963. *The Structure of Politics at the Ascension of George III*. 2nd ed. New York, NY: St. Martin's Press.

Nash, Gerald D. 1957. "Origins of the Interstate Commerce Act of 1887." *Pennsylvania History* 24 (3): 181–90.

Nichter, Simeon. 2008. "Vote Buying or Turnout Buying? Machine Politics and the Secret Ballot." *American Political Science Review* 102 (1): 19–31.

Nossiter. 1975. *Influence, Opinion, and Political Idioms in Reformed England: Case Studies from the North-East, 1832–74*. Brighton: Harvester Press.

Novak, William J. 1996. *The People's Welfare: Law and Regulation in Nineteenth-Century America*. Chapel Hill, NC: University of North Carolina Press.

2008. "The Myth of the 'Weak' American State." *The American Historical Review* 113 (3): 752–72.

O'Dwyer, Conor. 2006. *Runaway State Building: Patronage Politics and Democratic Development*. Baltimore, MD: Johns Hopkins University Press.

O'Gorman, Frank. 1984. "Electoral Deference in 'Unreformed' England: 1760–1832." *Journal of Modern History* 56: 391–429.

Ostrogorski, Moisei. 1903. *Democracy and the Organization of Political Parties*. Garden City, NY: Anchor Books.

Overacker, Louise. 1932. *Money in Elections*. New York, NY: Macmillan.

Palmowski, Jan. 2002. "Liberalism and Local Government in Late Nineteenth Century Germany and England." *The Historical Journal* 45 (2): 381–409.

Pares, Richard. 1963. *King George III and the Politicians*. London: Oxford University Press.

Parris, Henry. 1965. *Government and the Railways in Ninteenth-Century Britain*. London: Routledge.

Peltzman, Sam. 1976. "Toward a More General Theory of Regulation." *The Journal of Law and Economics* 19 (2): 211–40.

Phillips, John A., and Charles Wetherell. 1995. "The Great Reform Act of 1832 and the Political Modernization of England." *American Historical Review* (April): 411–36.

Piattoni, Simona, ed. 2001. *Clientelism, Interests, and Democratic Representation*. New York, NY: Cambridge University Press.

Pierson, Paul, and Theda Skocpol. 2002. "Historical Institutionalism in Contemporary Political Science." In *Political Science: The State of the Discipline*, edited by Ira Katznelson and Helen Milner, 693–721. New York, NY: W. W. Norton.

Pinto-Duschkinsky, Michael. 1981. *British Political Finance 1830–1980*. Washington, DC: American Enterprise Institute for Public Policy Research.

Pollock, James K. 1932. *Money and Politics Abroad*. New York, NY: Knopf.

Pollock, Sir Frederick. 1883. *The Land Laws*. London: Macmillan.

Porritt, Edward. 1909. *The Unreformed House of Commons: Parliamentary Representation before 1832*. Cambridge: Cambridge University Press.

Posner, Richard A. 1974. "Theories of Economic Regulation." *Bell Journal of Economcis and Management Science* 5 (2): 335–58.

Przeworski, Adam, Susan Stokes, and Bernard Manin. 1999. *Democracy, Accountability, and Representation*. New York, NY: Cambridge University Press.

Pugh, Martin. 2002. *The Making of Modern British Politics, 1867–1945*. 3rd ed. Malden, MA: Blackwell Publishers.

Purcell, Edward A. 1967. "Ideas and Interests: Businessmen and the Interstate Commerce Act." *The Journal of American History* 54(3): 561–78.

Rallings, Colin, and Michael Thrasher. 2009. *British Electoral Facts, 1832–1999*. 6th ed. Burlington, VT: Ashgate.

Rauch, James, and Peter Evans. 1999. "Bureaucracy and Growth: A Cross-National Analysis of the Effects of 'Weberian' State Structures on Economic Growth." *American Sociological Review* 64 (October): 748–65.

Reid, Joseph D., and Michael M. Kurth. 1988. "Public Employees in Political Firms: Part A. The Patronage Era." *Public Choice* 59: 253–62.

 1992. "The Rise and Fall of Urban Political Patronage Machine." In *Strategic Factors in Nineteenth Century American Economic History*, edited by Claudia Goldin and Hugh Rockoff, 427–45. Chicago, IL: University of Chicago Press.

Renda, Lex. 1997. *Running on the Record: Civil War–Era Politics in New Hampshire.* Charlottesville, VA: University of Virginia Press.

Reynolds, John. 1980. "The Silent Dollar: Vote Buying in New Jersey." *New Jersey History* 98: 191–211.

Richter, Donald. 1971. "The Role of Mob Riot in Victorian Elections, 1865–1885." *Victorian Studies* 15 (1): 19–28.

Ridings, Eugene. 2001. "Chambers of Commerce and Business Elites in Great Britain and Brazil in the Nineteenth Century: Some Comparisons." *The Business History Review* 75 (4): 739–73.

Riordan, William L. 2005. *Plunkitt of Tammany Hall.* New York, NY: Signet Books.

Riper, Paul P. Van. 1958. *History of the United States Civil Service.* Evanston, IL: Row, Peterson.

Rix, Kathryn. 2008. "The Elimination of Corrupt Practices in British Elections? Reassessing the Impact of the 1883 Corrupt Practices Act." *English Historical Review* 123: 65–97.

Robb. 1992. *White-Collar Crime in Modern England: Financial Fraud and Business Morality, 1845–1929.* London: Cambridge University Press.

Robinson, James, and Thierry Verdier. 2013. "The Political Economy of Clientelism." *The Scandinavian Journal of Economics* 115 (2): 260–91.

Roniger, Luis. 2004. "Political Clientelism, Democracy, and Market Economy." *Comparative Politics* 36 (3): 353–75.

Rueschemeyer, Dietrich, Evelyn Stephens, and John Stephens. 1992. *Capitalist Development and Democracy.* Chicago, IL: University of Chicago Press.

Sack, James J. 1980. "The House of Lords and Parliamentary Patronage in Great Britain, 1802–1832." *The Historical Journal* 23 (4): 913–37.

Salmon, Philip. 2009a. "The English Reform Legislation, 1831–32." In *The House of Commons, 1820–32*, edited by D. Fisher, 374–412. London: Cambridge University Press.

 2009b. "The House of Commons 1801–1911." In *A Short History of Parliament*, edited by Clyve Jones, 248–69. Woodbridge, UK: Boydell Press.

Samuels, David. 2002. "Pork-Barreling Is Not Credit-Claiming." *Journal of Politics* 64 (3): 845–63.

Sanders, Elizabeth. 1999. *The Roots of Reform: Farmers, Workers, and the American State, 1877–1917.* Chicago, IL: University of Chicago Press.

Scheiner, Ethan. 2006. *Democracy Without Competition in Japan: Opposition Failure in a One-Party Dominant System.* New York, NY: Cambridge University Press.

Schonhardt-Bailey, Cheryl. 2006. *From the Corn Laws to Free Trade: Interests, Ideas, and Institutions in Historical Perspective.* Cambridge, MA: MIT Press.

Schmidt, Steffen, ed. 1977. *Friends, Followers, and Factions: A Reader in Political Clientelism.* Berkeley, CA: University of California Press.

Scott, James. 1969. "Corruption, Machine Politics, and Political Change." *American Political Science Review* 63(4): 1142–58.

1972. "Patron–Client Politics and Political Change in Southeast Asia." *American Political Science Review* 66: 91–114.

Seager, J. Renwick. 1909. *Corrupt and Illegal Practices at Parliamentary Elections, as Defined in the Judgments in Election Petitions from 1886–1906*. London: Liberal Publication Department.

Self, Robert. 2000. *The Evolution of the British Party System 1885–1940*. Harlow: Longman.

Seymour, Charles. 1915. *Electoral Reform in England and Wales: The Development and Operation of the Parliamentary Franchise 1832–1885*. New Haven, CT: Yale University Press.

Shannon, H. A. 1931. "The Coming of General Limited Liability." *Economic History* 2: 267.

Shefter, Martin. 1976. "The Emergence of the Political Machine: An Alternative View." In *Theoretical Perspectives on Urban Politics*, edited by Willis D. Hawley, 14–44. Englewood Cliffs, NJ: Prentice-Hall.

1977. "Party and Patronage: Germany, England, and Italy." *Politics and Society* 7: 403–51.

1983. "Regional Receptivity to Reform: The Legacy of the Progressive Era." *Political Science Quarterly* 98 (3): 459–83.

1994. *Political Parties and the State: The American Historical Experience*. Princeton, NJ: Princeton University Press.

Sikes, Earl. 1928. *State and Federal Corrupt-Practices Legislation*. Durham, NC: Duke University Press.

Silberman, Bernard. 1993. *Cages of Reason: The Rise of the Rational State in France, Japan, the United States, and Great Britain*. Chicago, IL: University of Chicago Press.

Silbey, Joel H., Allan Bogue, and William Flanigan. 1978. *The History of American Electoral Behavior*. Princeton, NJ: Princeton University Press.

Sklar, Martin J. 1988. *The Corporate Reconstruction of American Capitalism, 1890–1916: The Market, the Law, and Politics*. New York, NY: Cambridge University Press.

Skocpol, Theda, Marshall Ganz, and Ziad Munson. 2000. "A Nation of Organizers: The Institutional Origins of Civic Voluntarism in the United States." *American Political Science Review* 94 (3): 527–46.

Skowronek, Stephen. 1982. *Building a New American State: The Expansion of National Administrative Capacities, 1877–1920*. New York, NY: Cambridge University Press.

Smith, Mark. 2000. *American Business and Political Power*. Chicago, IL: Chicago University Press.

Smith, Rogers M. 1993. "Beyond Tocqueville, Myrdal, and Hartz: The Multiple Traditions in America." *American Political Science Review* 87 (3): 549–66.

Stigler, George. 1971. "The Theory of Economic Regulation." *The Bell Journal of Economics and Management Science* 2 (1): 3–21.

Stokes, Susan. 2005. "Perverse Accountability: A Formal Model of Machine Politics with Evidence from Argentina." *American Political Science Review* 99 (3): 315–25.

2007. "Political Clientelism." In *Oxford Handbook of Comparative Politics*, edited by Carles Boix and Susan Stokes, 604–27. New York, NY: Oxford University Press.

2013. "What Killed Vote Buying in Britain and the United States?" In *Brokers, Voters, and Clientelism: The Puzzle of Distributive Politics*, edited by Susan Stokes, Thad Dunning, Marcela Nazareno, and Valeria Brusco 200–44. New York, NY: Cambridge University Press.

Stokes, Susan, Thad Dunning, Marcela Nazareno, and Valeria Brusco. 2013. *Brokers, Voters, and Clientelism: The Puzzle of Distributive Politics*. New York, NY: Cambridge University Press.

Stone, Clarence N. 1996. "Urban Political Machines: Taking Stock." *PS: Political Science and Politics* 29 (3): 446.

Sturges, Kenneth. 1915. *American Chambers of Commerce*. New York, NY: Moffat & Co.

Summers, Mark W. 1987. *The Plundering Generation: Corruption and the Crisis of the Union, 1849–1861*. New York, NY: Oxford University Press.

2002. "'To Make the Wheels Revolve We Must Have Grease': Barrel Politics in the Gilded Age." *Journal of Policy History* 14 (1): 49–72.

Swenson, Peter. 1991. "Bringing Capital Back in, or Social Democracy Reconsidered: Employer Power, Cross-Class Alliances, and Centralization of Industrial Relations in Denmark and Sweden." *World Politics* 43 (4): 513–44.

1997. "Arranged Alliance: Business Interests in the New Deal." *Politics & Society* 25: 66–116.

2002. *Capitalists against Markets: The Making of Labor Markets and Welfare States in the United States and Sweden*. New York, NY: Oxford University Press.

Sylla, Richard. 2000. "Experimental Federalism: The Economics of American Government, 1789–1914." In *The Cambridge Economic History of the United States*, vol. 2: *The Long Nineteenth Century*, edited by Stanley L. Engerman and Robert E. Gallman, 483–541. New York, NY: Cambridge University Press.

Tarr, Joel A. 1984. "Evolution of the Urban Infrastructure in the Nineteenth and Twentieth Centuries." In *Perspectives on Urban Infrastructure*, edited by Royce Hanson, 4–66. Washington, DC: National Academy Press.

Tarrow, Sidney. 1967. *Peasant Communism in Southern Italy*. New Haven, CT: Yale University Press.

1977. "The Italian Party System between Crisis and Transition." *American Journal of Political Science* 21 (2): 193–224.

Teorell, Jan. 2017. "Partisanship and Unreformed Bureaucracy: The Drivers of Election Fraud in Sweden, 17191908." *Social Science History* 41 (2): 201–25.

Thayer, George. 1973. *Who Shakes the Money Tree?* New York, NY: Simon and Schuster.

Thelen, Kathleen. 2001. "Varieties of Labor Politics in the Developed Democracies." In *Varieties of Capitalism*, edited by Peter A. Hall and David Soskice, 71–103. New York, NY: Oxford University Press.

Tichenor, Daniel J., and Richard A. Harris. 2002. "Organized Interests and American Political Development." *Political Science Quarterly* 117 (4): 587–612.

2005. "The Development of Interest Group Politics in America: Beyond the Conceits of Modern Times." *Annual Review of Political Science* 8: 251–70.

Tilly, Charles. 1998. *Popular Contention in Great Britain, 1758–1834*. Cambridge, MA: Harvard University Press.

Treisman, Daniel. 2007. "What Have We Learned about the Causes of Corruption from Ten Years of Cross-National Empirical Research?" *Annual Review of Political Science* 10: 211–44.

Troesken, Werner. 2009. "Patronage and Public-Sector Wages in 1896." *The Journal of Economic History* 59 (2): 424–46.

Trounstine, Jessica. 2006. "Dominant Regimes and the Demise of Urban Democracy." *Journal of Politics* 68 (4): 879–93.

Truman, David. 1951. *The Governmental Process*. New York, NY: Knopf.

Vogel, David. 1987. "Political Science and the Study of Corporate Power: A Dissent from the New Conventional Wisdom." *British Journal of Political Science* 17 (4): 385–408.

Walker, Jack. 1991. *Mobilizing Interest Groups in America: Patrons, Professions, and Social Movements*. Ann Arbor, MI: University of Michigan Press.

Walle, Nicholas van de. 2007. "Meet the Old Boss, Same as the New Boss?" In *Patrons, Clients, and Policies*, edited by Herbert Kitschelt and Steven Wilkinson. New York, NY: Cambridge University Press.

Wallis, John Joseph. 2006. "Federal Government Employees, by Government Branch and Location Relative to the Capital: 1816–1992." In *Historical Statistics of the United States, Earliest Times to Present: Millennial Edition*, edited by Susan Carter, Scott Sigmunt Gartner, Michael R. Haines, Alan L. Olmstead, Richard Sutch, and Gavin Wright, table Ea894–903. New York, NY: Cambridge University Press.

Wantchekon, Leonard. 2003. "Clientelism and Voting Behavior: Evidence from a Field Experiment in Benin." *World Politics* 55 (3): 399–422.

Webber, Michael J., and G. William Domhoff. 1996. "Myth and Reality in Business Support for Democrats and Republicans in the 1936 Presidential Election." *American Political Science Review* 90 (4): 824–33.

Weitz-Shapiro, Rebecca. 2012. "What Wins Votes: Why Some Politicians Opt Out of Clientelism." *American Journal of Political Science* 56 (3): 568–83.

2014. *Curbing Clientelism in Argentina: Politics, Poverty, and Social Policy*. New York, NY: Cambridge University Press.

Werking, Richard. 1978. "Bureaucrats, Businessmen, and Foreign Trade: The Origins of the United States Chamber of Commerce." *Business History Review* 52 (3): 321–41.

White, Leonard D. 1954. *The Jacksonians: A Study in Administrative History, 1829–1861*. New York, NY: Macmillan.

White, Richard. 2012. *Railroaded: The Transcontinentals and the Making of Modern America*. New York, NY: W. W. Norton.

Wickwire, Franklin B. 1965. "King's Friends, Civil Servants, or Politicians." *The American Historical Review* 71 (1): 18–42.

Wiebe, Robert. 1967. *The Search for Order*. Westport, CT: Greenwood Press.

Wilkinson, Steven I. 2007. "Explaining Changing Patterns of Party-Voter Linkages in India." In *Patrons, Clients, and Policies*, edited by Herbert Kitschelt and Steven Wilkinson, 110–40. New York, NY: Cambridge University Press.

Williams, O. Cyprian. 1948. *The Historical Development of Private Bill Procedure and Standing Orders in the House of Commons*. London: His Majesty's Stationery Office.

Williamson, Chilton. 1960. *American Suffrage: From Property to Democracy, 1760–1860*. Princeton, NJ: Princeton University Press.

Wilson, Edward. 1866. "Principles of Representation." In *Fortnightly Review*, vol. 4, edited by George Henry Lewes, 421–36. London: Chapman and Hall.

Wolfe, Archibald. 1915. *Commercial Organizations in the United Kingdom*. Washington, DC: Government Publication Office.

Wolfinger, Raymond E. 1972. "Why Political Machines Have Not Withered away and Other Revisionist Thoughts." *The Journal of Politics* 34 (2): 365–98.

Yarmie, Andrew. 1980. "Employers' Organizations in Mid-Victorian England." *International Review of Social History* 25: 209–35.

Ziblatt, Daniel. 2009. "Shaping Democratic Practice and the Causes of Electoral Fraud: Theory and Evidence from Pre-1914 Germany." *American Political Science Review* 103 (1): 1–21.

　2017. *Conservative Political Parties and the Birth of Modern Democracy in Europe*. New York, NY: Cambridge University Press.

Zeitlin, Jonathan. 1987. "From Labour History to the History of Industrial Relations." *Economic History Review* 40 (2): 159–84.

Zunz, Olivier. 1990. *Making America Corporate 1870–1920*. Chicago, IL: University of Chicago Press.

Index

CPSIA information can be obtained
at www.ICGtesting.com
Printed in the USA
LVHW092011121120
671536LV00004B/73